A Beginner's Primer of Where to Look and Wh

Begin by looking for good signs:

1. Matching color throughout
2. Signs of wear indicating the piece has been used for generations, even for a couple of centuries

But don't stop there. Repairs and replacements devalue a piece, and there are some out-and-out fakes awaiting the unsuspecting. Remember, objects do not lie! If you know where to look and what to look for, you'll be better able to uncover a problem piece—whether it is an honest, but heavily restored, antique or one of those wannabe antiques that just doesn't make it.

Furniture Part	Look For	Beware Of
Drawers	Look for handmade dovetails; feel underneath surface for rippling hand-planing marks; check to make sure the hardware post holes match up on the inside and outside	Machine-cut dovetails; sharp, straight edges; rough, splintery drawer bottoms; unexplained holes on the drawer inside and outside
Apron or skirt	Feel for irregular hand chiseling marks; look carefully for new wood cuts that indicate reshaping	Sharp, straight edges; perfectly smooth underneath surface; a difference in patina on the underneath wood indicating new cuts
Backboard	Look for up-and-down and crosswise saw marks; check for different patinas if looking at a two-part piece—secretary/bookcase, highboy, and so on	Any strange holes, stains, paint, or tool marks on the backboard may indicate a made-up piece
Feet and legs	Look for the leg (on chairs) and foot (on chests, and so on) to be carved from one piece of wood; examine for good signs of decades of wear	Signs that any of the feet or legs have been replaced; long, hairline marks that indicate the leg has been spliced and replaced; any differences in color from the rest of the piece
Chair backs	Examine carefully for cracks and repairs	Extensive patching and repairs to breaks—they'll just break again under the weight of the body
Chair arms	Look for mortise-and-tenon or peg; examine to be sure the color matches the chair frame	Round dowels which indicate post circa 1850 construction; different colors or different wood suggests the arms were added at a later date
Tabletops/ bottoms	Examine to be sure the top and bottom have always been together—check color, any unexplained holes, paint, stains, or marks; look for genuine signs of normal wear; stand away and look for good proportions	Unexplained holes, different color, poor proportions may indicate a replaced or reshaped tabletop

alpha
books

Silver

Always check out the marks on silver. They will tell you whether a piece is sterling or plate, English or American.

English Silver

Look for these hallmarks:

- **Lion**, facing left, for sterling
- **Letter**, in a shield or cartouche, telling the date
- **Initials**, identifying the maker of the piece
- **Symbol or icon**, identifying where the piece was made
- **Profile** of the reigning sovereign

   Beware! When a piece has individual parts, be sure the hallmarks correspond. Also, fill any silver container (teapot, pitcher, vase, and so on) with water. Tiny holes or splits can escape the naked eye.

American Coin Silver

American coin silver was made until circa 1860 to 1865. It can be marked many different ways. Check for these possibilities:

- *Coin*, or *C* (for coin)
- *D* for dollar
- *S* for standard
- **Name or initials** to identify the maker
- **Address** where the maker worked
- **Pseudohallmarks** similar to English hallmarks

American Sterling Silver

After the benchmark date of 1860 to 1865, America switched from coin to sterling (925/1000). These marks are quick indications that a piece is sterling:

- "Sterling"
- "925/1000," or sometimes just "925"
- The manufacturer's name, but always with either the word "sterling" or the number "925"

   Beware! Check silver carefully for pitting in the silver metal. Also, not all sterling silver is antique. Many outstanding American sterling silver pieces were made in the 1910s and 1920s.

Silver Plate

Don't discount silver plate. Victorian silver-plated items are rapidly disappearing from the marketplace. Look for interesting and unusual pieces.

Some of the marks used to identify Victorian silver-plated pieces of the 1850 to 1900 era are …

- A1.
- Quadruple plate.
- NS (nickel silver).
- EPC (electroplate on copper).
- EPNS (electroplate silver on nickel base).
- EPWM (electroplate silver on nickel/white metal mounts).
- EPBM (electroplate on Britannia metal).

   Beware! Old Sheffield plate is never marked "Sheffield." Also, the cost of replating a badly worn piece of silver plate can be extremely high.

THE COMPLETE IDIOT'S GUIDE® TO

Buying and Selling Antiques

by Emyl Jenkins

alpha books

Macmillan USA, Inc.
201 West 103rd Street
Indianapolis, IN 46290

A Pearson Education Company

This book is dedicated to a good friend and collector, Sharyn McCrumb, who insists that she doesn't know how I could possibly have written a Complete Idiot's Guide *on antiques without consulting her first.*

And to the newest member of my family, Benjamin Nicholson Hultzapple, who has all the right genes from his mother, Joslin Jenkins, and father, Michael Hultzapple, to turn into a real antiques aficionado.

Copyright © 2000 by Emyl Jenkins

International Standard Book Number: 0-02-863930-8
Library of Congress Catalog Card Number: Available upon request.

02   01   00   8   7   6   5   4   3   2   1

Interpretation of the printing code: The rightmost number of the first series of numbers is the year of the book's printing; the rightmost number of the second series of numbers is the number of the book's printing. For example, a printing code of 00-1 shows that the first printing occurred in 2000.

Printed in the United States of America

Publisher
Marie Butler-Knight

Product Manager
Phil Kitchel

Managing Editor
Cari Luna

Senior Acquisitions Editor
Renee Wilmeth

Development Editor
Michael Koch

Production Editor
Christy Wagner

Copy Editor
Diana Francoeur

Illustrator
Jody P. Schaeffer

Cover Designers
Mike Freeland
Kevin Spear

Book Designers
Scott Cook and Amy Adams of DesignLab

Indexer
Tonya Heard

Layout/Proofreading
Mary Hunt
Gloria Schurick

Contents at a Glance

Contents

14 Brave New E-World   115

Appendixes

Foreword

Some years ago I was sent a very tongue-in-cheek advertisement that was printed to look like a wanted poster one sees at the post office. It read:

WARNING!
Antique Pox
Very Contagious to Adults

Symptoms: Patient has blank expression, continually swivel-headed looking for roadside shops, continually seen to be checking auction catalogues, hangs out in all sorts of odd places, makes frequent nighttime telephone calls, mumbles to self, sometimes lies to spouse about contents in back of car after "road trip."

No Known Cure

Victim should be treated with frequent visits to shops and auctions; frequent buying and/or selling helps a great deal.

This was an advertisement for a shop or a paper of some sort, and of course it was very funny. Like all good humor, to be truly funny it has to have a basis of truth to it. And it does.

My own experience with antiques bears a similarity. I went to work temporarily for an antiques dealer in the early 1970s. I was going to stay only for four months—no more—and then back off to school—to law school. Well, two months later I went to the owner of the shop—who was my father—and said, "Gee, I really like this. It's fun! I'd like to stay." The antiques "bug" had bitten me, and I stayed, running the shop for the next 22 years, at which time I closed it and thought I was retiring to a life of quiet dealing to the trade. Chubb's *Antiques Roadshow* came calling a year and half later. Three years after being named host of the show—and in the midst of taping the fourth season of the show, in 1999, Sotheby's enticed me back to a daily commute to New York City and the exciting new world of the Internet. So the bug bit me hard, and the antiques world still excites me.

For many years, I haven't really worked; I've just been having a bit of fun. I have had the chance to be doing something I was passionate about. It's almost like religion when it's a calling rather than a career: "Chasing goods" as we say in the trade, running an antiques shop in New York City, travelling all over the world. There isn't a city in the world that doesn't have an antiques shop in it somewhere I've discovered—I've even found things in small towns in the Caribbean Islands.

If you think you're susceptible to the antiques bug yourself, Emyl Jenkins' latest book tells it all—and guides you through the so-called mysterious antiques business. What fun the trade is: the chase, buyer beware and caveat emptor, the dealer and the auctioneer, the runner and the picker, the antiques, and the stories, always the stories.

We touch history every day and have a tactile experience with the men and women of the past when we connect ourselves to them through antiques. Buying can be great fun this way, and that's the most important thing in life—having fun. And the best way to have fun in antiques is to know what you're dealing with.

Early on in my career as an antiques dealer, I had an amusing experience while "on the road." I had been travelling through New England and, very late in the day, called on a shop that was just about to close. The proprietor, a grouchy old fellow, barely even looked up when I walked in. He just figured I was another "tourist." He certainly didn't hop up and greet me with the usual awful question, "Anything you're looking for?" As I looked around the shop, I noticed a rather pleasing wooden sign, white with black lettering, in a good hand (I like old signs a great deal). The legend said: "The only person who was interested in what your Grandmother had was your Grandfather." I laughed out loud at this and got chatting with the grouchy old proprietor. We had a nice chin-wag about trade once we established we were both dealers. He had obviously seen way too many tourists during the course of the summers in New England, hence the sign. After a bit, I was finally invited to see some better things in the proverbial back room, and bought a jolly nice little mirror, which I took back to New York and later sold in the shop at a handsome profit.

We had about 18 million viewers watch the premier show of *Antiques Roadshow* this year, and I suppose we have now proved there are a lot of grandfathers out there!

My late partner once said to me that a dealer needs a daily "fix"; they've either got to buy or sell every day. *The Complete Idiot's Guide to Buying and Selling Antiques* will help you learn how to do this and have a "bit of fun" doing it.

Happy buying, happy collecting, happy hunting, and travel safe my friends.

Chris Jussel

Chris Jussel is a Senior Vice President of Sotheby's Online Auctions Associate Program. He is also the host of the Public Broadcasting Service (PBS) television series *Antiques Roadshow*, the most popular show on public television. Prior to hosting *Antiques Roadshow* in 1996, Mr. Jussel spent more than 20 years as the owner of Vernay & Jussel, which he closed in 1994.

Introduction

Every day it seems you hear about some fabulous find—a priceless antique that no one had a clue about until an expert examined it and voilà! Suddenly the very piece that was destined for the thrift shop, the neighborhood yard sale, or worst of all, the garbage dump, is proclaimed as rare, important, and, of course, valuable.

You're green with envy. Could you find such a piece? How do those experts learn so much?

This book can't guarantee that you'll magically and mysteriously uncover the million-dollar treasure, but it does promise to start you on the road to becoming knowledgeable and well-versed in many aspects of antiquing—buying, selling, and best of all, learning about and understanding the objects themselves. Who knows? Along the way, you may even uncover a long-forgotten family treasure in your own home.

If there is one major problem with antiques, it is that there are so *many* different types and kinds of them—virtually everything made during the eighteenth and nineteenth centuries can be called an *antique*. No one book could cover everything from soup (bowls) to nuts (the type that hold screws in place).

However, most general antiques shops carry an inventory of furniture, silver, ceramics, and glass—those traditional categories sought out by antiques collectors. And usually it is some object in one of these categories that catches the beginning antiquer's attention. Therefore, it is these areas that are explored in this guide. What may surprise you, though, is how you can apply what you learn about say, a corner cupboard, to a glass tumbler, because all antiques can be explored through an understanding of age, quality, rarity, and condition.

That's why, throughout this guide, I throw in painless history and sociology lessons, sprinkle a bit of easy-to-understand technology here and there, and try to appeal to your common sense. When you mix these together, along with the benchmark dates and quick reference sections, you'll have the tools and the confidence you need to give those "old things" a good once-over.

This is an antiques primer designed to dispel many of the mysteries associated with the antiques world. Antiques, themselves, aren't that complicated, though some people (the ones who want all the good stuff for themselves) would have you think they are. Truth is, if you know a little history, enjoy mysteries, love pretty things, and have a reasonable amount of common sense, you, too, can be the one who gets the "steals."

Speaking of steals, there's more to the grand and mysterious world of antiques than just the objects themselves. There's knowing where to find the quality pieces and how to make a good deal. That's why you also find chapters on both the traditional and the new-fangled ways of buying and selling antiques in these pages.

Knowing What to Expect

Because the world of antiques is so multi-faceted, there are five parts to this beginner's journey:

Part 1, "Is It or Isn't It Antique," explains what makes an antique an antique—something most people couldn't tell you.

Part 2, "The Thrill of the Chase," prepares you for making purchases in the usual onsite setting—shops, malls, house sales, and so on.

Part 3, "Antique Auctions: Offline and Online," delves into the fascinating world of antique auctions—real and virtual.

Part 4, "Getting Down to Brass Tacks," gets down to the nitty-gritty—the objects themselves, and explains what you should be looking for.

Part 5, "Here Today, Still Here Tomorrow: Protecting Your Investment," wraps the trip up by providing information on protecting your antiques and discussing some options available to you if and when the time comes to dispose of some of them.

To Help Speed You Along

Within the chapters in each part, helpful guides and tips are included to speed you along.

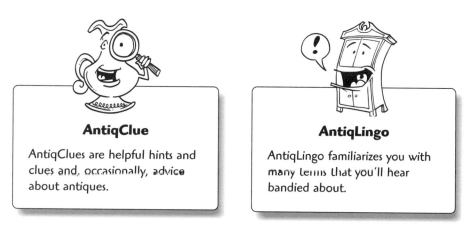

AntiqClue

AntiqClues are helpful hints and clues and, occasionally, advice about antiques.

AntiqLingo

AntiqLingo familiarizes you with many terms that you'll hear bandied about.

AntiqInfo

AntiqInfos provide background information and some intriguing facts to bring you up on the antiques learning curve.

Before You Buy

Before You Buy boxes are gentle warnings and tips for you to contemplate and remember, especially before you buy.

Acknowledgments

A special thank you to everyone who has shared time and knowledge with me, not just for this project, but over the years, especially friends and colleagues at Neal Auction Gallery, Sloan's, Freeman's, Sotheby's, Ken Farmer Auctions, Christie's, Robert Brunk, Skinner's, Winterthur, and Garth's. Thank you Sammi Flynn, Marshall Falwell, Dan Farrell, Janella Smyth, Hillary Holland, Dale Mitchell, Kathy Kamnikar, Neal Alford, Augie Fetcho, Joe Wilkinson, Jim Craig and Sam Tarlton, and of course, Annique Dunning, who makes every job easier. Thank you Jeanne Fredericks and to the editors who worked on this project with me: Renee Wilmeth, Michael Koch, Christy Wagner, and Diana Francoeur, and especially Chris Jussel who always brings knowledge and enjoyment to antiques buffs. Special thanks go to my step-daughter, Erika Sexton, and to my son, Langdon Jenkins, for their drawings; to my husband, Bob Sexton, for his immeasurable encouragement and patience; and most of all, to Charlotte Sizer, who lent her many talents and wry humor to this project when they were sorely needed.

Trademarks

Part 1

Is It or Isn't It Antique?

You need a new chest of drawers. You want an antique.

But you just heard about someone who plunked down thousands of dollars for an antique chest, only later to discover that, well, the drawers were antique but the pulls had been replaced. Then the top was old, but only about 60 or 70 years old. And the feet, it turns out, were brand new. In reality, that "antique" chest was a piece made up of composite parts, some old, some middle-aged, some new. It was anything but a true antique worth thousands.

What should you do? Abandon your dreams?

But wait! Week after week on The Antiques Roadshow *you've watched amazed owners learn that great-granny's favorite teacup really belongs in a museum, and that the silver candlesticks picked up at a yard sale for $2 are worth $2,000. Could you be that lucky?*

It's said that luck comes to the prepared mind. That's what these pages do—prepare you to find the piece of your dreams and avoid the wannabe antique.

So, put your fears aside and let's go antiquing!

Age Before Beauty

Say "antique," and just as sure as night follows day, everyone thinks "old." After all, age is what distinguishes the piece you lust after from that brand-spanking-new piece—be it china, silver, furniture, or a painting—that you can buy in triplicate off the showroom floor.

Of course age is *not* the only thing you should consider when buying an antique. Condition, quality, and design are extremely important, and we'll learn about those as we go along. But first and foremost, remember that this is one time when older really is better.

When Age Matters

Now that we're living in the second millennium, knowing exactly how old an antique is before buying it has become more important than ever before. That's because there's nothing new under the sun, and modern technology has made it very easy to create new things that look deceptively old.

To further complicate matters, the word *antique* has come to mean different things to different people. The question is, how old does something have to be to qualify as an antique?

Time and again when you're antiquing, you'll find that the people you talk to use three basic definitions. The problem arises when the person you're talking to is using one definition and you're using another. Misunderstanding may be the result.

What the Connoisseur Knows

Let's begin with the oldest of the old.

When antiques connoisseurs talk about antiques, they're referring to old, handmade—not manufactured—objects. More specifically, they refer to objects that predate the Industrial Revolution, a period that brought about sweeping changes in both the New and the Old Worlds and eventually led to the gradual decline of the individual workshop.

By about 1820 the Industrial Revolution, with its mass-production manufacturing and rapid transportation, had taken hold in Europe and America. Of course, furniture makers all over the world didn't suddenly stop making chairs by hand on December 31, 1819; nor did all the silversmiths throw out their hand tools. The demise of hand craftsmanship occurred gradually rather than on an exact date. That's why connoisseurs use broad *benchmark* dates—1820, 1830, or even 1840—to toll the death knell of antiques.

The famous Hitchcock chair: The product of nineteenth-century technology.

The Time-Honored Legacy of Craftsmanship

The Industrial Revolution certainly didn't bring an end to the making of fine and beautiful things after the 1820s, 1830s, or 1840s. It also didn't preclude paying a king's ransom at auction for some objects that date to 1875 or even 1955. What the connoisseur's definition of antiques does is to give credit to individual craftsmanship, which began dying out when manufacturing companies began taking over.

Legally Speaking

But wait, you say. Does the connoisseur's definition of an antique mean that the object had to have been made before 1840 to be a real antique? Not at all, legally speaking.

The legal definition of an antique states that to be an antique, the object has to be 100 years old. This legal definition is the second definition you need to know—especially if you're trying to bring something you've purchased abroad into the United States without paying customs duty on it.

AntiqClue

In 1825 Lambert Hitchcock began cutting and processing chair parts on the first floor of his factory. On the second floor, the parts were glued together, dried, and then finished, painted, and decorated. Hitchcock turned out some 15,000 chairs per year.

AntiqInfo

Think about it. It took about 80 years (1760s–1840s) for the Industrial Revolution to change the world from horse-drawn carriages to steamboats and railroads; and change came slowly, one invention at a time. That was more than two centuries ago. Little wonder that handcrafted antiques are so highly treasured today.

AntiqLingo

Antique: Definition No. 2: Legally, according to U.S. Customs, an antique must have been made "prior to 100 years before the date of entry."

AntiqInfo

In this book, when you see the word "antique," know that it is referring to the 100-year "legal" definition.

Before You Buy

Most antiques wear their age well, even proudly. But an antique in poor condition and of inferior design, made from cheap materials and put together with shoddy craftsmanship, comes up short—especially when it comes to value.

Reeling in the Years

The legal definition of an antique is generally accepted by the public. However, this definition gives no consideration to the quality, style, and condition, to say nothing of the craftsmanship, of a piece. The connoisseur justly complains that this definition, if used as a hard-and-fast rule, permits anything that is 100 years old to be given the hallowed title "antique." However, here is where your discrimination as an antiques collector and buyer comes into play: Stuff is still stuff even if it's antique stuff!

What a Difference a Year Makes

Remember that the 100-year rule is a "sliding" rule. Under this legal definition, a 99-year-old piece that is snubbed by the antiques collector in November will magically become a desirable, hallowed "antique" at the stroke of midnight on December 31. Still, the legal definition of what makes an antique an antique is the one you'll most likely encounter, and you can't go wrong using it. The courts will back you up, even if the connoisseur disagrees.

Nevertheless, as you continue to read these pages, you'll discover that quality, style, condition, and craftsmanship really are important—always, even when a piece barely makes the cut at 101 years old. You see, it's the whole package, not age alone, that makes an antique valuable or valueless.

The Grandmother Theory

To the dismay of connoisseurs, customs officers, and even lawyers, another definition of antiques has stealthily crept into our vocabularies. Blame it on the Space Age, real-time stock trades, or just longevity, but the Grandmother Theory of Antiques is alive and well.

This theory claims that anything old enough to have been around since your grandmother was a little girl is "antique." That definition may be fine for young folks, but some young (and old) grandmothers don't like it one bit. Since when does grandmotherhood confer antique status on one's possessions?

Like Good Wine, Objects Must Age

Antiques are expected to have something special about them—something that sets them apart from the rest of the pack. That can be rarity, quality, style, or history. But unless these objects have been around long enough to age gracefully, they are just that—objects.

Where does all this clutter go? Up in the attic, down in the cellar, or out on the curb for garbage pickup. And that's when things become "stuff."

On the other hand, give that stuff sufficient time and, like good wine, it becomes treasured and saved because it's special.

So beware the next time someone tells you: "It's got to be valuable because it's an antique. My granny bought it when she was a girl." Be suspicious. Do a little quick math. Unless that person's granny bought the piece over 100 years ago, which would probably mean granny's dead by now, the numbers just aren't there.

Collectibles vs. Antiques

Okay. You're getting it down. You know the connoisseur's definition of an antique. You know the legal definition of an antique. You know to look with suspicion on the Grandmother Theory. Now enter a word you hear a lot these days: *collectible*. Though collectibles are fun to collect and they have their own market and following, be forewarned. To the antique lover, these new kids just don't fit the bill.

Too Soon

As any antiques buff will tell you, the first problem with collectibles is age—they're just too young. The collectibles craze that's so popular today began for real in the 1960s with things like Coca-Cola trays, Jim Beam bottles, and Mickey Mouse watches—all just two or three generations (not centuries) old, and many too young even to qualify for the Grandmother Theory.

But age, or lack of it, isn't the only problem antiquers have with collectibles.

AntiqLingo

Antique: Definition No. 3: An antique is anything that belonged to your grandmother. *Don't bank on it.*

AntiqClue

The big push in collectibles began in the 1960s—partly because there weren't enough real antiques for all the wannabe collectors. What you learned in Economics 101 about supply and demand is as applicable to objects as it is to stocks and bonds. Conclusion: There are fewer antiques than collectibles. Go for the long term.

Collectibles: the new kid on the block.

Too Many

Collectibles were born in factories, not workshops. They rolled off assembly lines. Sometimes human hands never touched them except to pack them off to the retailer. In a word, from the get-go, collectibles were mass-produced for a mass market.

Hold on. The same thing can be said about some objects made at the end of the nineteenth century, objects that are hoarded by today's serious collectors of antiques (legally speaking). What's the difference? Age and plentifulness.

First, even if those nineteenth-century pieces were manufactured, they have lived past the golden-century milestone. Second, over the years, many of the original number of those objects have been lost to breakage, accidents, and the garbage dump. This means that the few remaining pieces are now hard to find. And, as you'll quickly learn, a big motivator in antique collecting is the thrill of the hunt!

AntiqLingo

A **collectible** is less than 100 years old, was mass-manufactured, and was inexpensive when it was originally produced.

Too Cheap

Then there's the price factor. The items we term collectibles—such as baseball cards, Barbie dolls, and that early collectible staple, Depression glass—were all cheap when they were first made. That's one reason why so many of them were produced. The man on the street could afford them. So now you've added a third criterion to the definition. The collectible is distinguished from the antique by age, plentifulness, and original cost.

Interestingly, by the 1970s, entire books dedicated to individual categories of collectibles were being published. This added a certain prestige to their status.

Look, eventually, some of today's collectibles undoubtedly will make the antiques shortlist. But they'll have to wait their turn.

The Least You Need to Know

➤ When you see an item labeled "antique," find out its exact age.

➤ Craftsmanship is important to antiques connoisseurs.

➤ In the life of objects, 100 years is a major milestone.

➤ Ultimately, there is more to an antique than just age.

➤ Collectibles are not antiques.

Chapter 2

Antiques.
Period.

> ## In This Chapter
>
> ➤ Learn how to speak AntiqLingo with the big boys
>
> ➤ Discover why savvy collectors seek period antiques
>
> ➤ Get a grip on what age—real age—has to do with value
>
> ➤ Wake up to the fact that fakes are all around us

Years ago (we antiques buffs love to talk about the past), a delightful and very sharp 90-year-old woman who had been in the trade for some 60+ years said to me, "When you're interested in antiques, you can learn something new every day." I shrugged off the comment at the time. But now that I'm a lot older (but not yet a legal antique, though I am a grandmother), I know she was right.

Take the word *antique*. You've already learned that "antique" can mean different things to different people. As if this weren't confusing enough, you may have noticed that the pros often speak of "period antiques." If you didn't know what they were talking about, never fear. You're going to learn something new today.

In fact, in just a few minutes you're going to be on your way to talking the lingo like a pro. You may even be mistaken for a connoisseur. Remember, perception is everything.

There's Nothing Like the Real Thing

The distinguishing characteristic of antiques is that they've been around for a long time. And, over the years, decades, and centuries, the old saying, "imitation is the best form of flattery," has been alive and well.

So how do you distinguish between a piece that was made hundreds of years ago and one that was made last year to look like the really, really old one?

Keep in mind, it doesn't matter whether you're talking about mahogany chair, a sterling silver fork, or a bone china bowl—all things that have been copied over the years. Throughout these pages, particularly in Chapter 18, "Chipping the Old Block, or the Chip Wood?" we'll look at each specific category of antiques to learn how to tell a fake, an altered piece, or a reproduction from the real thing. First, however, let's learn an important bit of AntiqLingo.

Understanding the Oldie Goldie

Take for example that popular furniture form, the Queen Anne chair. Today, we call this chair a "Queen Anne" chair because the style was popular almost four centuries ago during the reign of Queen Anne, from 1702 to 1714. (Don't worry if you don't know the dates of the English monarchs. This is not a history test. You can even cheat a little and use the chart in Appendix A, "A Guide to Furniture Periods and Styles.")

Now follow along closely.

Though the Queen Anne chair originated in the early 1700s, it is a popular antique today.

Limiting Circumstances

Obviously, on the day Queen Anne died, Queen Anne furniture didn't suddenly become "old fashioned" and go out of style. One of the main reasons was that things were made by hand, not machine, and therefore couldn't be easily and quickly replaced.

Consider also that Englishmen were moving to America at this time. Once these pioneers cut down some forestland, built a home, and started making a little money, they wanted chairs like the ones they had left behind in England. Enterprising local craftsmen soon began producing Queen Anne chairs that looked as much as possible like the ones found in England.

Remember, these were the early years of the eighteenth century, say 1710. By today's standards, transportation and communication moved at a snail's pace. So when a new style came along, it took a long time to travel from England to the Colonies (which were a little backward anyway). This meant that "new" styles came later to America and lasted longer than they did in England or Europe.

Given this short history lesson, we have the following visual result:

(Left) English Queen Anne chair made sometime between 1720 and 1730; (right) American Queen Anne chair made sometime between 1750 and 1760

13

What's in a Name?

Jump ahead some four centuries to the present. There is one magic word that identifies the proper age of a really old piece—in this instance, eighteenth-century chairs. That one word will also distinguish a true, original piece from later copies that may look like the genuine one.

AntiqLingo

Period is the term used in the antiques world to denote that a piece was made during the original time frame of the design.

AntiqLingo

Circa (also written as **ca.** or **c.**) is a term liberally sprinkled about in AntiqLingo. It means "approximate date," as in: The teapot was made circa 1830. When "circa" is used to cover a series of years, the numbers following are usually given in round numbers, or in multiples of fives, for example, "circa 1780 to 1785," or "circa 1790 to 1800." You will seldom see a date like "circa 1782 to 1784."

The magic word is *period*.

Thus, when an antique of whatever sort is called "a period piece," the piece can be dated to the period that it represents—like the two chairs illustrated in the previous figure, both of which, in a shop or an auction catalogue, would properly be referred to as "Queen Anne period chairs."

A Fading Beauty That Just Misses

Life and fashions change and so must your AntiqLingo.

Back in England, a new monarch came to the throne in 1714—George I. On both sides of the ocean, King George's reign inaugurated a new style of furniture called Chippendale. Appearing in England around 1750, Chippendale didn't reach America until about 1760.

In the Colonies, Queen Anne period chairs were slowly fading from the scene. However, let's suppose that in the Philadelphia home of the Jones family, their Queen Anne chair was still in use. In say, 1795, the Joneses' chair wasn't a prized antique but rather a piece of, well, … used furniture.

Time Makes the Heart Grow Fonder

Over time, that out-of-date, old chair took on a special meaning. After all, it was a family piece. Let's say that in 1815 John Jones inherited the chair (which was now 65 years old), but his brother Sam really wanted it. Sam asked the local cabinetmaker to duplicate the chair. He did.

A Chair by Any Other Name ...

Now the problem is, what do people in the twenty-first century call this 1815 chair made in the Queen Anne style?

It certainly can't be called a Queen Anne *period* chair. That design faded out around 1750. In 1815, or over a half century later, the design that was all the rage was what today is called Federal, or Hepplewhite. (Identification of all the styles is found in the furniture section.) Antiques experts refer to this later-made chair as an "antique Queen Anne chair, *circa* 1815." The reason the date is given as part of the chair's identification is to give proper credit to its age and craftsmanship.

Another way to correctly identify this 1815 chair would be to call it "an antique, but *out-of-period*, Queen Anne chair." This would explain that although the chair is not a mass-made reproduction, it's not a 1750 Queen Anne period chair either.

Some Knockoffs Are, Legally Speaking, Antiques

Back in 1815 not many copies of Queen Anne chairs were being made, except in some special cases—like the chair owned by the Jones family.

However, it's human nature to long for "the good old days" after enough time has passed, just as Sam Jones did back in 1815. When people look to the past, designs from an earlier time start looking pretty good. Good enough to copy.

And copy they did at the end of the nineteenth century. They copied Queen Anne, Chippendale, Hepplewhite, Sheraton, and even the relatively new (back then) Empire designs.

AntiqLingo

Out-of-period is the term used in the antiques world to denote a piece that is an antique but was made several years *after* the original time frame of the design had passed. The term can be considered an exalted synonym for "style," as in the "Queen Anne style."

AntiqInfo

By the late 1870s and 1880s, an entire set of living room, dining room, or bedroom furniture could be made in less time than it had taken an eighteenth-century craftsman to make just *one piece* of furniture by hand. The same thing can be said about most china, pottery, silver, and bric-a-brac.

By the 1870s and 1880s, the new machines of the Industrial Revolution had made the job of copying period pieces quicker and easier. Things "new" were suddenly looking like things "old." The problem is that *today* many of the copies that were made in the late nineteenth century are, yes, over 100 years old! Which means, of course, that they're antiques.

AntiqLingo

Style is the term used in the antiques world to denote a piece made several years after the original time frame of the design had passed. "Style" is the everyday word for "out-of-period."

In describing these later-made pieces, it is very important *not* to identify them as period pieces. Instead, use the word *style,* as shown in the next figure.

When the correct shorthand (style) is used to describe the chair on the right, and the date is included (ca. 1890), the knowledgeable antiquer knows that this piece meets the legal definition of "antique" but is not a period antique.

Why go to all this trouble? The difference in age—whether a piece is a "period" piece or a "style" piece—can mean a difference of hundreds, even thousands, of dollars.

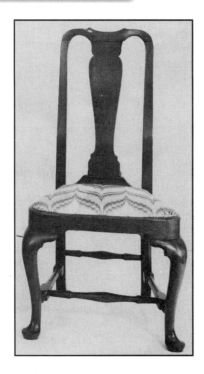

(Left) American Queen Anne period chair, circa 1750 to 1760; (right) American Queen Anne–style chair, circa 1890.

Beware the Clones

This chapter began by talking about imitation being the greatest form of flattery. In literally every category of antiques, copies have been made. Some are acknowledged as copies or reproductions, and even marked that way. Others are out-and-out fakes and frauds. How to identify these problem pieces will be discussed later in this book under each category. But as you start your antiquing adventures, you need to know that there are differences among these impostors.

AntiqInfo

America's 1876 Centennial introduced the old designs to the public again. Suddenly, everything "Colonial" became popular and copies of the old were made. Soon these copies had cornered a large part of the furniture market.

The company's markings are a clear indication that this is a faithful copy of an earlier piece.

Enter the Repro Man

The most frequently encountered antique "look-alike" is the *reproduction*—a copy that is of recent manufacture (not to be confused with the much older, "style" pieces just discussed). But just as there are "antiques" and "antiques," there are good and bad classifications of "reproduction."

In Good Faith

Let's begin with the good reproduction—the copy intended to look like the original piece and actually based on the original, period design. In other words, let's begin with the *faithful reproduction.*

These days, faithful copies are turned out by the truckloads in furniture factories, *and* they are also

AntiqClue

When talking about a particular piece that was made out-of-period, but is a faithful copy of an earlier style and has passed the magical century mark, casually mention its date. "How much are you asking for the late-nineteenth-century Queen Anne–style chair?" Mentioning the date shows everyone that you know what you're talking about.

made by individual craftsmen using the same techniques and materials as those of the original artisans.

The Not-So-Faithful Copy

Not all copies are faithful copies, however. Stores, shops, and auction sales are full of copies that have taken great liberties—extreme liberties—with the original antique designs. These pieces stand out like a sore thumb to the knowledgeable antiquer, and often even to the novice. You'll learn more about these pieces in the specialty chapters that follow, but to get you going, look at the following figure of a poorly designed circa-1920 reproduction of a Queen Anne chair. Then compare this "Queen Anne" chair with the other Queen Anne chairs I've shown you, and you get the picture.

The Great Pretenders

You're starting to get the hang of the traps that await the uninformed antiques treasure hunter. Like every other area of life, the antiques world has its share of dishonest masqueraders: the con artists who sell con pieces.

AntiqLingo

A **reproduction** is an honest, recently made piece that has been copied from an earlier design and that was never intended to deceive the public into thinking it was an antique. A **faithful copy** is one that follows the original design line for line, inch for inch, material for material, decoration for decoration. These pieces are generally of fine quality and hold their value through the years.

This reproduction is a poor excuse for a Queen Anne chair.

Unlike roses, which, we are told, would smell as sweet by any other name, these fake or fraudulent antiques stink. To begin with, once they are discovered, they lose their value.

Money is, of course, the reason that fakes are made. There is big money to be made in fake antiques, and fakes exist in every category. Further, they've been around for a long, long time. As a beginner in the wonderful world of antiques, you need to realize that lots of fakes were made at the turn of the twentieth century, when collecting antiques became a fashionable, interesting, and profitable pastime.

AntiqLingo

A **fake** or a **fraud** is a piece made with the specific intent to deceive the purchaser.

For the Lion-Hearted and the Lamb-Hearted

One of the most often-used phrases in the antiques world is "caveat emptor," which means let the buyer beware. With so many antiques, reproductions, and fakes lurking around every corner, you now know why this phrase is relevant. Sometimes it's even used to frighten off the faint of heart. Not here.

In this book, the message is *let the nonreader beware.*

These pages are written to show you where to look and what to look for so that *you* can be the one to distinguish the genuine antique and the period antique from the fake or the faithful (or faithless) reproduction.

Think about it this way. No one is born with an antiques gene. If I can learn it, you can learn it.

Read on!

AntiqInfo

Even the experts have been tricked by charlatans. In the early twentieth century, when Henry Francis du Pont, founder of the Winterthur Museum, was in his collecting heyday, fake pieces of early-nineteenth-century glassware were made and carefully planted for sale.

The Least You Need to Know

➤ Serious collectors prefer period antiques.

➤ Many "legal" antiques still don't make the grade for a period piece.

➤ An object can look old, and even be old, yet not be a genuine antique.

➤ Reproductions are not fakes.

➤ Even antiques experts have made mistakes.

Chapter 3

Some Antiquing Pitfalls and How to Avoid Them

In This Chapter

➤ Learn why common sense is a good shopping companion

➤ Discover why too little learning is a dangerous thing

➤ Find out what your sales receipt should include

So here's the scene. You're getting a grip on what to expect when you go antiquing. You're ready to begin testing your wings. But once you're in the shop—or at the flea market—or at the auction about to raise your paddle—or wherever, there are still a few more factors to think about.

Some of these are part of your individual makeup. For example, a "gotta-have-it" mindset or the degree of emotion or sentiment that you bring to antiquing are factors that differ from person to person. Yet other factors, like coping with a dimly lit shop or with a dealer who knows even less than you, the novice, do, are just part of the antiquing big picture.

This chapter will make you aware of these tricky situations. How you handle them is up to you.

Hey, Good Lookin'!

You don't have to be a rocket scientist to figure out that people like pretty things. Although it's true that beauty is in the eye of the beholder—which, in AntiqLingo, translates into "one person's junk is another's treasure"—beauty alone doesn't cut it in the antiques world.

Beauty Is More Than Skin Deep

The truth is that the real guts of a genuine antique, whether a period piece or a legal antique, often lie beneath its alluring surface.

Take a beautiful, circa 1900 cloisonné vase that looks perfect on the shelf. But when you examine it and run your fingers around on the inside, you discover a serious dent on the backside.

Or how about the charming, circa 1785 cherry candlestand with the tilting top. You can already picture it in your living room. But when you tilt the top from its upright (vertical) position to its tabletop (horizontal) position, you discover that the top is warped.

Only a careful examination would have revealed the imperfection of this period Hepplewhite candlestand.

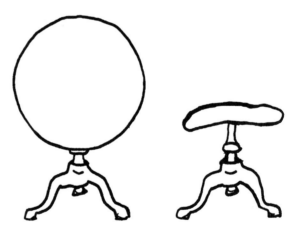

The seasoned antiques expert uses this kind of caution to evaluate a piece, no matter how beautiful it is at first glance.

Inside, Outside, Upside Down

The preceding cautionary tales are why the first rule, the one that every antiques collector needs to remember, is one you learned as a kid reading Dr. Seuss books. Look "inside, outside, upside down" before you buy. You'll learn where to look and what to look for in Part 4, "Getting Down to Brass Tacks."

Dark Corners

Back in the old days, before fluorescent-lighted antiques malls and Internet shopping, everyone's favorite antique haunts were dark and dingy hole-in-the-wall shops—the dustier the better.

Sure there were treasures to be uncovered, but with little light shed on the silver coffee pot or the wicker chair, many a dollar was plunked down for damaged, or less than perfect, merchandise.

Seeing the Light of Day

Even today, it's not a bad idea to take along a pocket flashlight or, if you're a serious porcelain collector, a trusty black light. All sorts of unexpected nicks, repairs, alterations, and even out-and-out replacements show up when you take the time to give a piece a thorough once-over.

You might even be pleasantly surprised and find a magical maker's mark or signature that you'd never have uncovered without taking the time to look carefully.

AntiqClue

Common sense has more to do with successful antique collecting than you might imagine. Caution is always advised. When passion is ready to overtake you, say to yourself, "Be still my heart." Then go about your job methodically, but always hoping for the best.

The Gotta-Have-It Mindset

The beginning antiquer often falls into another pit, one best described as the "gotta-have-it" mindset. This is quite different from the burning passion that the seasoned collector feels upon successfully locating the object of his or her quest.

The difference is that the beginner often wants the piece simply because he or she has "never seen another like it." This thought is usually followed by another: "I'll never find another one like it."

In contrast, the connoisseur *has* seen another one like it—exhibited in a museum, pictured in a book, or maybe even displayed at a shop or auction. The connoisseur knows whether the piece is rare or plentiful, whether to snap it up or bide his or her time until a better example comes along.

AntiqClue

Think about it. Question 1. Who's your favorite detective? Poirot, Holmes, Magnum, Jessica Fletcher, Simon Templar, James Bond? The guys on *NYPD Blue?* Question 2. What puts them ahead of the competition? *They see things other people miss.* Make it your goal to become a detective of the decorative arts.

Look Before You Leap

So if you, the beginner, find yourself champing at the bit to own something you really don't know much about, *stop!* Look before you leap.

Bide Your Time

In the meantime, be patient. Go to other antiques shops. Surf the Net. Do the research necessary to find out whether the item is …

➤ Really rare.

➤ Fairly priced.

➤ Genuinely an antique—not a copy or reproduction.

AntiqClue

Not sure whether a piece is a true antique? Look around. If the same piece shows up in lots of different places, you can be almost positive that it's a copy.

Put a Hold on It

Afraid it will get away? If you want to be sure that this piece of your dreams will be there when (and if) you come back for it, put a hold on it. That works. Most dealers will happily hold a piece for 24 hours, or longer, if you leave a deposit.

So Dear to My Heart

If there were one word I wish I could wipe out of every antiquer's vocabulary, it would be "grandmother." Now don't hang me as a heretic. Remember, I'm a granny, too. Furthermore, I've got some pretty worthless things around the house that belonged to my grannies that I wouldn't sell for a million dollars (as the saying—not the truth—goes). A few bucks, no. A million dollars, yes.

But there's a difference between hanging on to something for sentimental value and buying something at a *premium price* because it's "old and granny had one just like it."

The Cold, Hard Facts

Over the years, I've learned that when "sentimental attachment" comes into the picture, even rational people act irrationally. How often have you heard someone say, "This quilt is priceless. It can never be replaced. My Great-great-aunt Maude made it"?

The cold, hard facts are that some pieces really are special, and even unique. A hand-made quilt is a good example. When your Great-great-aunt Maude made it, she put her time, ideas, and talent into it.

However, chances are that her next-door neighbor, Jane, was also making a hand-made quilt. So was her best friend, Margaret. It's what all the girls were doing. Their mothers and grandmothers, too. In other words, there is no end to the number of handmade quilts that have been made over the years.

The art of quilting is popular in modern times, as well. Want proof of how many quilts have been made over the years? Just visit some antique shops that specialize in the "country look." And when on vacation, drop into a craft shop in any popular mountain tourist town.

A Fistful of Dollars

While you're at both places, look at the price tags on the quilts—old and new. One will be priced at $100. Another one, $10,000. Why?

When you're dealing with an antique, its value is heavily based on its age, quality, craftsmanship, condition, and design—for starters.

Moral: You can put a price on an antique, but you can't put a price tag on sentiment, so don't even try.

Ticket, Please

Speaking of price tags, they should reveal more information than just the price. After all, the merchandise in some antiques stores can range anywhere from born yesterday to a couple of centuries old, or older.

Where's the Info?

The minimum info given on any antique's price tag should include an approximate date—circa 1890, or circa 1790, for example. None of these vague "antique" labels. If a specific time frame, say 1880 to 1890, isn't given, the least you should expect is a starting-point date like "mid-nineteenth century" or "late eighteenth century."

You can then use this approximate date to open up a discussion about how old the piece might actually be.

AntiqClue

The information printed on a price tag can be a real clue as to how much the shop owner knows about the piece. When the description is as sparse as "old chair," you can bet that you probably know as much about the chair as the seller. And after you finish this book, lots more.

What Dealers Don't Tell Can Hurt Them

Sometimes, especially in mom-and-pop antique shops (where, incidentally, many treasures may await your discovery), the dealer simply doesn't know how old a piece is. That's where your expertise will keep you from getting taken. It can also make it possible for *you* to get a good deal.

What Dealers Don't Write Down Can Hurt You

Even more important than the information written on the tag is what the dealer writes down on the bill of sale (your receipt).

During this learning period, when you're not as knowledgeable as the antiques dealer (and even when you are as knowledgeable), you can protect yourself from making a bad buy by getting a complete sales receipt. To do this, ask the seller to write on the bill of sale a full description of whatever you've bought. Here again, none of this "old chair—$450" stuff.

If It's in Print, It Is

Insist on a written description that tells …

➤ The kind of chair.

➤ The age of the chair.

➤ The condition of the chair.

➤ The price of the chair.

AntiqClue

Reputable dealers will take back any item that is found to be other than what it was stated to be. This is no different from a retail store accepting a return on faulty merchandise.

This information might translate into a description such as: "Mahogany Queen Anne–style side chair, circa 1875, in good condition. $450."

With this sort of written receipt, should you later find a label on the chair that reads, "L & W Chair Company, Founded 1922," you'll be able to return the chair with the receipt and get your money back. You hope.

Added Insurance

During this learning period, before you're really positive that your own judgment can be trusted, ask the dealer whether you can return the merchandise. If the answer is no, be wary.

Knowledge—the Ultimate Tool

Ultimately, the most important tool you can take with you when you go antiquing is what you know—your knowledge. And the great thing about what you know about antiques is that it's cumulative. Right now, page by page you're gathering knowledge about antiques that you thought only other people had. And you're soon going to realize that once you know how to look at and analyze, say, a piece of furniture, you will be able to apply those same general principles to a piece of china or to a brass candlestick.

At this point you've seen how knowledge alerts you to the pitfalls that await you in the antiques world. Add a little bit more knowledge and you'll know how to avoid those very same pitfalls.

The question for you is, where do you find that knowledge? For antiques you can go to the same places you've gone to learn about other things you're interested in—books, periodicals, lectures, even the Internet.

One fact sets antiques apart from many other fields of study: The real source of information about antiques is … the objects themselves.

Know Where to Look

The secret to your antiquing success is knowing *where* to look for those telltale clues that reveal what you need to know.

For example, eighteenth-century furniture makers joined the front of a drawer to its sides by making dovetails—by hand. Later, by the mid-nineteenth century, there were machines that could cut dovetails. Once you know this information, you will instinctively open all drawers to see if the dovetails were made by hand, or by machine.

Know What to Look For

Once you know where to look, you must know *what* to look for.

It's those telltale clues that declare to the knowledgeable antiquer how old something is, what

AntiqClue

Glance around an antique shop and you'll see how many different types of antiques there are. There's no way one book can answer every question about every antique. That's why you'll find Appendix C, "What to Read," packed full of great reference books and sources where you can get the answers you're looking for.

AntiqInfo

In 1775 Dr. Samuel Johnson wrote: "Knowledge is of two kinds; we know a subject ourselves, or we know where we can find information upon it." This statement is as true today as it was then.

material it's made of, what condition it is in, what its quality is, and, in some instances, that basic question, what is it?

Yep. The antiques dealer who told me that you can learn something new every day when you're interested in antiques was right on.

The Least You Need to Know

➤ Many pitfalls await the blasé antiquer.

➤ To capture the good piece, you can't go by outward appearance alone.

➤ Savvy collectors proceed cautiously when making a purchase.

➤ Insist that your sales receipt contain a full, written description of your purchase.

➤ It may sound trite, but knowledge really is the key to getting the good buy.

Chapter 4

Quality vs. Quantity

In This Chapter

➤ Find out how materials affect value

➤ See how value depends on quality

➤ Learn what distinguishes the connoisseur from the everyday shopper

➤ Begin looking at things with a new eye

Among seasoned and successful collectors, there's a generally accepted rule that goes like this. Buy what you like. Buy what you can afford. But most important, buy the best you can afford.

What makes the best the best? Quality, not quantity.

It's Old, But ...

Without proper aging, a piece isn't an antique. It's just an old piece.

However, age doesn't automatically confer value. An old piece isn't always more desirable than a new one. Write this in concrete: A brand new piece of superior quality is preferable to an old piece of inferior quality, no matter what its age.

The Sum Is Equal to the Parts

When you look at an object, you see the lump sum—a chair, a picture, a fork, a vase. Then you begin breaking down the piece into its components: the materials, the design, the proportions, the condition, and so on.

Materials Equal Quality

Anyone who furnishes a home needs a few essential pieces of furniture, such as a table, chairs, or a bed. Other items, like a silver tea set or matching china for 12, are luxuries that, while nice to have, really aren't necessary. But sometimes these two types of items can meet. Let's use a simple table as an example of how the line can be crossed, making a necessity into a beautiful item whose quality makes it a luxury.

The year is 1815, and the Smiths need a table. The local cabinetmaker gives them some choices. He asks, "Do you want a mahogany, a cherry, or a pine table because it's going to make a big difference in the price?" The Smiths have deep pockets, so they choose mahogany.

Design Equals Quality

That's settled. Now the Smiths must decide on the design. The cabinetmaker gives them some more choices. Do they want drop leaves on the table? How about drawers?

What about proportions? How high should the table be? How wide? If the table is too wide for its height, it will look top heavy. If it is too narrow for its height, it will look spindly.

The cabinetmaker returns a week later with a basic design, and the Smiths think they are good to go. Except …

Good proportions directly affect quality.

Decoration Equals Quality

The cabinetmaker is anxious to show off his skills, and perhaps to increase the bill a little. Wouldn't the Smiths like a little inlay around the drop leaves? How about some bellflowers on the front legs? The proper amount of decoration, beautifully executed, will certainly add to the table's quality, he suggests. The Smiths agree to all his suggestions. We leave the Smiths now, happily contemplating the beautiful table they'll soon own.

It takes expert craftsmanship to produce fine decoration.

Quality Craftsmanship—the Ultimate Test

No matter the materials, no matter the design, no matter the proportions, no matter how elaborate or beautiful the decoration. Without fine craftsmanship, all has been for naught.

So, while you're looking at all these component parts, keep craftsmanship front and center. A poor craftsman can use the best material and still turn out a lousy piece. But when the best craftsman uses the best and creates the best, a masterpiece is born.

Quality Is Evergreen

The simple exercise with the Smiths, showing how the right choices affect quality, applies to all categories of antiques. You'll learn more about quality in the chapters dedicated to the different types of antiques. But this is a beginning.

Here is something else to remember. High-quality standards apply to objects no matter when they were made.

Let's say that you're in the market for an 1850 to 1860 Victorian étagère (which is a fancy word for a whatnot). When Victorian étagères were being made, the wood of choice was rosewood, although

AntiqInfo

"Some of the chairs produced by the lesser Georgian makers, or perhaps by country joiners, are positively graceless and clumsy, and it would be foolish to acquire such objects. They had better be consigned to oblivion, and the sooner the better, despite whatever claim of antiquity they may have." *The Practical Book of Period Furniture*, 1914.

some were also made of mahogany. And one that was elaborately turned was considered preferable to a plainer one. That's why the étagère shown here, was estimated to sell for as much as $12,000. You see, quality carries over from decade to decade.

A fine quality mahogany étagère, circa 1850, typical of good craftsmanship and interesting design.

(Photo courtesy of Neal Auction Company)

AntiqInfo

The Henry Francis du Pont Museum houses over 89,000 objects in 115 period rooms and three exhibition galleries. The collection includes 2,885 tables and 3,429 chairs. No wonder it is America's finest museum of the decorative arts.

Museum Quality, Fact and Myth

In your search for antiques, you'll hear one phrase used over and over again: "museum quality." This overused phrase is often misused, as well. Does a connection with a museum guarantee quality? Let's see.

The Facts

No doubt about it. Museums are filled with wonderful, sometimes priceless, antiques, and there's no better place to see the cream of the crop. Take, for example, Winterthur, the home of Henry Francis du Pont that houses literally thousands of the finest period antiques in America. Pieces in the Winterthur collection range in value from just a few dollars to literally millions of dollars for some rare pieces.

The Myths

But there are museums, and then there are museums. Very interesting and important local and regional museums can be real gems. However, their collections may fall short when it comes to *exceptional* quality. After all, most of these smaller museums depend on the generosity of local donors for their collections. That's why the comment most often heard in a small local museum is, "Oh look! Your grandmother had one just like this. I wonder what ever happened to it?"

Another way to look at the idea of museum quality is this. Museums are always buying pieces on the open market—from auction houses, shops, and even perhaps the Internet. Many pieces found in museums were once in private homes.

So what does this do to the term "museum quality?" It simply means that the term should be used carefully and advisedly and only when speaking about the truly exceptional piece.

AntiqLingo

Museum quality refers to rare and extremely valuable pieces of the finest craftsmanship that would be suitable for a major museum.

Telling the Turtle from the Mock

So far you've only been reading about quality. To get a handle on this all-important aspect of antiquing, you have to do more than just read about it. You've got to see the good and the bad— together. You've got to compare the shoddy piece with the quality one.

There's no better place to compare than at an antiques auction where you're allowed to examine every piece to your heart's content. In the meantime, keep reading, keep looking at museum pieces, keep going to antiques shops, keep surfing the Internet. But remember, there's nothing like getting up close and personal with the real thing to help you recognize the mock when it comes your way.

AntiqInfo

Of all the thousands of books written about antiques, one stands at the head of the class when it comes to understanding quality: Albert Sack's *The New Fine Points of Furniture Early American: Good, Better, Best, Superior, Masterpiece* (Crown Publishers, 1993).

The Least You Need to Know

➤ When examining antiques, think quality.

➤ Quality must be evident in every aspect of a fine piece: in its materials, design, decoration, and craftsmanship.

➤ Down through the years, quality lasts.

Chapter 5

Luck Comes to the Prepared Mind

In This Chapter

➤ Learn how rarity adds to desirability

➤ Discover why it doesn't matter whether or not George slept there

➤ Find out why you, too, should always "brake for antiques"

➤ Learn when not to follow the herd

You've heard the question as many times as I have. "How were you so lucky?" That's the question you ask the one-time winner—not the serious collector whose home looks like you wish yours did. Anybody can hit it big one time, just by chance. But it's the person who knows what to look for—and what to walk past—who hits the jackpot time and again.

You're getting closer. You're acquiring the lingo. You're learning what to look for. So, moving right along, here are a few more common-sense cautions and easy-to-remember tips to add to your list.

When Less Is Really More

One of the big differences between collectibles and true antiques can be summed up in one word: rarity.

Isn't rarity why you prefer the antique to the mass-made, easily obtainable object? You crave something different—something that won't be in every store and every home

you visit. When you think about why you like an-tiquing, isn't one reason your deep-seated hope that you're going to find a hidden treasure?

Want proof of how important rarity is in the antiques market? It's a word the major auction houses love to throw about. Rarity brings in the dollars because it sends out the message, "Buy this piece now, or never."

Everything's Relative

So how do you know whether a piece really is rare? First, listen to your common sense. It'll tell you …

➤ The older the piece, the less chance that lots of them still exist.

➤ The finer the piece, the fewer that were made originally.

➤ The more fragile the piece, the less chance that many of them have survived.

AntiqInfo

Auction houses know the power of good press. When the Neal Auction Company declared a 1718 Guillaume DeLisle map of Louisiana to be "rare," collectors fell all over themselves for a chance to own it. The top bidder happily paid $9,900 for the priv-ilege. Another lesson to be learned: Rare doesn't have to mean $1 million.

Good, better, best should often read common, hard-to-find, rare.

(Photos courtesy of Neal Auction Company)

Then do a little research: in books, on the Internet, and in shops and auction houses. Note how often the object you're looking for pops up. You'll quickly learn just how rare, and how commonplace, certain antiques are.

What the Market Can Bear

You're starting to realize that economics plays a big part in the antiques world—the same way it does in stocks and bonds and real estate. When an antique is genuinely rare, and lots of people want it, the price runs up. It's called supply and demand. Savvy collectors know this—especially when it comes to selling.

Economics can also control the way in which a collection is sold. To keep from flooding the market with too much of a good thing, a collection will sometimes be dispersed slowly, just one or a few pieces at a time.

When Birthright Matters

There's a million-dollar word that rolls off collectors' tongues—*provenance*. Lots of people have trouble pronouncing it, but they definitely know what it means: $$$$. *If* the provenance is true, that is.

Provenance is a fancy word for background or history. To many antiquers, however, it conveys a cachet that somebody famous once owned this piece or, for certain pieces, that the piece passed through the right hands.

George Washington Slept Where?

For provenance to mean big bucks, it has to be proved. To say that Robert E. Lee had tea served from your great-great grandmother's silver teapot (my mother was a Southerner), or that Ulysses S. Grant sat in your great-great grandfather's favorite chair (my father was a Yankee), isn't provenance, just a nice story. There has to be proof positive (a photograph, a diary entry, and so on).

Before You Buy

Make sure that something stated to be rare, really is. In Chapter 3, "Some Antiquing Pitfalls and How to Avoid Them," you learned about the "gotta-have-it" mindset, how people impulsively buy something because they've never seen another one. Recently, an Internet auction listed a "rare" coin-silver ladle marked "R & W Wilson." The ladle was nice. It was worth buying. But it wasn't rare.

AntiqClue

What makes a soup tureen or a large platter more expensive than a dinner plate? It's more than size. It's rarity. Fewer were made to begin with. Fewer are around today.

The Proof Is in the Object, Not the User

What does it matter, though, who may have come in contact with the teapot or the chair if they were cheaply and poorly made back in the 1850s?

The proof of a piece's value lies in its age and its quality first. Its history may be important, but the piece, itself must still be significant.

Here's another example. You have a hand-drawn Civil War map dated 1862 showing a minor scrimmage fought in Northern Virginia. Robert E. Lee fought in that scrimmage. Family myth says that the General drew the map. Sure the map has value, but without his signature, the proof just isn't there. The moral of this story? It always comes down to proof.

The Maker's Mark

While we're dropping names—Lee, Grant, Washington—let's drop a few more. What's all this talk in the antiques world about Paul Revere bowls and Thomas Chippendale chairs? What about all those stories you've heard about signed pieces?

They happen. And when they do, they make headlines because a little bit of lost history has been re-found.

When Many Heads and Hands Were Better Than One Name

Today we're more conscious of the importance of knowing the maker of a piece than our ancestors were. In the eighteenth and nineteenth centuries, craftsmen tended to work together in shops, especially in the large towns where the best craftsmen were. (Naturally, that's where they could get the most work and the most pay.)

When the shop received an order, let's say, for a chest of drawers, one craftsman might start making the frame. Another would start making the drawers—a tedious task considering that the fronts and backs were attached by hand-cut dovetails.

Supervising the project would be the master craftsman, who might, or might not, actually contribute to the making of this specific piece.

Long-Term Memory— Long Forgotten

When the piece was finished, a label (paper in the early days) would sometimes be attached. Occasionally, a piece would actually be signed. But most often, the person who signed and dated the piece would be the proud, new owner.

Once that piece has gone through several generations of owners, often passing out of a family's hands, the label is usually long gone and no one knows for certain whether the maker or the owner signed the piece.

So if you see initials, a signature, a date, or the name of a city or town scribbled somewhere on a piece of furniture, chances are it will be information left by the owner, not the maker. To find out for sure, you may need an expert to help you with the research.

In short, much of what is known about the past has been forgotten—especially when it comes to individual craftsmen who were content to pass their skills on to others and didn't leave much of a written record.

Before You Buy

When you're buying, make sure the object is worth its price. Provenance, if not proven, adds interest but not necessarily value.

AntiqClue

Warning! Fake eighteenth-century labels have been put on furniture by the unscrupulous who want to cash in on a famous name. If you find a labeled eighteenth-century furniture piece, call in the experts.

The Big Changeover, or Why Benchmark Dates Are Your Friends

By the 1840s and 1850s, furniture manufacturing companies were beginning to spring up across the country. At the same time, quicker and easier transportation made it possible to deliver those companies' goods to faraway places. (Remember the history lesson in Chapter 1, "Age Before Beauty"?) As a result, companies began putting labels on their pieces so customers would know who made them. By the 1870s and 1880s, makers' labels were the rule, not the exception.

AntiqClue

If you learn only one thing about antiquing, make sure it's this. Look for an identifying mark or label, first! Finding a label often immediately tells you if a piece is a reproduction and you need look no further.

AntiqClue

Two benchmark dates and phrases are indelibly etched in every antiquers' book of knowledge: 1891, when the name of a country begins appearing on imported objects; and 1918, when the words "made in" begin to accompany the country's name.

Other help for manufacturers and their customers was on the way, too. This time in the form of Uncle Sam.

When the Government Came to the Antiquer's Aid

Thanks to the 1890 McKinley Tariff Act, objects coming into the United States from 1891 forward must bear the name of the country where they originated.

This is good news. It means that when you turn a plate over and you read "France," you can be reasonably sure that the plate came from France and was made after 1891.

A few years later, the words "made in" were required to be added to the country's name. So when you see those additional words used with the country's name, "Made in France," the *benchmark date* to remember is 1918—the end of World War I.

That marking system is still being used today, some three quarters of a century later. Although "Made in France" on the back of a plate may tell you that the plate doesn't date from the eighteenth century, you may still wonder whether it's a 1920s plate or a 1990s one. In Chapters 22, "Coming Out of the China Closet," and 23, "The China Collector's Cabinet," you'll see how digging a little deeper can sometimes help you establish a more accurate date.

But all the news isn't good news. The bad news is that paper labels or other easily removable labels can fall off or disappear. Then the proof of age is gone with the wind. Without any identifying information left on an object, you might think that you're looking at a really old, legal antique.

(Left) The name of the country dates this plate sometime between 1891 and 1918. (Right) Add "made in" to a country's name, and the benchmark date to remember is 1918.

BERNINA

That's where familiarity with craftsmanship and knowledge of how objects were made before the twentieth century become essential to the antiquer. Does that frighten you? Don't let it. You'll read more than once the friendly reminder: If I can learn and know it, so can you.

Proof Positive, or Attributed To?

I've warned you to watch out for the overuse of "provenance" and boastful claims that a piece was made by some well-known name in the antiques world. Only when it can be *proven* that a piece was made by a particular maker does its value increase.

Sometimes a piece will be *attributed to* a maker or a workshop. This claim usually starts when a knowledgeable person identifies something about a piece—design, construction, decoration, and so on—that is reminiscent of a particular maker. With lots of research, this "attributed to" claim will either hold or fold. If the hunch is right, the payoff is big bucks.

When Homegrown Is Best

There's something else that eagle-eyed antiquers are always looking out for—pieces with local appeal. It's like a friend of mine pointed out: He watches TV to keep up with international news, but he turns on the radio to find out what's happening down the street. So antiques have both a wide, and a narrow, appeal.

For example, almost everyone, almost everywhere has liked Rose Medallion china since the Chinese began exporting it in the eighteenth and nineteenth centuries. Prowl through fine antique shops in London, Rio, or Savannah, and you'll find a piece or two of Rose Medallion. Chances are that the prices in all three places will be pretty similar, too.

But who in Rio gives a hoot about Newcomb Pottery? For that matter, who in Savannah gives a hoot about it?

What, in fact, is Newcomb Pottery?

AntiqInfo

A lot of research goes into attributions. When the Neal Auction Company attributed a circa 1880 chair to the famous Herter Brothers, they did so because the exotic woods, hairy paw feet, and bold anthemia (a classical leaf design) carving were related to chair number 39 of the Herter Brothers' catalogue and other known Herter pieces. The chair sold for $14,300.

Why It Pays to "Brake for Antiques"

Newcomb Pottery was first made in 1895 at Sophie Newcomb College in New Orleans. In its heyday, this art pottery won awards at major exhibitions. Since much Newcomb Pottery was still being made in the mid-1940s, only those pieces that are over 100 years old are true antiques. But the artistic quality of its pieces puts

Newcomb Pottery in that respected category of "art pottery," and every year more and more of its pieces become "antique."

Now, if on your trips you find a piece of Newcomb Pottery in a Goodwill Store in, say, Bangor, or Fargo, grab it. It has escaped identification, and you've found a treasure.

Sell Homegrown Back Home

But don't take your prize home to Marin, California. Do your homework. Send it straight off to New Orleans. That's where pieces of Newcomb Pottery sell for hundreds, thousands, and tens of thousands of dollars.

The lesson to be learned is simple. Antiques that can be associated with a particular geographical area have their greatest value when they go home to a captive, and knowledgeable, audience.

No one in the family had any idea that this Newcomb vase would bring $30,000 at a Neal Auction sale.

Beware Media Hype

Perhaps most important of all, though, is this advice: Beware media hype. Or, put another way: Turn off Oprah. At least if her celebrity guest is talking about antiques.

As soon as a popular star begins touting, for example, Shaker furniture or Tiffany lamps or American furniture, the media hype follows and prices soar. Oprah herself flirted with Shaker furniture. Barbra Streisand fell in love with Tiffany, and Bill Cosby even used period pieces (or copies of them) on the set of *The Cosby Show.*

Buck the Trend

To avoid contributing to the instant inflation that follows, stick to your own tastes. Follow your own heart, not someone else's. In fact, if you've bought this book because your favorite star's antique-filled house has just been featured in *Architectural Digest* or *House Beautiful,* jump to Chapter 8, "Accumulator or Collector."

The Least You Need to Know

➤ Rare items become even rarer as time goes by.

➤ Family stories and unsubstantiated claims of provenance may be fascinating, but they seldom hold water to the serious collector.

➤ There are many golden names in the world of antique furniture, but few pieces were marked by these superstars.

➤ When you're familiar with important regional antiques, you can profit from their value and perhaps save a bit of history for posterity.

Chapter 6

Right as Rain

In This Chapter

➤ Learn why acceptable condition varies from piece to piece

➤ Discover that a less-than-perfect piece can really be a great buy

➤ Start thinking about some of the choices you'll encounter

➤ Become aware that condition means more than whether or not a piece is broken

Okay, so you're only buying a plate, or a tray, or a bed—not a house. But "condition, condition, condition" is just as important to the antiquer as "location, location, location" is to the potential home buyer.

Yet, over and over again you hear the comment, "This has to be valuable. Look how old it is. Look how rare it is. Look how nice the quality is."

Yes, but if the piece is in poor condition, that takes away some of its bloom—especially if there are others of the same item that are in good, fine, or even excellent condition.

Condition, Condition, Condition

Because the general term "antique" covers such a large variety of items—everything from glass toothpick holders to wrought-iron fireplace andirons—and encompasses such a vast time frame—from time immemorial to just one hundred years ago—obviously there has to be some give-and-take when it comes down to condition.

AntiqClue

Great condition adds value to a piece that is rare to begin with.

Before You Buy

If you remember only one rule about condition, make it this one. The more damage there is to a piece, the lower its value.

A good rule to keep in mind is this. The rarer the piece, the more acceptable an imperfection.

A Nick Here, a Ding There

To see how this works, let's go to a virtual tag sale.

You've just spied a Queen Anne period silver teapot made in England in 1715. Over the years this treasure was often used by its proud owners, and invariably it received a few dents.

At some point in time, the teapot was packed away. Now, years later, here it is, waiting for you with a $500 price tag on it. (That's because there's a coat of arms engraved on the side and the tag sale conductor, even though unknowledgeable about silver, figures it's "valuable.") Luckily you have a prepared mind and know that this is a period piece. (You'll find out how you know in Chapter 19, "Heavy Metal: Understanding Silver." That's where, in the twinkling of an eye, you'll learn how to read English silver hallmarks.)

Still, the dents bother you. They shouldn't. An expert silversmith can take those out.

What you really need to be concerned about is any other damage. How do you look for that?

Thinking It Through

You ask the person in charge of the tag sale if you may fill the teapot to be sure it holds water. It does.

Next you examine the teapot carefully where the spout, the handle, and the top are joined to the body. Any repairs or evidence that these might be "younger" than the body? Nope.

You don't have all day. You've got to make a decision. Hmmm … $500. Since most Queen Anne teapots of this age and quality begin at around $5,000, this is a good deal. You decide to buy it even though its condition isn't perfect.

The Other Side of the Coin

While you're mulling over the teapot, you spy a nice-looking, medium-sized blue-and-white platter in the china cabinet. It's old—about 1860. Looks good.

But when you take it down, you see a large chunk on the front that you didn't see earlier because of the cup and saucer in front of it. The platter is marked "English Staffordshire platter. $50.00."

Should you buy it? I'd say no. You'll find another platter, priced higher, without damage. Probably in the $200 to $300 range. But you won't have to put something in front of it, and its value will hold, perhaps even go up.

AntiqClue

How much condition affects the value of a piece depends on what the piece is. Acceptable condition for a period Chippendale tea table is different from acceptable condition for a late Victorian tea table.

When Imperfect Is Good Enough

But wait. Over in the corner of the china cabinet is another nice blue-and-white piece—a plate. You know it's a Delft plate. (How? You've read Chapter 22, "Coming Out of the China Closet.") And you know that the tin glaze that makes Delft, Delft, chips easily.

Sure enough, this plate has some chips where the pottery base is showing through, but that's to be expected. Even Delft plates on exhibit in museums will sometimes have a small chip here and there along the rim. Best of all, the $35 price tag makes this $375 plate a real bargain. Certainly a far better bargain than the $50 platter.

The minor chips around the edge do not obstruct the major decoration of this early-nineteenth-century Delft platter.

The Big Picture

All in all, condition is relative. If you say, "I'll buy only pieces in perfect condition," frustration will be the result. You have to bear in mind the general guide—condition, condition, condition—and *combine* that with information you know about specific pieces and categories of antiques before deciding whether to buy or not to buy.

The Big Break

Up to this point, we've been talking about pieces that aren't in perfect condition, but they're not actually broken either. Although a broken piece can have some archival or historical value, the place for such an item is usually a museum, not your living room.

AntiqClue

Before opening your wallet for the broken piece, find out how much an unbroken one costs and how much the repairs will cost.

Making It Whole

Of course there are other times when you will want to buy something in "as is" condition, especially when you think you can have it repaired.

Remember, though, by the time you've put money into buying the broken piece and then paid to have it repaired (which can be expensive), you may have spent as much—or more—than you would have paid for the same piece in good condition. Consider, too, that the repaired piece is just that. A repaired piece.

If, on the other hand, you don't expect to *ever* find the piece in great condition, and if you can afford the repairs, and if you can live with the repaired piece (until you find the perfect one), go for it.

Leaving Things Well Enough Alone

"Are there times when you shouldn't repair a piece?" is a question often asked at antiques seminars and lectures.

Absolutely. Especially if you're on the selling end.

For this example, let's take a piece of furniture—say a nice early-nineteenth-century Pennsylvania corner cupboard that you've recently inherited. Your great-grandfather bought it in the early twentieth century from a neighbor who was moving. The dentil molding around the top left side has been missing ever since you can remember. Now you want to sell the piece. (Your taste is for more formal, English pieces.) Can you get more money for it if you get it fixed?

The chest on the left sold for considerably more than the one on the right. Why?
The one on the left had not been restored, while the one on the right had been
spiffed up.

Good Intentions Gone Bad

The local furniture guy in your area tells you he can carve the replacement molding, but he can't match the finish of this new part with the rest of the piece. "Gonna have to refinish the whole thing," he says.

Later, in Chapter 18, "Chipping the Old Block, or the Chip Wood?" you're going to learn about patina and how refinishing a piece can be the same as setting fire to thousand-dollar bills. But for now, suffice it to say that a really, really serious antique collector will not want to buy the refinished piece. That collector would rather have the corner cupboard with its old finish and a portion of the molding missing.

When Worse Is Better

In this situation, repairing and refinishing the piece will decrease its value and cost you the sale. That's why, to many an antiques aficionado, the grungy piece that proudly shows its age is the one to have. It's a simple case of worse being better— which is the same thing as saying, there are times when the better-looking piece is the worse choice. Now you know why the experienced antiques collector often walks right past a pristine piece and goes for the grimy one.

Fix It Up or Throw It Out?

Everybody knows that age takes a toll. Your overweight friend sits in a period Hepplewhite chair and breaks the back. (Hepplewhite chairs tend to have weaker backs than Queen Anne and Chippendale chairs.) Your cat breaks your grandmother's Haviland chocolate pot. You put the Imari plate too close to the edge of the shelf, and it falls off and breaks in half.

I've warned against letting sentiment rule the day when you're in a buying mood. Nonetheless, when tragedy befalls a treasured piece that you already own, well, that's different. You should still use your common sense and calculator, however, to figure out whether it is cost-effective to fix the broken item. Only you know how much your own pieces are worth to you.

Just remember, should you ever decide to sell a mended piece, a repaired and restored piece is not an investment-quality antique.

AntiqClue

When is good condition bad? When it disguises an "improvement" or, worse yet, a fake.

AntiqInfo

It's easy to skip over the important step of examining a piece to check its condition. After all, who expects a 200- or 300-year-old piece to be perfect? But a careful examination can lead you to uncover a real treasure, or an out-and-out fake, or something in-between.

Those *Other* Kinds of Condition

So far we've looked at the usual, straightforward kinds of condition you expect to encounter in any piece that's lived, not just for a few years, but perhaps through centuries. Such pieces are subject to breakage and repair. But beware, other kinds of condition lurk in the shadows of the antiques world.

Enter the Bad Guys

Over the years, many an antique has been changed—added to, altered, improved, enhanced, made more "fashionable." Oh you can use lots of fancy words, but what it comes down to, is somebody with ill-intent monkeyed with the piece along the way.

We usually associate these changes with furniture. A chest of drawers is turned into a desk. The four large bed posts on a simple Empire bed are shaped, whittled down, carved, and the bed is passed off as a delicate, highly desirable Sheraton bed. The possibilities go on and on.

Changes also occur in valuable silver pieces that can be reworked. Famous makers' hallmarks have even been cut out and "lifted" from one piece and put onto another when there was money to be gained from doing so.

A Word to the Wise

The following caveat is posted to alert you to the situation, not to frighten you: Condition is important, and when you detect something about a piece that doesn't look quite right, seek more information before you take it home. This chapter isn't the place to detail what the fraudulent craftsman can do, but I will describe these practices in Chapter 18.

The Least You Need to Know

➤ When you're thinking about buying, condition is right up there with age and quality.

➤ Condition can greatly affect value.

➤ What is acceptable condition in one piece may not be in another.

➤ Condition covers a whole realm of situations including alterations and faking.

➤ If you're buying a piece, it's worth your time to check condition carefully.

Chapter 7

The Summing Up: Objects Do Not Lie

In This Chapter

➤ Learn what makes an antique a perfect 10

➤ Discover where to find comparable prices

➤ Find out why you can't compare antiques to stocks

➤ Get ready to make an honest steal

Learning about antiques is really so easy. The reason more people don't do it is that all the highfalutin, multisyllabic, and often foreign words used to discuss them are intimidating. At least that's what I've concluded.

Add to that the fact that antiques are o-l-d. Weren't you always taught that things from the far past should be revered?

In this kind of elitist environment, many people are a little afraid to step into the antiques world. The pretty table that they yearned to own or the ivory figurine that was absolutely fascinating slips into the realm of the unobtainable. An invisible, impenetrable shield puts these objects seemingly out of reach. The truth is that a little caution and common sense will go a long way toward making you an assured antiques collector and buyer.

You already know more than most folks. This chapter is all about wrapping up your new-found knowledge into a usable package.

The Best Formula

You now have a nodding acquaintance with the factors that antiques experts take into consideration every time they consider a piece: age, craftsmanship, design, condition, rarity, and, most of all, quality. Think of these as the component parts that make up the whole. If any of these is missing, or only partly there, the piece will fall short of getting a 10 or an A+.

AntiqClue

Repeat after me. Age + Quality + Rarity + Condition = Value.

AntiqInfo

Price guides are just that—guides. Antique experts who keep up with the market don't need to check a price guide. They know. But most people can get helpful information from these well-researched annual price reports: *Kovels' Antiques and Collectibles Price List, Miller's Antiques Price Guide,* and *Antique Trader's Antiques & Collectibles Price Guide.*

You've also learned that a dash of provenance, regional appeal, and even sentiment can be part of the big picture.

Extenuating circumstances may also play a part in your decision to buy a piece or pass it up. Those can include practicality, space, and priorities. But most important is usually price. How much something costs.

Money on Your Mind

Money is often the determining factor in a decision to buy a piece. This is when you need to remind yourself that the pieces that hold their value get high points for, yes, repeat after me, age, quality, rarity, and condition. The money you pay for a top piece is not wasted because the piece will hold its value over time.

That's what makes the rule I gave in Chapter 4, "Quality vs. Quantity," so important. *Buy what you like. Buy what you can afford. But buy the best you can afford.*

Getting Your Money's Worth

Best is the key word here.

When you let doubtful stories of provenance, the merchant's sales pitch, or your own sentiment get in the way, this is when you fall for the inferior piece at an inflated price.

How do you know what you ought to pay for something? Look before you buy. Look where? At the pieces that are for sale in antique shops. In price guides. In auction catalogues. On the Internet.

Comparison Shopping

Comparison shopping is one of the many fun aspects of antiquing. You get to go shopping, see other items, and look into various markets. Who knows, you may find an object that you like better than the one you're researching.

This Isn't Wall Street, Boys and Girls

The whole antiquing process is quite different from checking a stock price on the Internet or on CNBC. First, every common share of AOL or Coca-Cola or GM is identical to every other common share of that stock. They all look alike. They all represent the same value at any given frozen moment. Further, the difference between the asking price and the latest bid falls within a narrow margin—usually anywhere from a $1/16$-point to a 5-point spread. (The 10- or 20-point spread can happen, but it isn't commonplace.)

Antiques, though, are altogether different. Take candlesticks. To begin with, all candlesticks are not alike. They don't look alike. They differ in age, quality, material, and condition.

Further, the cost spread you encounter for any given antique can run the gamut. Let's look at a pair of brass candlesticks for this example. A pair of nineteenth-century, brass beehive-motif, eight-inch-tall candlesticks will probably cost somewhere between $150 and $350. Now that's a big spread.

AntiqClue

Comparison shopping is not a waste of time, and it's fun, too. What could be better news? Even the most prudent and experienced antiques collectors love to shop till they drop.

These coin silver spoons are almost identical in every way—age, quality, rarity, condition, even size. But there's a $75 difference in their price. Why the difference? It's the market they're in.

(Photos courtesy of the North Carolina State Archives)

Passion Says Buy but Prudence Advises Caution

How do you get your money's worth? The secret is to do your homework ahead of time. You want to buy a pair of brass candlesticks? Hit the books before you hit the pavement.

But what if while you're looking for a great pair of andirons, you discover a beautiful pair of candlesticks. You haven't a clue whether the price is right. These are the options:

➤ Put them on hold.

➤ Take them home on approval.

➤ Take your chances that they'll be there when you come back.

➤ Go ahead and buy them anyway.

While you're deciding what to do, think about it this way. You wouldn't buy the first stock you ran across would you?

The Price Is Right

Ultimately, the choice is yours. But when getting a good buy is important to you, remember, it isn't a good deal unless the price is right. And knowing when the price is right comes from understanding the current market for the piece you're considering.

Waiting for Godot

Everyone knows that you can't sit on a stock certificate or eat off a CD. Trying to compare antiques and investments falls into the old apple-and-oranges fallacy.

We like our stocks and bonds because they create real, tangible cash money. We love our antiques because they are beautiful, full of history, and speak to us of craftsmanship and aesthetics.

Yep. There are lots of differences between stocks and antiques. But let's talk cold, hard facts. So forget beauty, history, craftsmanship, and aesthetics.

If, heaven forbid, you should ever need—or just want—to sell a piece that you've bought, you may not be able to sell it quickly. The stock market's built-in buyer-seller mechanism doesn't exist in the antiques market. Sometimes an antique sits in a shop for months, even years, before someone who wants, loves, and needs it comes along. Which, of course, is why auctions are a good option when you need to close a deal quickly.

When a Deal Is Too Good to Be True ...

You know how the story ends: it probably is.

If you don't know values before you shop, then you won't know whether you're paying a fair price—especially if you can be bowled over by an impressive sales pitch. Which leads me to a good example of how the unknowing antiquer can be misled when some impressive numbers are thrown around. It happened this way in a shop out in the western reaches of Virginia ...

Roped Off

The ropes around the sofa caught my eye first. They sent the message that the sofa in question either was about to collapse or was terribly valuable. Either way, the message was the same—don't even think about sitting on it.

Then I noticed that prominently displayed on the sofa's seat cushion was an auction catalogue from Sotheby's or Christie's showing another sofa that bore some, but not much, resemblance to this sofa. The sofa shown in the catalogue had sold for around $25,000. On the sofa behind the ropes was a price tag of $2,500.

The Bigger Sucker Theory

Seeing he had a potential "live one," the shop owner rushed over and began his spiel. "Lady, that sofa is just like the one that sold in New York for $25,000. But I got this one out of a house where the people were moving and since I didn't have to pay much for it, I can let it go for $2,500."

Mistaken identification is nothing new in antiques. When this eighteenth-century Philadelphia tea table became the first American antique to sell for $1 million at Christie's in 1986, Christie's American furniture department created a rogues' gallery of look-alikes that were later productions sent in by hopeful owners.

Hold Everything

At this point, I ask you, What's wrong with this picture—even if you haven't seen the two sofas?

First, what difference does it make how much he paid for the sofa if it's worth $25,000?

Second, if the sofa really is worth $25,000, how much would it cost to transport it approximately 450 miles to New York City and sell it there? And why isn't the dealer taking it there?

Before You Buy

When getting ready to close a deal, use your common sense and do the math.

Third, even after the auction house's commission, insurance, and advertising costs are subtracted from the $25,000 that the sofa is supposedly worth, how much is left? A lot. Even taking into account inflated New York prices, there is too much of price difference between the one in New York and the one here in Virginia.

I never found out whether the dealer really thought he had a period sofa or not, but it doesn't matter. A sofa worth $25,000 that is selling for $2,500 just doesn't add up.

So Far, So Bad

Of course, the problem lies in the sofa itself. It only vaguely resembled the sofa that had sold for $25,000. That one was a period piece, in excellent condition, of fine craftsmanship and great quality. Its value was $25,000. How do I know? The underbidder proved it—but more about that in Chapter 13, "Playing for Keeps."

The $2,500 sofa, on the other hand, was a 1940s reproduction of mediocre quality when it rolled off the assembly line. Over the years it had been used and abused, and at this point in its history was little more than a piece of secondhand furniture. It just happened to be of similar shape and design to the period piece. *Its* value? Probably what the fellow paid for it—$700 to $900, not $2,500.

How do I know that? This was a case where experience was the teacher. I have seen so many 1940s reproductions like this sofa that I immediately recognized what it was. You'll reach this point yourself—sooner that you might imagine. But back to the question, Why isn't that sofa worth $2,500, to say nothing of $25,000?

The answer is age, quality, rarity, quality, condition, and craftsmanship. Now you understand why I say, objects do not lie.

Why did the dealer try to sell this wannabe sofa for $2,500? Could it be that he was betting that a buyer would be blinded by the "evidence" in the catalogue? Was this a case of the Emperor's new clothes? Or was the dealer just not in-the-know?

It doesn't matter. What does matter is that *you* know.

Getting the Honest Steal

At times, though, the shoe is on the other foot, and you can be the one who gets the honest steal. It happens everyday.

A Chinese Export plate is bought for $5 at a yard sale and is sold to a dealer for $250. A simple side chair is picked up for $25 and at auction brings $750. A customer plunks down $250 for a Victorian silver-plated tray in an antique shop and sells it to a collector for $1,500.

The question is, How do you make it happen? It's a two-step process. You have to know the object. You have to know the market.

AntiqClue

When it comes to antiques, never settle for the "it looks like a duck, it must be a duck" mentality. Outward appearances are only part of the equation.

Don't Forget the Middleman

Even if you are sorting through and picking out the cream of the crop to make a profit, always remember that the antiques dealer is a merchant. To stay in business he or she has to make a profit. At the end of the month, the dealer must be able to pay the bills and have enough profit left over to buy fresh merchandise.

So when the middleman tells you, "This is the best I can do," respect his or her statement. That's part of knowing the market, too.

AntiqClue

In today's busy world, you may not have lots of shopping time. In that case, getting a "steal" isn't your main motive. Getting the object for your collection at a fair price is.

The Least You Need to Know

➤ To get the best piece, you've got to keep your wits about you.

➤ Considering just one aspect of an antique—its age, quality, rarity, or condition—isn't enough.

➤ Good news! Comparison shopping is fun and advisable.

➤ The antiques dealer deserves an honest profit.

Part 2

The Thrill of the Chase

Ask seasoned antiquers what makes them tick, and in a weak moment they'll confess: the thrill of the chase.

There's nothing like it. You've set your sights, or maybe you're just out for an afternoon's adventure. Your pockets are full, or maybe you just have a little leftover at the end of the month. You're on your way to the New York Armory Show, the crème de la crème of antique shows, or maybe you're just going to try potluck in Des Moines. Regardless ... some treasure awaits you at the end of the chase.

Chapter 8

Accumulator or Collector

In This Chapter

➤ Discover how to find out what you really like

➤ Learn some secrets of seasoned, successful antiques collectors

➤ Make wish lists to dream about

You're ready to mount up and begin the chase. After all, look how much you've learned up to this point. But *what* are you going to buy and, equally important, *why* are you going to buy these things? The answers to these questions can distinguish the accumulator who buys higgledy-piggledy from the focused collector.

Accumulating lots of things can be fun, but it can also be expensive and eventually you may run out of space. That's why, if you are just getting interested in antiques, taking the time to define your interests and tastes can save you money and time in the long run. As the old saying goes, "Buy in haste; repent in leisure."

The Taste Test

Faced with the choice of accumulating or collecting, try asking yourself a few questions before you leave home.

Let's begin with your reasons for beginning the search:

1. Do you want to furnish your home or apartment with antiques?

2. Do you want to create a stylish "look"?

3. Do you want to build a large collection?

4. Do you want to be surrounded by a few fine investment pieces?

Since you're a novice at the game (you're no longer a complete idiot, mind you), how you answer those questions will help you more than you know.

Fessing Up

If you skirted questions 1 and 4 but answered a resounding yes to questions 2 and 3, you'll be tempted to buy lots of things on the spur of the moment.

On the other hand, if you said yes to 1 and 4 but skipped over 2 and 3, then chances are you'll proceed cautiously when you make a purchase.

Now get this straight. There's no right or wrong answer to the quiz. It's just a way of probing more deeply into why you're interested in antiques.

Don't feel guilty if you find you're in the spur-of-the-moment category. Even I occasionally throw all caution to the wind when I come upon a piece that speaks to me. It happened just the other day when I found a wonderful pair of chinoiserie knife boxes. Were they period pieces? I didn't care. Were they even antique? Probably not. Did I want them? Yes! Could I afford them? No. Am I still dreaming about them? You bet.

Figuring Out Why You Like What You Like

Part of your development as an antiques aficionado is figuring out *what* to buy. When you think about all the options—all the furniture pieces in all the furniture styles, all the silver, all the china, all the glass, all the rugs, all the bric-a-brac and accessories, on and on—it's mind-boggling. But deciding may be easier than you think.

I still remember overhearing a cute young couple's conversation at a Florida antiques show. They were in the mood to buy. Trouble was, she wanted a silver epergne for the dining room table and he wanted a nice Chippendale-style armchair to use at his desk. "You always want a piece of silver," he said. "Well, you're always looking at furniture," she replied.

Little did they know how much their comments revealed about them.

Spying on Yourself

So, why don't you spy on yourself? Go to a large antiques mall. Begin wandering around with no specific purpose. See where you go. Along the way, you might even jot down some prices and a few notes about your "favorite" pieces (there'll be more about that later). At the end, look back over what you were attracted to. China accent pieces? Desks and chests? Paintings? Chances are you'll see a pattern starting to emerge.

Zeroing In

Now go back to one piece that you particularly liked. Force yourself to answer this simple question: Why do I like it? Don't shy away. You're not being graded on this taste test. And don't settle for the easy answer, "It's pretty." (Though that is a perfectly valid reason.) Right now you're stretching your mind. You're expanding your horizons.

Having trouble? Try these possibilities for starters:

➤ For furniture—the wood is deeply figured.

➤ For rugs—the pattern draws me in.

➤ For silver—the form is interesting.

➤ For a china figurine—the colors are beautiful.

Now let's go a little further. Dig a little deeper:

➤ For furniture—the inlay on the legs caught my eye.

➤ For rugs—the pattern is tightly woven.

➤ For silver—the intricate design along the border is interesting.

➤ For china—the pose makes the figure intriguing.

The closer you look, the more you'll see. I guarantee it. And each time you do this, you're one step closer to becoming an antiques collector—and eventually, an antiques connoisseur.

What Collectors Know

Why go through this exercise? Because in my conversations with collectors who have grown into connoisseurs, they confess that their biggest regret is that they bought too hastily at the outset. They grabbed up this piece and that without knowing why they were buying it.

A Little of This, a Dab of That

Many connoisseurs will admit that they were trying to get a good deal and that their budgets were limited at first. Still, looking back, they say they wish they had proceeded more carefully and bought just one really nice piece in great condition rather than buying lots of things in haste.

Building a Strong Foundation

Do you have dollar signs rolling around in the back of your mind when you're buying antiques? If so, a well-formed, interesting, and *focused* collection of one category or area of antiques usually has greater monetary value if, and when, you decide to dispose of it than does a hodgepodge accumulation. For example, a collection of Hepplewhite furniture or English sterling silver will always attract others interested in these collections. But one piece of Hepplewhite furniture or English sterling silver can get lost in the crowd.

Learn from the Mistakes of Others

We can all profit from the mistakes of others. Here are some tips based on those mistakes:

➤ **Measure before you buy.** Good auction catalogues cite measurements—height, width, depth—so that the buyer can be sure the piece will fit in its new home. Check a piece's measurements before you buy it.

AntiqClue

Why are period rooms in museums so appealing? Because they've been arranged to show off each piece. Fine antiques, like great pictures, need their own space.

➤ **Bigger is not necessarily better.** Some of yesterday's pieces are overpowering in today's homes. It takes a tall ceiling to accommodate a seven-foot-plus Empire armoire. This can affect price. If you can use some large pieces, you may get great values (more for the inch).

➤ **Keep focused.** Many connoisseurs have told me that even they get sidetracked at times. But once you become genuinely interested in building a substantial collection, chances are you'll stay focused. In the early stages, you can be led astray by another pretty or interesting object. Try to keep focused.

➤ **Let passion rule.** One highly esteemed (even famous) antiques connoisseur had this advice: The best buys are the pieces that you buy because you love them!

To Thine Own Self Be True

Unquestionably, the best advice for a novice antiquer is as old as the hills: To thine own self be true.

Don't follow the pack. Don't fall for the fads. If you buy something because it's fashionable or you've heard it will be a great piece down the road, or you've watched someone else admire it and that's made you want it, chances are you'll grow tired of it eventually. The pieces you choose to have around you, to live with, to enjoy, are an extension of your personality. Don't cheat yourself. Give in to your passion and your likes.

AntiqClue

Fads are just that—fads. That's why rooms shown in 1950s magazines look so, well, 50-ish!

Think about it this way. You have to have a table to eat at, a chair to sit on. You have to have a bed to sleep in. If you have to have these things anyway, you might as well buy a table, a chair, and so on that you enjoy. What you choose to have around you truly enhances your life and speaks volumes about you.

Make a Wish List

You've taken a quick taste test. You've thought about why you like what you like. Now it's time to be practical again, or at least as practical as you can be when making out a wish list. Writing down a list of the antiques you'd like to have, short and long term, will help keep you focused. In this section you'll find wish lists of furnishings and accessories that you might choose for the various rooms in your home. For each list item, I've included tips and information to help you make a wise choice. There are separate lists of furnishing and accessories for the living room, dining room, and bedroom.

When you make up your own list, remember that there's always room for your own specialized collections. They are what make your home a mirror of your interests and personality, whether they are old books or glass door knobs or silk fans. I haven't included these types of collections since they fall into a category all their own and often do not fit into one room's "furnishings."

Adding a Personal Touch

Accessories, those small pieces that are often called bric-a-brac, are the finishing touches to a room. They are where your personal tastes can really dominate. The wish lists of accessories gives you possible choices and ideas for accessories that you might place in your home. There is a separate list for the living room, dining room, and bedroom.

Be Careful What You Ask For

I'm reminded of the saying, "Be careful what you ask for … you may get it!" If you believe that dreams can come true, making a wish list is for you.

Every collector has a story about some elusive piece that almost magically and mysteriously popped up when least expected. Some people would say it's not magic but rather a matter of luck coming to the prepared mind. Whichever school you belong to, keep the faith. Treasures are everywhere.

AntiqInfo

It helps to have some idea of the market before you jump in. You'd feel pretty stupid if you asked to see a set of 12 eighteenth-century *period* chairs in the $10,000 range. Why? Christie's sold 17 George II dining chairs for $1,888,729 in July 1999, and 12 American Chippendale ones for $585,550 on January 16, 1999.

Before You Get Started

I've included some tidbits of info in the list that may also appear in later chapters. The way I see it, who knows when you'll have the time to finish reading this book? What if you get the chance to go antiquing this weekend? In that case, these "sneak-peak" tips will keep you on your toes, or send you ahead to the chapters you think will be most helpful to you, according to your needs and plans.

Thinking Things Through

To see how these tips work, let's pretend that a coffee table is high on your living room wish list. You should be aware that there's no such thing as a period, or even "legal antique," coffee table because coffee tables didn't exist until the late 1910s and early 1920s.

This fact doesn't mean that you shouldn't buy a coffee table when you find the right one at the right price. But it does mean that you shouldn't think that you're buying a period one, no matter what the sales pitch. And it could mean that you might opt to buy a great pair of nineteenth-century candlesticks for your mantel instead of a mid-twentieth-century coffee table.

Wish Lists of Antiques for the Living Room

This first wish list covers antiques for the living room, den, study, or library and includes tips for a successful search.

Wish List of Antique Furniture for the Living Room

Sofa	Eighteenth-century sofas are for the Vanderbilts. Most people are happy with a good reproduction of an eighteenth- or early-nineteenth-century style. If your taste is for the mid- and later-nineteenth-century Empire or Victorian periods, take heart. Period sofas from these eras abound.
Wing chair	Here, too, eighteenth-century wing chairs are for the Vanderbilts. Old reproductions are usually good buys, but remember what new fabric and labor are going to cost.
Occasional chair	There are lots of nice eighteenth- and early nineteenth-century period chairs on the market. Even a Chippendale chair—if it's simple, not fabulously carved—can be surprisingly inexpensive. Period chairs from the mid- and late-nineteenth century are even more plentiful. Realize, though, that many occasional chairs should be sat in only occasionally. They can be fragile and may not hold up to heavy use.
Comfy chair	Forget an antique. This item is a twentieth-century one and is usually best purchased new, though some old reproductions have great styling to them.
Coffee table	Available only in old reproductions that are based on earlier styles. There was no such thing as a coffee table in Chippendale's day.
End tables for sofa	All "low" tables are products of twentieth-century modern design, when plushy, comfy chairs and sofas became popular. To find suitable antique tables, think sturdy candlestands or Pembroke tables.
Pembroke table	A timeless piece, be it period, antique, or old repro. Said to have been named for either the ninth Earl of Pembroke who might have designed it, or the Countess of Pembroke who reputedly ordered one. They've been around since the 1750s and deservedly so. They look great in any room.

continues

continued

Secretary/bookcase	Every room needs one eye-catching area. A fireplace and mantel can provide this; but if you're into antiques, what could be better than an elegant and useful secretary/bookcase? Good, but not exceptional, ones are expensive but well worth it. Check to see whether the top and the bottom match. See Chapter 18, "Chipping the Old Block, or the Chip Wood?" for more about this.
Slant-front desk	An alternative to the tall secretary/bookcase is a slant-front desk with an attractive mirror or a piece of art placed above it, or even a hanging shelf adorned with lots of curios. Slant-front desks are much less costly and more easily found than secretary/bookcases.
Writing desk or table	A flat-topped writing desk takes up much more room than a slant-front desk and is generally better suited for a formal library or study than for a living room. Eighteenth-century writing tables will be English, not American. But by the later nineteenth century, Americans adopted this form and made lots of really big writing desks. The market for these pieces may increase as home offices become more commonplace.
Chest of drawers	Chests are usually reserved for bedrooms or dining rooms—someplace where storage is needed—but a good-looking chest of drawers can be as practical as a slant-front desk. They're about the same size, more plentiful, usually reasonably priced, practical, and adaptable to any room should you move.
Highboy, tall chest, chest-on-chest	These great-looking pieces are up there in price. They usually start in the high thousands and move quickly into five figures; of course, exceptional examples go through the roof. Highboys are American. Chest-on-chests are English. Tall chests can be either. These versatile pieces are also suitable for dining rooms and bedrooms. But watch out for mismatched tops and bottoms.

Lowboy	Always a desirable piece, an eighteenth-century lowboy—called a dressing table at that time—can move from room to room. But lowboys are pricey and many a highboy base has been turned into a "lowboy." For more details, see Chapter 18.
Center table	Very popular in the Empire and Victorian eras, center tables run the gamut from very affordable to very costly. They are fairly easily found.
Tea or silver table	In Chapter 7, "The Summing Up: Objects Do Not Lie," you learned that a Philadelphia tea table was the first American antique to sell for over $1 million, and that tells the story on the price of antique American tea tables. Nevertheless, many great-looking copies were made in the late nineteenth century—yes, they are now "legal" antiques—plus there are lots of respectable old reproductions. The English sometimes called their tea tables "silver tables," because this was the place of honor for the silver teapot. Whether English or American, the tea table is a formal piece and would be out of place in a New England country antiques setting.
Drop-leaf table	This staple has been around since the eighteenth century. Drop-leaf tables range from the type called a "harvest table" in New England to the popular, smaller Victorian "breakfast" table. In other words, they are found in all sorts of shapes, sizes, and designs. A good piece to begin with since they're plentiful, versatile, affordable, and practical.
Sofa table	This dressed-up city cousin of the simple drop-leaf table and a relative of the center table is usually placed behind a sofa when the sofa is placed out in the room, not pushed up against a wall. A piece suitable for the more formal or sophisticated room.
Pier table	This is another formal piece. Sometimes called a petticoat table, the pier table was originally intended to be placed between two windows. When the original mirror in the bottom center portion is still present,

continues

continued	the value goes up. Wondering where the "petticoat" name came from? The story goes that ladies used these mirrors to see if their petticoats were showing.
Candlestand	Candlestands were essential pieces in the days before gas and kerosene and electric lamps. These really great small tables have lots of possibilities. They are plentiful, not too expensive, and equally at home in almost any decor and in any room.
Gaming or card table	Many of these fun pieces have tops that fold over. The ones that have a fold-over top are sometimes called handkerchief tables. Those types of card or game tables are small and easily moveable. Other game tables are larger and less portable. Game, or gaming, tables were made in England and America and are often reasonably priced. They are also great conversation pieces.

Wish List of Antique Accessories for the Living Room

Mirrors	It wasn't until the mid-nineteenth century that most families could afford large mirrors. Glass was expensive in the eighteenth century. Plus, the technology to cut a large piece of glass without breaking it didn't exist. Thus, a *period* eighteenth-century mirror can be more expensive than much period furniture! Most people settle for old reproduction Chippendale mirrors. On the other hand, nineteenth-century mirrors are much more affordable. Do remember that a good-looking mirror can bring a room to life.
Porcelain	Vases, plates, small platters, bowls, urns, figurines. Sevres, Haviland, Wedgwood, Chinese Export, Imari, Spode, Majolica, Delft. There's no end to the possibilities, combinations, and price ranges. Your color scheme can be a big factor in selecting porcelain accessories.
Lamps	Like mirrors, lamps can really make a room come to life. Obviously, electric lamps are of modern vintage, but antique pieces from vases to figurines have long been a favorite prey for lamp makers. By the 1910s,

great lamps of all sorts of materials were being made by notable companies. Does Tiffany ring a bell? Good lamps are expensive and worth it.

Crystal and glass	Like porcelain, decorative crystal and glass pieces were made in all varieties, from vases to candlesticks to boxes, and they can be found in all price ranges. You may be familiar with names like Waterford and Sandwich glass, but Victorian-era glass pieces can be colorful, fun, and affordable. (For more details, see Chapter 24, "The Glass House.")
Silver	True, silver is usually associated with the dining room, but a pretty silver candy dish or chamber stick, even a silver letter opener or ink well on the desk is quite attractive. After you read Chapters 19 through 21, you'll be a silver expert.
Brass and bronze	Say brass and you think candlesticks. Say bronze and you think sculpture. Brass candlesticks are almost a must in any home decorated in any period design. Bronze sculpture is more a matter of taste. Bronze statuary is also tricky—fakes abound!
Textiles	Think textiles in home decor and rugs pop into your mind. Choices abound: Persian, Aubusson, and Chinese, for starters. But there are other textiles worth considering. A Victorian shawl tossed over a chair back or an Oriental obi artfully used on a table or chest of drawers top can be a lovely effect.

As you prepare your wish list, you might also consider including wooden tea caddies, cloisonné vases, inlaid tilt-top tables, and other fine accessories. Wooden tea caddies are right up at the top of the list of wanna-have antique accessories. Cloisonné vases brighten any room. A mother-of-pearl inlaid papier-mâché tilt-top table or even a sewing table is as pretty as can be. For the less-formal room, you might consider a historically interesting bandbox, a pewter salt shaker, an intricately carved wooden butter mold—the list goes on and on. Here's where you are limited only by your imagination and pocketbook—and, of course, the availability of the object of your desire.

Wish Lists of Antiques for the Dining Room

Not only does the dining room need the usual table and chairs, it's the room where collectors can display their treasures in a variety of ways.

Wish List of Antique Furniture for the Dining Room

Dining room table	Surprisingly, period dining room tables are obtainable and won't break the bank. Why? Because often they aren't very usable in twenty-first-century dining rooms. They are too low for the modern person's knees and legs to fit comfortably. Nice old reproduction tables that are an inch or so higher are better suited to today's homes and everyone's dining comfort.
Dining room chairs	Finding a large set of 8, 10, or 12 *period* chairs is frequently like searching for a needle in a haystack. Usually sets have been split up among family members over the generations. Often, when you find a single period Chippendale or Hepplewhite chair, it was part of a larger set. Most large sets of Queen Anne, Chippendale, Hepplewhite, or Sheraton dining room chairs will date from the later nineteenth or early twentieth century.
Sideboard	Considered by many the choice antique dining room piece, both English and American period sideboards come on the market with great regularity. But beware, the sideboard was not a furniture form until the end of the eighteenth century. There is no such thing as a period Queen Anne or Chippendale sideboard.
Serving table	Smaller than the usual sideboard, a well-proportioned Hepplewhite or Sheraton serving table is an attractive alternative for many of today's dining rooms. Empire and Victorian serving tables tend to be larger.
Corner cupboard	Serviceable storage pieces, corner cupboards have been favorite pieces in Pennsylvania and the mid-Atlantic and Southern states since the late-eighteenth century and on down through the years. They come plain and fancy, and in one or two pieces. Hanging cupboards are more apt to be from England than America.

Breakfront	Breakfronts might be said to be the corner cupboard's English cousin, since most of the period ones were from England. By the twentieth century, these were widely reproduced by American companies. Why are they called breakfronts? Because of the center drawer that "breaks down" to become a small desk.
Welsh cupboard	An English furniture form, the Welsh cupboard is less formal than a sideboard, great for displaying pewter and blue-and-white china. It was widely copied by American furniture manufacturers in the early twentieth century.

Wish List of Antique Accessories for the Dining Room

Silver	Start with candlesticks—what could create more ambiance than flickering candlelight reflected in silver? Add the ever-popular silver tea service, a beautiful and remarkably practical silver basket, some fanciful Victorian silver pieces—the Victorians loved silver—and you've built an enjoyable and lovely collection!
China	Move the porcelain from the living room into the dining room, and it becomes "china." The possibilities grow, too. In addition to the usual dining china, there are tureens, pot de crèmes, platters, individual nut dishes, and chocolate pots. If you have a corner cupboard or breakfront, the choices for filling it are deliriously exciting.
Crystal and glass	Ditto the china comments. This is your chance to fill every inch with different specimens of pressed glass—patterned salts, celery holders, pitchers, ice cream dishes, on and on. Or go for equally varied opportunities in cut glass.
Linens	From damask napkins almost large enough to cover a small table to exquisitely detailed cutwork placemats, antique linens add an elegant touch to any dining experience. Because most people don't want to take the time to properly care for them, antique dining room linens can be a real steal.

Wish Lists of Antiques for the Bedroom

Chests, chairs, tables, and mirrors are pieces that are at home in both the bedroom and the living room or den. A few pieces, though, such as beds and dressing tables, are found exclusively in the bedroom.

Wish List of Antique Furniture for the Bedroom

Bed	Early period beds are scarce, but beds from the mid- and late-nineteenth century are much more plentiful. If you've room for a grandiose, highly carved, mid-, or late Victorian bed, buy one. And don't forget the bedsteps if they're available. More practical for most folks are the country-type "cottage" beds also from the nineteenth century. Many eighteenth-century and early-nineteenth-century beds have been adapted to today's standard double, queen, and king sizes. This cuts down on their value as pristine antiques but makes them a lot more usable in today's homes. This is one of those times when you may fudge a little and go for the original piece in less-than-perfect condition.
Armoire or wardrobe	Inch for inch, these portable closets from the nineteenth century are great buys—if you have wide walls and high ceilings. If you're tempted to turn one into an entertainment center for your den, please keep the original parts for the next owner.
Blanket chest	The actual forerunner of the chest of drawers, the simple, hinge-top blanket chest has never gone out of style. That means there are lots of them and they are reasonably priced. These look good in a den, too. Incidentally, cedar chests are twentieth-century items.
Dressing table and dresser	If you're fortunate enough to find and afford an eighteenth-century period dressing table or lowboy, chances are you'll show it off in your living or dining room. By the mid-nineteenth century, though, a new type of dressing table came along. As mirrors became less expensive, furniture companies took a basic chest of drawers and attached a mirror to it. Voilà, the dresser was born. These pieces are everywhere and readily affordable. They come in little, medium, and large sizes, too.

Rocking chair	A few rockers date from the 1820s or 1830s, but most come from the later nineteenth century, or even twentieth century. Warning! Many a throw-away chair was given new life by chopping off part of the legs and adding rockers.

Wish List of Antique Accessories for the Bedroom

Silver	Nail files, mirrors, glove stretchers, clothes and hair brushes, jewelry boxes, button hooks, curling irons—yes, curling irons—perfume bottles, hair receivers. If you can think of it, they made it in silver, or silver plate, for the dressing table. The sky's the limit.
Glass and crystal	The obvious items are cologne and perfume holders, but you'll also find crystal-handled clothes brushes, powder jars, and hat pins, just to mention a few of the possibilities.
China and porcelain	Speaking of hat pins, how about a wonderful hand-painted hat pin holder? And that's just the tip of the iceberg.
Linens and textiles	If you didn't get your fill in the dining room, here's your chance to really indulge. There are bedspreads, coverlets, dresser scarves, wonderful Victorian quilts, priceless samplers, hooked rugs, lingerie holders, and more. For the adjoining bath, acquire monogrammed and embroidered hand towels.

Other Furniture Items to Look For

One of the wonderful things about the hunt for the perfect piece is the vast selection that awaits you. Here, for your perusal, are additional furniture pieces that might strike your fancy. If you don't know what they are, never fear. Part of this educational process is learning to talk the talk. (For more information, check out Appendix E, "Glossary.")

Here goes:

More Antiques for Your Wish List

Canterbury or music stand	Coat rack
Cellerat	Corner stand or washstand
Cheval mirror	Étagère or whatnot

Meridienne	Secrétaire à abattant
Ottoman	Settle
Pedestal	Tête-â-tête
Prie-dieu	Trestle table
Récamier	Work or sewing table

Remember—Aim High

Have you noticed how value keeps creeping into our discussion of antiques? And so it should. These treasures have always been part of world economics. Why else would thieves risk all for a Fabergé egg, a sixteenth-century silver standing salt, or a nineteenth-century bronze?

That's why, as this chapter winds down, here's a gentle reminder. Even as a novice collector, aim high and buy the very best you can afford.

The Least You Need to Know

➤ The accumulator buys whatever strikes his or her fancy. The collector builds a well put-together collection.

➤ When you identify your passions, you'll make the best buys.

➤ It is wiser to make one good purchase than several lesser ones.

➤ Follow your tastes—not someone else's.

➤ Dream. Dream. Dream.

Chapter 9

Antiquing the Old-Fashioned Way

In This Chapter

➤ Learn who the shopkeepers are

➤ Discover where to look for shops

➤ Find out how to have fun and learn at the same time in antiques shops

---

Freestanding, little-bit-of-everything antiques shops and highly specialized shops are still the backbone of the traditional antiques scene. Sadly, though, they are slowly disappearing.

Twenty-five years from now, they may be a thing of the past. I hope not, but to ensure that you'll have memories to share about "the good old days of antiquing in the early twenty-first century," visit these shops now.

The Traditional Shop

In the good old days, antiques shops were often dusty, dimly lit places, crammed with a variety of items. Sometimes these traditional shops were merely the front or back room or two in a large house. In today's new world, when antiques shops are as close as your computer, these shops may be hard to find. Still, antiques are "old things," and some traditional people like to shop the traditional way. But it can take some hunting to find the stand-alone antiques shop. Try checking the Yellow Pages in the telephone book, the classified ads in local newspapers, and the advertisements in antiques trade journals and magazines.

Browsing these traditional antiques shops can be a profitable way to spend your time because of the amazing range of the stock. And the more overcrowded the shop is, the better, according to some antiquers. To narrow the hunt, however, and save time, you might ask at the outstart, "Do you have any *whatever?*"

A nice advantage of the traditional shop is that the shopkeeper often keeps a want list for customers. Should the desired item come in, the dealer will notify you either by postcard or a telephone call.

Specialty Shops

When you're looking for that unique or special antique, especially when time is of the essence, you'll do best if you go straight to a specialty shop. These shops can be easily tracked down through their ads in antiques publications or listings on the Internet. There's no end to the list of items that dealers specialize in—from art glass to eighteenth-century English flatware.

Specialty shops offer several advantages. They usually carry a wide selection of items in their specialty and provide an excellent education for you along the way. Also, many dealers will search for a specific item that you want, either by utilizing their contacts in the trade or by keeping you in mind as they travel to various shows.

Tapping the Shopkeeper's Resources

One of the joys of antiquing is finding people who are walking encyclopedias of knowledge. That's what you're apt to find in the traditional antiques shop. These folks are often scholars who have spent their entire lives studying and exploring the fascinating world of antiques. Many times they are characters in their own right.

AntiqInfo

For a good reference book that lists lots of antiques shops and other invaluable sources, see *Mahoney's Antiques & Collectibles Resources Library* (Wallace–Homestead Book Company, 1999).

Over the years I have found traditional shopkeepers are the ones most likely to have a large library of antiques books. They may even have inherited these books from their parents who were also shop owners. Ask this shopkeeper a simple question, and he or she will rush to the bookcase and *show* you the answer. What could be more fun than this sort of painless learning?

Though the traditional shopkeeper is your best bet for a broad range of information, don't neglect the specialty dealer for detailed information about an item that falls within his or her area. These dealers have a wide range of contacts and can dig up the specialized information you need when it can't be found elsewhere.

Location, Location, Location Equals $$$

Antiques dealers are just like other shopkeepers when it comes to selecting a location for their shops: Money is a big consideration. It makes sense that the more expensive the rent, the more expensive the antiques will be. But remember this, antiques dealers are a special breed of people. Many shop owners take great delight in choosing an offbeat location just for the fun of it. Many like to select a building that has as much character as the antiques they sell. Warehouse districts and Victorian neighborhoods are great hunting grounds for antiques shops.

The High-Rent District

Let's say that you're in an antiques shop on East 58th Street in New York, or on Royal Street in New Orleans. Chances are that you're going to be paying top dollar for any item you buy in this sort of location because rent is expensive there.

But there are exceptions. Take the Persian rug dealer who happens to have bought a few pieces of brass and silver in order to get the rugs that he wants. Now he can either sell these pieces to another dealer or add them to his own inventory just because they look nice. Odds are that if he decides to offer the pieces in his own shop, he won't know how to price them, so he may price them low. This is when a great steal can be made even in the high-rent district.

AntiqClue

Most store-front specialty shops are in the high-rent district. Don't expect to find a specialty item in a specialty shop for an especially low price. These dealers know what they have and what their values are.

Off the Beaten Track

By and large, the really great buys are found off the beaten track. In the days before *The Antiques Roadshow*, people said, "There are no good buys left in the antiques shops." Now they know differently.

What's the secret to being the one who gets the good buys? As the bumper sticker says, "Brake for antiques shops." In other words, put on your thinking cap, take the time to look around, know the price ranges, and remember that it is possible to find anything, anywhere.

The Antiques Dealer as Professor

I mentioned earlier that antiques dealers can be excellent teachers. How can you learn from their years of experience? Show that you are an eager student.

But as they say, timing is everything. Wait until there are no other customers around and then begin asking questions, especially if you're just looking and not really in the market to buy. In other words, be considerate of the shop owner's time.

AntiqClue

The best antiques dealers-teachers are often the ones who have been in business for the longest length of time. They've learned from their own experience and from the many questions their customers have asked them.

The Shop Floor

If antiques dealers are good professors, their best classrooms are the floors of their antiques shops.

The Open Classroom

It's the *things* on the floor that make the antiques shop the perfect classroom.

Let's pretend that you're looking for a slant-front desk and that the shop you're browsing in has three slant-front desks. Now the buzzword here is "comparison."

The three slant-front desks are: an old reproduction mahogany desk; an eighteenth-century, English-made mahogany desk; and an eighteenth-century, American-made walnut desk. You have a chance to compare the woods, the English-made desk with the American-made desk, and the old reproduction desk with the two period desks. And don't forget to compare the high prices!

Please Touch

Best of all you can touch all three desks to your heart's content. And when I say touch, I mean you can almost take the pieces apart. In a shop it's okay to pull the pieces away from the wall so you can see the backs. You can even remove the drawers from the desks to check the construction. If necessary, you can turn each desk upside down. You can't do that in any museum that I know of.

Furthermore, most really good antiques dealers will help you do all this and will answer your questions along the way.

Inquiring Minds Want to Know

Good dealers are interested in spreading the word about antiques and will immediately recognize a customer who genuinely wants to learn. The advantage isn't all on the customer's side, however. The dealer gets the chance to share his or her love for antiques and, just as important, to gain a potential client.

Okay. You've got a great antiques dealer-teacher. You're in the best classroom imaginable. Here's your chance to shine—to score an A+ in the course.

Twenty Questions? Start with One

As you become more expert in the field, you'll have many more then 20 questions. Nevertheless, start with just one. What is a good first question to ask? Try this: How can you tell how old this piece is?

AntiqClue

Found a great antiques dealer who is also a great teacher? Why not suggest that he or she teach an antiques class in the shop?

Another good approach is to ask the dealer's advice or opinion. Let's say that there are two Pembroke tables in the shop that appeal to you. Ask the dealer, "Which one do you like better?" (You don't have to take the dealer's advice, but this opening gives you the chance to pick his or her brain.)

Other questions you might ask are, "Which one is the better quality?" Or, "Which one will hold its value in the long run." Questions like these invariably open up an entire discussion.

Your question will probably open up a barrage of comments and instructions, so be prepared for a lecture.

The Least You Need to Know

➤ A shop's location can be an indication of its pricing.

➤ Good deals can be found almost anywhere.

➤ Go to specialty shops when you have a special need.

➤ Take advantage of the experienced dealer's knowledge.

➤ Serious antiquers ask questions.

Chapter 10

On the Road Again

In This Chapter

➤ Discover the array of shopping choices that await the antiquer and the differences between them

➤ Pick up tips for antiquing in the different arenas

➤ Learn the unwritten rules of house sales

Part of the excitement of antiquing is heading down the road and not having the vaguest idea exactly where you're going to stop first. It's the choices that make for so much fun—antiques malls, flea markets, yard sales, estate sales, thrift shops. Knowing that you haven't a clue what treasures await you at any of these stops adds to your sense of adventure.

The antiques world is your oyster. My advice is to leave home with an open mind and lots of free time to enjoy your antiquing experience.

Antiques Malls: The Tip of the Iceberg

Once upon a time, antiques malls were considered an oxymoron. But times have changed. These days antiques malls are a wonderful and convenient way to see lots of pieces spanning many centuries. But if you have adopted the concept that an antique has to be at least 100 years of age, then you will probably have to sort through lots of wannabe antiques to make a great find in the usual mall.

Leave Your Stopwatch at Home

The problem with antiques malls is that it takes time to sort through so many things. If you're in a rush, antiques malls are best saved for leisurely rainy days.

When you do find yourself in a mall and you're short of time—it's bound to happen—cut to the chase. Locate someone at the front desk. Tell that person what you're looking for. Most people who work in antiques malls love antiques themselves, so they are familiar with the variety of objects found in each different booth or stall.

AntiqLingo

A **picker** is a knowledgeable person who wanders about "picking" antiques out of unlikely places and then sells his or her treasures to dealers who know what they are.

AntiqClue

You can usually tell a lot about an antiques shop from its ads in trade journals and magazines. Most antiques malls' ads are pretty generic. However, more and more malls are going upscale and carrying genuine antiques. These malls are the ones you will want to go back to over and over again.

On the other hand, antiques malls have fabulous treasures lurking in dark corners and hidden under piles of magazines and old quilts, just waiting to be found. Because of the sheer quantity of stuff, there is bound to be a good selection in many areas. In fact, antiques malls are the favorite haunts of antiques *pickers*.

Variety Is the Spice of Life

Let's face it, the thrill of the hunt is one of the chief appeals of antiquing, and that's the lure of antiques malls. In fact, rummaging through all the stuff displayed in an antiques mall can open your eyes to something you never thought you'd be interested in.

Remember, too, antiques malls are where you can see many similar pieces. It isn't unheard of to find three slant-front desks in an antiques mall. When you're in a mall, don't think, "There's just too much here!" but rather think, "This is a great study place."

Mom and Pop Are Off at Work

Among the many differences between the freestanding antiques shop owned by maybe one or two people, and the antiques mall where lots of different shop owners have their individual booths, is the ease with which you can have your questions answered.

In an antiques mall, all Mom and Pop have to do is buy the antiques, price them, and get them to the mall. Daily supervision of the booth is mostly left to whomever is in charge of managing the mall that day, though the booth dealer may be in and out of the mall at various times. While the manager may be familiar with the objects throughout the mall, he or she may not know the nitty-gritty information you are looking for. That can work either for or against you. Without anyone to ask, you can make a bad choice. On the other hand, if you know what you're looking at and the piece has been incorrectly marked or labeled (and underpriced), then you're in luck!

Flea Markets

Flea markets have become a real family affair. Some people even use them as a weekly entertainment site. And why not? They are fun, you're likely to run into your friends and neighbors, you don't have to get dressed up to go, and, best of all, an endless variety of treasures awaits you. And the goods and the people and the weather change every week. Trouble is, in the summertime—the height of the flea market season—the sun rises mighty early. I've never known anyone to get a great flea market find in the late afternoon.

AntiqClue

Wondering whether a piece is an antique or a reproduction? Antiques malls are great hunting grounds for the answer. If the identical item pops up in lots of different malls or in different displays in the same mall, this is a definite clue that all these pieces are probably brand new.

Overlooking the Dogs

As in the larger antiques malls, you have to dig through untold amounts of things to find just one treasure at most flea markets. And to make it worse, many of the very best things are brought to flea markets packed in boxes that you have to go through yourself. These are usually items found when cleaning out the grandparent's house. The silver lining is that these pieces are usually marked at giveaway prices.

Come on Back

Like antiques malls, flea markets have an invisible "come on back" welcoming mat that's always out. The reason why antiquers keep going back is the ever-changing variety of goods.

AntiqClue

Really savvy flea market shoppers always head straight for the new kid on the block. It's the one-time seller who is most likely to bring treasures from the attic or basement to sell at the flea market.

And like antiques malls, flea markets come in many different varieties, from small to gigantic. Most novice antiquers begin by visiting their local flea markets. But if you get really hooked, you may soon pack your bag and head straight for the big boy— the Brimfield Outdoor Antiques and Collectibles Shows in Brimfield, Massachusetts.

Yard and Garage Sales

I don't even have to read the newspaper to find yard and garage sales. My car just seems to know which streets to take. But until you have your automobile as well trained, check the Thursday and Friday newspaper classified ads to find out which neighborhoods are having the most yard sales that weekend. Take out your city map, get a red pencil, and in no time you'll have your Saturday and Sunday activities planned.

Anything Goes

Once upon a time little old ladies ran neighborhood yard and garage sales. No more. These days, antiques dealers and auctioneers have joined their ranks. So now you have both amateurs and professionals conducting these popular sales.

Needless to say, you probably have a better chance of finding a real "steal" at the amateur-run sale. But when the professionals are conducting the "onsite" sale, the prices asked for the goods are usually less than those found in antiques shops and malls for the same pieces.

Weeding Out

Just as you have to do in your own home when you're doing your spring cleaning, yard and garage sale shoppers have to weed out the good from the bad. Usually some of this has been done for you by whomever is having the sale. This means that the better pieces will go to an antiques dealer—leaving the not-so-good pieces for the yard or garage sale. That's the bad news.

The good news is that this doesn't *always* happen, especially if an amateur is running the sale. Then, lots of good things may slip into the sale unnoticed.

Here's an example of how such lucky finds happen. The amateur sale conductor is cleaning out closets to get ready for the sale. She finds a flower bowl that has been pushed to the back of the closet shelf. Because it was in the back, the sales conductor assumes the bowl to be mediocre and prices it accordingly But you know differently. That's where your knowledge, your perseverance, and your eagle eyes will put you out ahead of the rest.

And speaking of flowers ...

Down the Garden Path

Some of the hottest items in the antiques marketplace today are objects related to the garden—statuary, urns, gates, benches, and so on.

As they say, take a walk on the wild side. There is always the chance that you'll find some treasure in the backyard or side yard that no one has even thought about or seen—and that you can take home for a song!

Estate Sales, House Sales, Moving Sales, Tag Sales

Estate sales used to be called house sales. Then sometimes house sales were really moving sales if the owners were moving—and not necessarily to the graveyard. And because the prices for the merchandise in these sales are often written on tags, a more or less generic name for all of these sales is "tag sale."

Estate, house, moving, tag—it makes little difference what the sale is called if there are antiques for you to take home.

A Worthwhile Pursuit

These sales have long been a part of the antiques world. They used to provide a quick and easy way of disposing of personal property without incurring a great deal of expense. But today, like their close relatives, the yard and garage sale, these "inside the house" sales are now often run by professionals. Regardless of who plans them and sets them up, these sales provide a badly needed service for the seller and great opportunities for the buyer.

It's Now or Never

Great buys are to be had at all these sales, but there are two major disadvantages. First, you have to make up your mind on the spot whether or not you're going to buy the pieces. (Granted, if it's a two-day sale, you can take your chances that the piece will be there when you come back. But that's iffy.) Second, once you've bought something, it's yours. That means you need to look over every piece carefully before you buy—or else just take your chances.

Those two reasons should inspire you to learn all you can about antiques before you buy.

AntiqClue

If your thing is porcelain and glass, head straight to the kitchen or wherever the flower-arranging bowls and vases are being displayed. Usually several of them will be put in one box and the entire lot priced at just a few dollars. Many fine quality antiques (art glass, good porcelain, and even sterling silver, tarnished, of course) can sometimes be in those boxes.

The Five Rules of the Game

Often, such good buys are to be had at these sales that lines will begin forming even before the sun rises. When a sale of this magnitude is held, there are certain rules you have to play by.

The following rules of etiquette apply to well-publicized and heavily attended sales. If you don't abide by them, you'll get a bad reputation among the house sale crowd.

1. No cutting in line. Getting to these sales early in the morning is inconvenient for everyone, and you'll find no sympathy in the ranks if you have overslept.

2. When two-part tags are used, once the tear-away part of a tag is pulled, the item is yours.

3. Don't ask the sale conductor to put certain items "back" or aside for you. Remember, this isn't an antiques shop where items can remain on the shelf. Everything has to be sold at the end of the day.

4. Cash and checks talk. If a professional is running the sale, credit cards may be accepted, but don't count on it.

5. Cash-and-carry is the rule of the day. Getting home what you have bought is your responsibility. The people having the sale almost always have a "cleanup day" the day after the sale. Usually any larger items can be picked up then.

AntiqClue

There are some very impressive house sales held in equally impressive neighborhoods. Occasionally these sales will even have preview parties or a presale day. On the other hand, the old saw, "You can't judge a book by its cover," is also true. Great things can come out of humble homes.

Other Options: Thrift Shops

What happens when the family wants to keep the majority of its possessions but has some things to get rid of? They often send these things to the Salvation Army, the Goodwill store, the church bazaar, or some other charitable group or thrift shop. If you have the time, never pass by any of these potential treasure chests without stopping and shopping.

A One Shot Deal: Classified Ads

Check the classified ads for all the local sale activity, and while you're checking them out, glance at the individual "for sale" listings. One woman bought an eighteenth-century highboy, which was advertised simply as an "old chest." You see, in the antiques world, *anything* can happen.

The Least You Need to Know

➤ Antiques shops aren't the only game in town.

➤ Antiquing at malls, flea markets, and sales can take a lot of time.

➤ Take sharp eyes and lots of cash with you to house sales.

➤ Be adventuresome!

Chapter 11

On the Spot: To Buy or Not To Buy

In This Chapter

➤ Know why it is appropriate to ask for a better price

➤ Learn why comparison shopping is so important

➤ Discover how savvy antique shoppers find what they're looking for

➤ Find out what your sales receipt must have on it

No matter where you like to shop for antiques, eventually you're faced with the dilemma: to buy or not to buy. This places the responsibility on you to have sufficient knowledge about what you're buying to make wise choices.

Some people opt to find dealers, auction house experts, decorators, or other experts to guide them in their decisions. But the greatest rewards come to the savvy antiquer who, at the end of the day, can proudly say: I found it!

The Waiting Game

You have found the antique you're looking for. You have the perfect spot for it. You even have a way to get it home. But you hesitate. There are probably one or two reasons that are keeping you from sealing the deal:

1. You're not sure that this is a true antique.

2. You're not sure that you can afford it.

So now what do you do?

What You Do Depends on Where You Are

If you are shopping at a flea market, tag sale, or thrift shop, you are pretty much going to have to make up your mind on the spot. You'll have to take the chance that the piece is what the seller says it is. The price may be somewhat negotiable, and certainly you can always try to get a better price. However, you still have to do it on the spot and then live with your decision.

At an antiques shop or an antiques mall, you have more options. If you're unsure whether or not the piece is a true antique, or a period piece, there are two approaches you can take.

The first is to ask questions:

➤ What makes this an eighteenth- (or nineteenth-) century piece?

➤ Are there any replacements on this piece?

➤ Has this piece been repaired?

The list goes on and on, and you will learn more about what sort of questions to ask when you become familiar with the different categories of antiques in Part 4, "Getting Down to Brass Tacks."

The second approach is to simply put the item on hold—either by requesting that the dealer reserve it for you for a day or so, or else by making a cash deposit—while you go off to do your homework.

Now if you are in doubt about whether you can afford the piece, the best thing to do is to take your chances that it will be there once you've made up your mind. On the other hand, if you're really serious about the piece, you can try to bargain, and even ask about partial payments. We'll discuss those options shortly.

In either instance—whether questioning the authenticity of the piece or the depths of your pockets—heed this advice: Shop around.

Shop Around

If you were an experienced antiquer, you would be able to make a decision on the spot. Why? Because you would *know* what the object was and what a fair price for it would be.

But at this stage you're still a novice. This is a learning time, and there is no better time to learn than when you're on the brink of buying a piece.

It works this way. You have found a piece you like. You know how much it costs in that shop. This gives you a specific item and price. It's comparison-shopping time. You may find a comparable piece for less money. Or, you may find that the one that sent you on this hunt is a fabulous buy. Either way, you will have added to your knowledge of antiques and their prices.

The Gentle Art of Bargaining

Speaking of prices, it's time to learn what you can expect when you are negotiating a lower price.

Everybody likes to get a good price, even an occasional steal. That's been part of the antiquing tradition since peddlers sold "old things" from door-to-door out of wooden carts. But to get the best price, it helps if you understand something about the antiques business.

The Shopkeeper Has Bills, Too

Funny thing, when its bargaining time in an antique shop, many customers forget that the antiques dealer has bills to pay, too.

Next time you're in an antique shop, stop and look around. All those chandeliers and the table lamps that are lighted are using electricity. The clerks who are there to wait on you have to be paid. Is the silver sparkling and shiny? Somebody had to polish it. Oh, and did I mention rent? And most important of all, somebody had to be paid for all those things, those very things that you'd like to have in your own home.

Bargaining is fine. It can even be fun. But it should be fair to the dealer.

Whose Bottom Line?

It's amazing what dealers will pay to get what they want. Sometimes, dealers will pay top dollar for an item of exceptional quality just to have it in their shop. In such instances there isn't much room for negotiation.

AntiqInfo

Heed this advice from a dealer, who ought to know! "People just don't comparison shop enough," my friend and antiques dealer Nina Klinkenberg told me. "Everyone expects the dealer to tell them everything. If they would just compare pieces, they could learn so much by themselves—from whether it's a real antique to whether it's a good price."

AntiqClue

Timid about asking for a better price? Don't be. It's almost expected these days.

At other times, dealers will buy out an entire household and be able to price the items individually at their whim.

The problem is that you don't know which is the case when you spy something you want. The only way to find out the dealer's "best price" is to ask. (Of course while the dealer is looking up the price paid in his or her little black book or checking the code on the price tag, it doesn't hurt to pray a little.)

If the dealer comes back with a price that is within your range, everything's fine. On the other hand, if the item is still too pricey for you, then the ball is in your court. Be honest. Tell the dealer what you can pay for it. (And pray again.)

When It's a Big Purchase

If the item you're interested in is very expensive, or if you're in a large antiques shop or mall, charge cards may be welcome. On the other hand, remember that many antique shops are still doing business the "old-fashioned way," and some dealers are willing to work with the young collector on a monthly payment basis.

The moral of the story is: It never hurts to ask.

Remember Your Manners

And while you're asking, remember that you catch more flies with honey than you do with vinegar. Sure, you will run into a crusty old dealer on occasion, but antiques dealers by and large are a pretty decent lot.

Clinching the Deal

Once you've settled on a price, you may think it's a done deal. Far from it if, for any reason, you should end up having second thoughts. That's why this next bit of information can be as important as learning how to distinguish a period Chippendale chair from a reproduction Chippendale chair.

AntiqClue

Antiques may be "old things," but antiquers don't want to see the *same* old thing every time they go into a shop. To move their merchandise and make room for new "old things," dealers are often happy to cut a good deal.

AntiqClue

There is a major difference between a retail store and an antiques shop. Retailers can often return unsold items. The antiques dealer can't. That's why you will often find negotiating room in the price of an antique.

Binding Contracts

The bill of sale that you receive when you purchase any item can be worth its weight in gold—or worthless. The importance of getting a good receipt has already been mentioned in Chapter 3, "Some Antiquing Pitfalls and How to Avoid Them." Now we'll examine the bill of sale more closely.

This is how it works.

If the receipt you're handed for an antique has a description that reads more like a generic prescription—chair, or plate, or spoon—then you have no recourse should you find out later that what you bought isn't what you *thought* it was.

If you're handed such a receipt, ask for a full description of the item—eighteenth-century, English chair; late-nineteenth-century Imari plate; nineteenth-century, English silver-plated stuffing spoon.

AntiqClue

If you are buying several things from one shop, the dealer will almost always knock a few dollars off the final price. That's the seller's way of thanking you. But in an antiques mall, various pieces come from different stalls or booths, so no such courtesy can be extended.

This sort of information serves two purposes. First, if you find out that the piece simply isn't what it was purported to be, then you have proof that you purchased the item in the full belief that it was an eighteenth-century, English chair; or a late-nineteenth-century Imari plate; or a nineteenth-century, English silver-plated stuffing spoon.

Second, having this information may help to identify an item if you need to file an insurance claim for it.

Either way, look at it like this. Getting specific information is the equivalent of getting a brand name and a serial number on a receipt for a piece of video equipment bought from Circuit City or Sears or any other retail store.

So before leaving the shop, look at your receipt. It should have the following information on it:

1. A full description (including the age) of the specific piece
2. A statement of the piece's condition
3. How much it cost

Buy, Buy, Buy!

Talk to the seasoned antiques collector and you'll often hear, "I have never regretted the things I've bought. It's the things I didn't buy that I regret."

That's because even pieces bought in haste, or while the collector was still an "accumulator," can be disposed of. The last few chapters have been filled with information about where to buy antiques. Dealers have to get their goods from somewhere. They can't make them up in their garages—or at least they aren't supposed to.

Further, you can always have your own yard sale or take a booth at a flea market—or even give away those unwanted items. So it's not that hard to get rid of the things that you've bought, though sometimes you may not get what you paid for them.

But finding the "one that got away" … well, that's the stuff that *bad* dreams are made of.

Making a Lasting Impression

You've looked, but come up empty handed. When you're unable to find the piece you're earnestly searching for, consider this tack. Ask the dealer to give you a call if one shows up. Better yet, you could leave a lasting impression.

Thanks to the personal computer and the ease of desktop publishing, you can make up a standard business card with your name, address (street and e-mail), and phone number. Title yourself "Serious Collector." Then, on the reverse side, list the items you're looking for. Pass out these cards to responsible dealers. Who knows what they'll turn up, or when. And they'll be sure to remember you.

The Least You Need to Know

➤ Most antiques dealers have some room for price negotiation.

➤ How *much* room there is for negotiation is an individual matter—piece by piece, dealer by dealer.

➤ Comparison shopping is a great way to learn.

➤ A sales slip with full information is of great importance.

➤ Smart shoppers leave their names and wish lists with responsible antiques dealers.

Part 3

Antique Auctions: Offline and Online

What a difference a year makes. It can turn a wannabe antique into the real, legal thing. And these days, ever-passing years bring more buying opportunities to the antiques lover's fingertips, literally.

With new Web sites popping up and even the traditional auction houses joining the electronic wave, choices abound. Thank goodness there seems to be room for both the traditional auction and the virtual auction. In fact, most traditional auctioneers have found that their business has increased as a result of the exposure Web auctions have brought to the public. Why? Because there's nothing like the real thing.

Chapter 12

Antique Auctions: In a Class by Themselves

In This Chapter

➤ Be introduced to the wonderful world of auctions

➤ Learn that Sotheby's and Christie's aren't so intimidating after all

➤ Discover the difference between a city and a country auction

Start with a rare blue plate, an elegant inlaid table, or a mysterious item that no one seems to give a hoot about. Throw in the curious, the serious, and the casual passerby. Add a dash of jealousy, a pinch of greed, and a hefty dose of avarice. Top it off with passion. Start the bidding. Watch the fireworks fly.

In a word, antiques auctions aren't just in a class by themselves. They're the best show in town. And they're free. But don't expect to leave without spending a bundle.

The City Mouse and the Country Mouse

Auctions are, and have always been, divided into two major kinds. The glamorous, highly advertised, high-rolling city auction contrasts with the understated, quickly thrown together, what'll-you-give-me country auction. Neither one should be missed.

Both have their share of good buys and rip-offs. It's your responsibility to get the former and leave the latter for the less wise.

The Truth About the Big Boys

Sotheby's and Christie's used to be the haunts of blue-haired ladies and titled gentlemen. But these days, when newspaper headlines are blaring the fabulous prices brought at auction sales for select pieces, both the rich and famous and the not-so-rich and not-ever-famous are frequenting the auction houses. Those once-hallowed halls aren't so sacred any more. Although the Barbra Streisands and Oprah Winfreys of the world may pay record prices for Tiffany lamps and Shaker furniture at the internationally known auction houses, other reputable but lesser-known auction houses are attracting buyers just like you and me. And as *The Antiques Roadshow* has shown, nowadays even the humble homeowner can walk away with a fabulous treasure bought at auction.

AntiqClue

Two basic ingredients make for a successful audience: the items being sold and the people buying them. Despite the sometimes exclusive and intimidating aura associated with big-name auctions, remember that without the bidders, the items will go unsold.

Sotheby's and Christie's Started It All

Sotheby's and Christie's trace their roots back to eighteenth-century England. Three hundred years later, they are still the highest stars in the firmament, but today heaven seems more approachable than it did in the past.

These days both Sotheby's and Christie's have offices and representatives worldwide. Their international presence, combined with their expertise and contacts, makes it possible for them to draw the merchandise and the audiences to keep them at the front of the antiques auction scene.

AntiqLingo

A **lot** is a numbered unit of merchandise sold at an auction. For example, a lot might be written up as "Lot 302—A scene of a New England farmhouse, signed A. Blake, 1889 in the lower left corner." Another lot might be "Lot 38—22 pieces of sterling flatware, plus 3 silver-plated trays." Both of these are lots.

In Hollywood's popular "caper movies," Sotheby's and Christie's are often the prototypes for the glamorous but staid settings where some of the action takes place. In this make-believe land, both business and bidding are conducted in a very orderly, genteel fashion. Don't let this quiet demeanor fool you, though. In the real setting, the competition to get the best goods makes for a cutthroat business. And at an auction itself, bids can go so fast that an item can soar into the hundreds of thousands of dollars before you know it.

Understanding Million-Dollar Sales

Did I say hundreds of thousands? How about the million-dollar sales we read about? And there are plenty of those these days.

There are two kinds of million dollar sales. The first occurs when a particular item, be it a rare painting (most usually) or another item, reaches that million-dollar threshold.

The other kind happens when the entire contents, or total *lots,* of a sale reach a combined total amount of over a million dollars. With multimillionaires being found in every town and city in America, that happens much more frequently now than in the past. It is in these sales that some perfectly good items can also sell for just a few hundred or even $25.

This entry from a Sloan's auction catalogue illustrates how a piece is offered as a "lot."

You see, aside from the exceptional, specialized auction where maybe 10 or 20 paintings will be offered with the anticipation of their selling for a total of millions of dollars, the auction house needs to have enough items to make up a good, full-day auction. People won't make the effort to come otherwise. That's why most auction houses try to have a variety of items that will sell in a wide price range.

The Big Names Aren't the Only Game in Town

While Sotheby's and Christie's may get the most headlines, don't think, even for a minute, that they get all the goodies. They may try, by having representatives across the country, but every large metropolitan area has its own fine auction houses. Just think of all the fabulous items that have come into the Washington, D.C., area over the years as foreign diplomats and ambassadors have settled there. Think about the treasures that line the rooms in Chevy Chase and Georgetown. What happens to many of these pieces? They go to Sloan's.

Or what about Los Angeles where many movie stars and moguls have megabucks and marvelous taste? Those pieces go to Butterfield's.

Or the heart of America's antiques land, Ohio? Garth's has built a remarkable reputation based on selling fine regional American pieces to serious collectors.

AntiqClue

Do you know when most people catch auction fever? When they make their first modest purchase.

In Appendix B, "Where to Go," you'll find a quick reference list of well-known and established regional auction houses. Also check listings and advertisements in the monthly *Art & Auction.*

And Don't Forget the Country Auction

Even city slickers know that some real action can be found outside those metropolitan-area auction houses. There's nothing more fun than spending the day in a hamlet or burg, or on the grounds of a country house, among things that were accumulated by a family over several generations. Just thinking about it makes your mouth water. Unfortunately, these events have become so popular among city folk that your neighbor may be standing next to you, even though you're 50 miles from home.

Fun and Frolics

Unlike the more refined atmosphere of the city auction, at the country auction talking and even shouting isn't just expected, it's part of the fun and friendly atmosphere.

But there are some drawbacks you need to know about. For example, at country auctions seldom do you have the chance to look over the items before the bidding starts. This is sometimes due to the location. Either you can't get there early enough to see the pieces before the auction, or the auction is being held on a site where there isn't room for people to mill around and check out the goods.

You Love Me, Take Me Home

Another drawback you may face is how to get the goods back home. Country auctions are so well known for their great furniture buys that you may be sorely tempted to grab up a piece just because it *is* such a great buy. But unlike a large city auction house with a permanent gallery, onsite country auctions are usually here today, gone tomorrow, and the items have to be removed the day they are bought.

Thank goodness, today's sport utility vehicles (SUVs) make it possible to haul off a lot. But keep this in mind before venturing out from your high-rise in D.C. or Chicago into the Shenandoah Valley or Wisconsin Dells in search of a little memento and coming back with a *houseful* of treasures to squeeze into your 750 square feet.

A Softer, Gentler Auction

Despite these drawbacks, most novices find country and small-town auctions less intimidating than the big name houses where so much money seems to be at stake. With that in mind, you might be more comfortable attending some of the lower-keyed auctions to observe, learn from, and yes, buy from.

Looking Ahead

So you see, knowing that an auction is going to be held is just the beginning. And getting there is just a first step. It's knowing how to buy *wisely* at an auction that is of major importance. That's what is coming up in Chapter 13, "Playing for Keeps."

The Least You Need to Know

➤ It takes bidders to make an auction successful.

➤ Most auctions will offer a variety of items that fall into a wide price range.

➤ You need to think before you buy.

Playing for Keeps

In This Chapter

➤ Learn how to approach the auction scene

➤ Be introduced to auction catalogues and learn how to decipher the item descriptions

➤ Explore different bidding techniques

➤ Discover how to bid for pieces when you can't be at an auction

---

If there's any place where you find more fabulous antiques and knowledgeable people in a more relaxed, casual atmosphere than at an auction, I can't think of it. There's an excitement, an anticipation in the air that's almost festive.

But the stakes can be high if you don't know the rules of this playing-for-keeps game.

Not for the Fainthearted

Auctions are not for the fainthearted. Final decisions must be made quickly. If you're thinking, "Yes, the decision to buy has to be made quickly," think again. The decision *not* to buy must also be made in the twinkling of an eye.

That's why the experienced auction-goer does lots of homework before the first piece is offered for sale—homework that comes in the traditional form of a book, the auction catalogue.

Auction Catalogues: The Key

Not long ago, only the high-rolling auction houses put out color catalogues published on slick paper. Now, virtually all auction houses have learned that collectors are so passionate about objects that when they can receive an attractive and accurate catalogue, they'll study it; and when they find a piece they really want, they will send in their bids, one way or the other.

AntiqInfo

If you're interested in becoming a serious collector, find out the names of the auction houses that sell the sort of items you want. Then take a year's subscription to their catalogues. You'll stay informed about what's coming on the marketplace while at the same time you're learning a great deal about rarity, quality, and pricing.

Before You Buy

In addition to the written descriptions given for each lot, many auction houses will add a tag line: "All items sold as is." This is a *caveat* telling you to thoroughly examine a piece before you buy it.

If you have never seen an auction catalogue, and don't live in an area where you can drop by an auction house and buy one, pick up a copy of *Art & Antiques* or *Art & Auction* and check out the auction houses' ads for upcoming auctions. You'll see that you can call the auction house, and for around $25 (usually) they will send you a catalogue. Get one. It's one of the best buys around—much better than many $50 or $75 books on antiques.

Read Before You Bid—or Buy

Once you have a catalogue in hand, you'll be drawn to the pictures. Go ahead. Flip through them. But to fully understand the catalogue, you must carefully read the terms and conditions section that appears at either the front or the back of the catalogue. Not only does this section explain the business agreement you'll enter into if you're a successful bidder, it explains how the auction house describes its merchandise. This is important information so you'll know exactly what you are bidding on.

To familiarize you with this process, here are some examples of how most descriptions read and what they mean:

➤ An entry that states "Chippendale Mahogany Side Chair, Philadelphia, circa 1760 to 1780" means that the house guarantees the chair to be all of those things.

➤ If the heading reads "Chippendale Mahogany Side Chair" (note the place and years are omitted), the auction house experts consider the chair to be from the eighteenth century. However, the chair has too many repairs or alterations for it to be considered a pure, period piece.

➤ Now when the description says "Chippendale Style Mahogany Side Chair," with the word "style" intentionally front and center, you can assume that the chair does not date from the eighteenth century but rather was made at a later time, in the Chippendale *style*. (For more details, see Chapter 2, "Antiques. Period.")

What the Numbers Mean

Included with each catalogue entry (or lot) are two very important sets of numbers. The first is the item's measurements. Pay attention to these. I will always remember the young couple who couldn't be at an auction but who left a high bid to ensure that they would win a prized eighteenth-century slant-front desk. They did. They paid for it. But when it arrived by UPS, they were extremely puzzled. When they opened the package, they found they had purchased a miniature. They hadn't checked the dimensions. Luckily they were wealthy and could live with their mistake.

The other numbers to check out are the presale "estimates" given at the end of the description.

An *estimate* is the auction house's educated guess of the price range within which the piece will sell, based on what other pieces similar to it have sold for. This estimate is published to serve as a guide to potential buyers. The price spread will fall within a reasonable range—for example, $300 to $500; $1,800 to $2,400; $10,000 to $12,000.

Auction Previews: Better Than a Museum

A catalogue is a reference tool. You can keep it and refer to it later on. But it doesn't take the place of firsthand examination. You do that at the auction showing or preview.

Some midsize auction houses may have an open-to-the-public preview that lasts only two or three days. Many large houses have a "patron's only" opening preview. This is usually a nighttime event where champagne flows, collectors rub elbows,

AntiqClue

It's an unwritten rule of thumb that the lower price in the estimate's range approximates the **seller's reserve,** or the price below which the item will be "reserved" for the owner—in other words, not sold. But this isn't always true, and many pieces do not have any reserve on them.

AntiqClue

What can you do in the case of the smaller auctions when there is no public preview and you're really interested in one advertised piece? Try calling the auctioneer beforehand and ask if it's possible to see the piece a few minutes before the auction begins.

and much scholarly discussion transpires. The following day, a several-day preview opens to the general public.

You can immediately spy serious collectors at auction previews. They are the ones reading their catalogues, comparing the catalogue's descriptions with their own observations, and making notes in the margins for later reference.

Auction previews afford the novice and the expert alike the best of all opportunities to compare one piece with another. You are actually *expected* to inspect any piece you're interested in—from top to bottom, and front to back.

AntiqClue

Don't forget to eavesdrop. You can pick up no end of invaluable information by listening in on other peoples' discussions at auction previews.

Help When It's Needed

When auction house experts see your interest in the merchandise, they may politely ask if they can tell you anything about the piece. Take advantage of this great opportunity. They're the ones who examine pieces to determine their age, authenticity, and condition. Often they assign price estimates and write the catalogue descriptions. These experts will often point out details you might overlook.

On the other hand, if you have questions, take the initiative. Seek out an auction house expert. That is what they're there for.

To Bid or Not To Bid, and How

Armed with information about the pieces you are interested in, you're now ready to decide whether to bid, or not to bid, and how to let your bid be known.

At a small auction, raising your hand may do the trick. But at most auctions, you'll need to register for a number and a paddle. This is done at the front desk on the day of the auction. Then, when you want to make a bid, you simply raise the paddle with your number on it.

At the end of the auction, you check out at the desk. You will be presented with a list of the items you have purchased and how much you paid for them. You will then be told when you can pick up the pieces, or you will make other arrangements according to circumstances.

But now back to the bidding itself.

Setting Your Limits

Seasoned auction-goers usually try to set a top price that they will pay for a piece before the bidding begins. This price is based on many factors, including but not limited to:

➤ The piece's own merits.

➤ The piece's estimate and the bidder's budget.

➤ How many other pieces in the auction the bidder is considering.

➤ When, during the auction, the piece is being sold.

➤ What the competition is.

In the Heat of the Moment

Needless to say, all good intentions can fly out the window in the heat of the moment—especially when you see that your main competition for a piece is a noted dealer who buys only the best!

Or, if it's late in the day and you've lost every other piece that you've bid on and you refuse to go home empty-handed, this is when you stretch your self-imposed limit and raise the top price.

Under those sorts of circumstances usually the only way to avoid breaking your vow is to leave the scene of the potential crime.

The Race Is to the Swift

But when do you begin bidding?

Some people jump in at the start of the bidding, hoping that their competition will be chatting with the person next to them, or be making a cell phone call, or be otherwise distracted. Better yet— maybe the competition will have stepped into the bathroom or gone outside for a breath of fresh air.

Then, the early bidder may get a steal. Especially if it's a fast moving auction, and most are.

AntiqInfo

It isn't unusual for a piece, any piece—from a $25 to a $2,500 item, or even a $25,000 item—to be sold in under two minutes.

AntiqClue

So how should *you* bid? It depends on you, your stress threshold, and your gamesmanship. Ultimately, you will decide whether you're the jump-in-early or the patient-type bidder. What's important is that you get the goods you want. And if you don't this time, there's always another auction coming up.

AntiqInfo

You may have heard about dealer rings in which a few dealers agree not to bid against one another, thereby keeping the selling price down. After the sale, the ring supposedly holds a private auction. This practice is illegal. Furthermore, most auctioneers want to get the most money they can for their goods and have ways of breaking up rings.

AntiqClue

Something you can't live without is coming up at auction. You don't trust yourself. Ask an experienced bidder-friend to bid for you, or pay a dealer or broker (usually 10 or 15 percent) to get the piece for you. That's a fairly common practice among major collectors who value a dealer's wisdom, knowledge, and experience.

Then Again, Patience Is a Virtue

Other auction-goers reason that they will let the bidding go along and then, when interest lags, jump in *if* the next bid falls within their acceptable price limit.

This kind of bidder holds back, rather than letting the early bidders know someone else is interested in the piece. The bidder's reasoning is that the more people who show an interest in a piece, the higher the bidding will go (the follow-the-herd instinct). But if just a couple of people are bidding, then other bidders may decide the piece isn't so great after all and lose interest.

This strategy works, too.

Learning the Competition

If you're new to the game, you probably won't be able to distinguish the dealers, the collectors, and the casual buyers from one another. Eventually, though, dealers will become identifiable to you.

They are the ones who, when they stop bidding, mean it. The auctioneer may try to tempt or even tease them into just one more, higher bid. They, the dealers, will sit on their paddles rather than give in and pay more than their preestablished limits.

The dealers are the ones who may pass out their cards to bidders who are interested in the same items they were bidding for. And the dealers are the ones who are found huddled together at the back of the room, discussing their mutual clients and what they've been buying lately.

Practice Makes Perfect

In the long run, the best way to learn the auction scene is to go to auctions and bid. Realize that you may not be successful in your first bidding attempts. But practice makes perfect; and after you've lost a few and won a few, you'll get the hang of it.

Not the Final Price

If you've never bought anything at an auction, it may come as a rude awakening that the final bidding price is *not* the final price.

The Buyer's Premium

Auction houses have to make money. To do this they have always charged the seller a percentage of the selling price. But several years ago, American auction houses took up the European custom of tacking on a buyer's premium to the final bid. The buyer's premium is usually 10 or 15 percent of the *hammer price*. Thus, if you pay $1,800 for a piece, you can expect either $180 or $270 to be added to your bill.

AntiqLingo

The **hammer price** is the price in effect when the auctioneer takes the final bid from the crowd and bangs down the hammer on the podium. This is a sign that the piece has sold and no more bids will be taken. Therefore, the hammer price is the price the piece sells for.

Other Charges

Other charges incurred at an auction are more typical of business transactions. They include tax (if applicable), packing, shipping, and insurance charges. If you've bought an especially fragile piece that needs special packing, you may want to tip the packer.

When You Can't Be There

You've had the chance to pour over the auction catalogue. You've found one or more pieces you want to bid on. You may have called the auction house to inquire more about those pieces—a normal procedure when you don't live in the same city as the auction gallery. Trouble is, you can't be there to bid on these objects of your desire.

If you can't attend the auction itself, never fear. The auction house will take your bid anyway.

AntiqInfo

Auction houses have pickup areas where sold items are held until after the sale. The whole pickup, payment, and shipping process varies from house to house. Some houses provide free wrapping materials and even packers to assist you. Other houses expect you to do everything yourself. Check the house's policies before buying.

Absentee Bidding

If you attend the auction preview, you can leave a bid onsite. An attendant will help you fill out the appropriate form if you haven't done this before. This is called an *absentee bid*.

What happens if a piece sells for less than the absentee bid you left? That's great. You pay only the price of the last bid, plus the buyer's premium, of course.

So let's say that you left this absentee bid:

Lot 32   Chippendale chair $1,800 plus one

The bidding on the chair stops at $1,200. The auctioneer then enters your bid at the next *increment*, which in this instance is a $200 increment. The bid now stands at $1,400. No other bids are made. You get the chair for $1,400 (plus the buyer's premium).

Ma Bell Goes to the Auction

If you really want a piece, though, you will want to be on the phone for the bidding.

Someone from the auction house will call you a few lots before the item comes up. (You will have discussed this earlier, of course.) The auction house person will then lead you through the bidding, and you will be able to tell the person when to *"Bid!"*

The auctioneer takes these phone bids along with all other bids from the floor, so it's just as if you were there. If the bidding goes over your limit, you stop. Or you can keep going until you get a piece.

Phone bids are popular and easy. Once you've actually observed how they work at an auction, you'll get the gist of it.

The Least You Need to Know

➤ Auction previews and sales are invaluable educational experiences.

➤ Buy and use auction catalogues.

➤ The price you pay for a piece will be higher than the hammer price.

➤ Absentee bidding is fair and efficient if you can't make it to a sale.

Chapter 14

Brave New E-World

In This Chapter

➤ Learn the advantages of using the World Wide Web to explore antiques

➤ Find out the hazards of using the Internet superhighway

➤ Discover what kinds of antiques and antiquing info can be yours once you are online

➤ Become comfortable with Web lingo

➤ Get ready to attend a virtual auction

The Internet is a collection of virtual communities, thousands of which are composed of talented specialists, scattered across the globe—and they're there for you if only you'll seek them out.

How can the Internet enhance your knowledge of antiques?

➤ It can provide you with journal articles, catalogues, and historical documents (such as price guides) from sources you did not even know existed.

➤ It offers a continuing education.

➤ It can place you on the front row at a virtual auction.

AntiqInfo

In your quest for more computer knowledge, check out *The Complete Idiot's Guide to Online Auctions* (1999) and *The Complete Idiot's Guide to Online Search Secrets* (1999).

The World of the Web

So much is going on in this brave new e-world—new developments and constant changes. A link to the World Wide Web can be your link to a better understanding of the antiques world. If you're a computer-type, you may find that cyberspace will inspire you to explore the "real" antiques world.

If you're not a computer-type, this book isn't intended to tell you how to use a computer. This is a book on antiques! But it will point you to some of the many options, sites, and opportunities that await the brave new cyberspace antiquer. Think of it as rummaging around in your grandmother's basement or attic. You never know what you'll discover.

Crank Up the Engine

Trying to finding your way around the Internet without getting lost can be mind-boggling. That's why you need to crank up your favorite search engine—to help you search for your prized antiques.

Here are some good search engines to get your search started:

    www.yahoo.com—most similar to roaming through a library

    www.google.com—similar to Yahoo; has received praise for being very intuitive

    www.northernlight.com—"armorial Chinese export teapot"

    www.hotbot.com—best all-around

Getting Where You Want to Be

Once you're connected, your mission is a quest for antiques. Type in an antiques-related item in the search box. Let's use "William and Mary."

Right away, you may learn that you have to be more specific than that, especially if the search engine gives you hundreds of thousands of possible references for "William" and then follows this up with hundreds of thousands of possible references for "Mary." So try again. Try typing "William and Mary furniture" (as a general topic) or "William and Mary gateleg table" (as a specific topic). Be sure to include the phrase you use in quotation marks. This will help prevent the search engine from breaking out "William" or "Mary" and sending you on a wild goose chase. Even so, you'll be amazed at the amount of information now available to you about William and Mary furniture or gateleg tables.

Not Just for Buying

You may have been enticed this far by the promise that the Internet will let you *buy* a piece of real English silver without flying to England or by the thought that you can shop for a Tiffany lamp from Sotheby's in your p.j.'s.

However, consider as well the resources that can be found at the click of a mouse: appraisal services and appraisers; advice on, and sources for, restoration; educational materials (books!); and lists of brick-and-mortar auction houses and museums. (That's the e-way of saying it is an actual store, not a virtual one.)

The Price Is Right ... or Wrong

The Web is also great for comparison shopping if you don't have an extensive personal library of auction catalogues and price guides. You can now use the Internet to do important research before you buy.

Go to virtual galleries or malls to check current prices of items you're interested in, or look at recent bids in online auctions.

But don't just check prices of similar or comparable pieces. Comparison shopping also means comparing the cost of a period piece versus a reproduction.

Let's say you want an eighteenth-century slant-front desk, but you've been told, "You can find a new reproduction for $3,800 that is just as good. You can't touch an eighteenth-century one for under $5,000."

Because you've done your comparison shopping, you know that a good, but not magnificent, period eighteenth-century desk does *not* have to cost $5,000. You found one that sold for $4,200.

AntiqClue

Remember, the Web is *big!* A search for a single word like "antique" can return tens of thousands of pages. Typing in "Eastlake oak bookcase" will get you much closer to what you're looking for.

AntiqInfo

Two auction sites that contain good reference and educational material are www.icollector.com and www.circline.com.

AntiqLingo

A **virtual gallery,** mall, or auction house/museum is one that exists online and offers e-commerce (online payment) for select inventory.

AntiqInfo

Don't forget the importance of verifying rarity, quality, and price when researching an antique. The Internet is a good place to start.

Leveling the World-Wide Playing Field

Another tough spot that novice antiquers find themselves in goes something like this:

You're looking at an English silver serving spoon made by Hester Bateman when the dealer says, "This is the only one I've ever seen outside of a museum." You crank up your search engine and in no time turn up a half dozen Hester Bateman silver serving spoons on the various cyberspace auction sites.

Armed with a world of knowledge, you are better equipped to make an informed decision before buying that rare and costly treasure.

Shop Anywhere, Anytime, Anyhow

A good catch phrase ... and it easily applies to sites on the Internet. But is *more* always better?

Getting Sucked In

Going to the Internet for a quick answer is sometimes the long way around. Have you ever tried to find a fast answer on the Net and two hours later realized that you'd almost forgotten your original search?

Truth is, you can waste a lot of time looking for a piece of Newcomb pottery at the sothebys.com site ... which has a link to their *Connoisseur* section (good to learn a little more before you buy) ... which has a link to their *Collecting Guide* (with a "selection of practical and insightful primers on many of the most popular areas for today's collectors of antiques") ... which is currently featuring silver (and your mother does have a beautiful tea service with a bowl) ... what is that extra bowl used for?

Now *what* was I looking for?

Get a Life

Nowhere in this discussion of cyberspace have I mentioned the benefit and enjoyment of seeing and touching an eighteenth-century piece of English sterling, or of meeting the fascinating owner of one of those few remaining dusty and dimly lit antiques shops. You miss a lot of life when you live it through telephone lines and a computer screen.

You may also miss tiny chips in porcelain, a scratch on the side of a blanket chest, or, most tragically, the chance to run your hand across the bottom of that Chippendale chair and feel the marks left in 1790 when it was hand-planed.

Understanding the New Kid on the Block

There are advantages and disadvantages in any marketplace. The trick is *knowing* how to use the tools at hand.

Risks and Rewards

Even as I write this book and you read it, new Internet sites are popping up daily. Considering this, and the fact that the majority of these companies have not been around long enough to build a reputation, there are obvious risks involved if you're an antiques novice or a Web novice, or both.

As for rewards, they can be great, should you find the right site. You now have the potential to find more inventory and information than ever before.

Buyer Beware

What are your antiquing words to live by? *Caveat emptor!*

They ought to jump off the page when you're considering purchasing from an online dealer or auction house that you're unfamiliar with.

To get more information on condition, age, or any other aspect of the deal, try sending an e-mail to the seller listed on the Web site.

AntiqClue

Don't know where to start when you've stumbled upon a new antiques Web page that's full of all kinds of yummy, informative links? Most Web sites have a special place for first-time visitors: "New to (and the name of the company)." Click there first.

AntiqInfo

In 1999 Sotheby's announced its plan to invest $25 million to develop Internet auctions. In that same year, 5-year-old eBay acquired Butterfield & Butterfield (the 135-year-old San Francisco auction house), and Amazon signed a 10-year agreement with Sotheby's. (Both Amazon and Sotheby's started out selling books!) Now Sloan's has joined forces with antiqnet.com.

Here Today, Gone Tomorrow

Struck by the urge to make an impulse purchase? The act of walking away from a piece to see if you are still thinking about it in 24 hours is a good trick. After all, by now you know that it's always smart to compare, question, and research.

Suppose that while browsing a country antiques shop, you find a pair of Sheraton beds. It can be scary to leave them after you've seen them, touched them, and examined them. But you may be able to put them on hold until your friend, who is more knowledgeable about antiques, comes to town the day after tomorrow.

AntiqClue

More and more, auction sites are offering personalized services under headings like "My Agent," "My Portfolio," or "My eBay." For registered users (and you must register), these sites will track items and e-mail a buyer/seller/bidder update. They may even help you find an item you are looking for, or track your account history.

However, this strategy won't work in a cyberspace auction. There is no "hold" button in cyberspace. And auctions are not scheduled for 11:00 A.M. February 21. Although online auctions do have starting dates and closing dates, much of the bidding takes place that last day—or often in the last few minutes—and that may be the very time you stumble upon this object of your desire.

So be forewarned: The next time you log on to check out the bed, desk, chair, or whatever, it might have been sold. But worse yet! You are now dealing with technology, and your ISP may be down, the Web site might be "under construction," or you might encounter software or hardware problems on your computer.

How Suckers Are Born

I've touched on problems specific to the Internet. But being the brave soul you are, you've learned the ropes and have relaxed in this new world. This is when it gets really easy to get sucked in. Let's look at some of the ways you can prevent this.

Seeing Is Believing

Do you see enough to buy on the Internet? You will, certainly, if you are purchasing Miller's *Pocket Antiques Fact File* from amazon.com or a current Sloan's auction catalogue from antiqnet.com.

But what happens when you've decided to enter a virtual auction, and you have narrowed your search, to say, decorative arts → furniture → American. Now you are faced with a list of all the lots in that category. This list typically includes a small picture of the item, a brief description, the time remaining in the auction, and the current bid.

If you click on one of the lots, you will find a more detailed description with date, dimensions, condition of the piece (hopefully), bidding details, a link to the selling company, and (again hopefully) close-up pictures of the item.

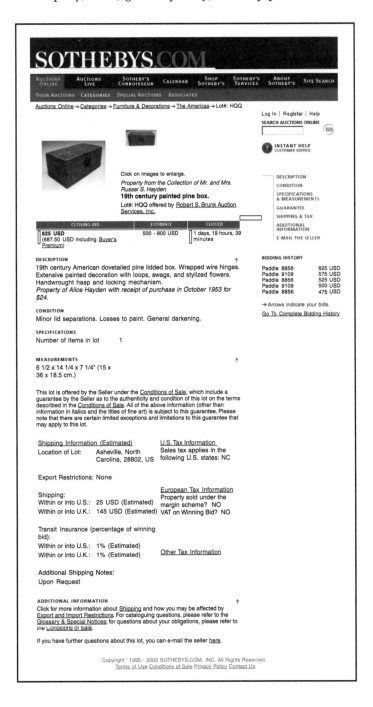

Notice the detailed description (including measurements and condition) that appears with this picture of a painted pine box up for bids at Sotheby's online auction.

You can e-mail or call the company, but, no matter how high the resolution of your monitor, you can't touch the piece. The photo may not show the back of the armoire (so that you can see whether the wood has darkened with age or has telltale circular saw marks) or may not show any internal dovetailing. Even if a photo does show the dovetails, they may not have enough detail for you to tell whether the cuts were made by hand or by machine.

AntiqClue

Some sites offer a feedback forum (found at eBay), or the like. This essentially creates a history on buyers and sellers, with readers' comments on reliability, punctuality and courtesy. If you've had a particularly good or bad experience, enter your comments. Or read those that others have made about an individual or dealer before you seal a deal.

Before You Buy

Whether purchasing from an online auction house or museum, find out the return policy before you buy—especially time constraints and associated costs. This is especially important when you plan to purchase an item sight unseen.

Honesty Is the Best Policy

To ensure that you know as much as possible before bidding, tell the individual or the company that you are a picky buyer and want "all the dirt." Be specific. Ask if a piece is monogrammed, or if the monogram on a silver-plated tray is on a sterling inset.

When the piece arrives, confirm that you got what you wanted. If not ... well, you know the return policy, right? Read on.

Return Policy

Which part of an auction catalogue were you advised to read and understand *before* getting too excited about the picture of the silver epergne? The *terms and conditions* section.

A similar business agreement is part of any reputable online auction house. Look for a link from a Web site's home page titled "services" or "information." From there, you should find another link to a section that will describe their conditions of sale.

Hidden Costs

You may recall the discussion in Chapter 13, "Playing for Keeps," regarding buyers and sellers fees. The situation is similar for online auctions. Although a few online auction houses do not impose a buyer's premium, you won't know until you read it yourself.

In cyberspace, when you purchase an item from a regular business site (for example, barnesandnoble.com), you know what the associated shipping, handling, and, possibly, insurance costs will be. However, in the case of person-to-person auctions (like those held on eBay), the seller will tell you what these services will cost. The seller should have investigated the cost of packing and shipping beforehand, but as an educated buyer, you should know the approximate cost of these things yourself.

When you take part in a business-to-customer transaction (as would be the case at eBay's Great Collections site), typically you will purchase an item under the dealer's conditions of sale, and that person will advise you of shipping costs.

Baby Step by Step

So, you've decided to make an online purchase of a piece of Georgian silver or a candlestand. Are you going to pay for it with your credit card? Many people feel that credit cards aren't safe on the Internet because your credit card number will be readily available to the world. Controlled purchase is a valid concern, and credit card numbers are required as part of the registration process for most companies. For this reason many people refuse to make purchases online and as I write, this is a hotly debated subject. But think about this: It's also pretty common to hand over a credit card as payment in a restaurant. What's the difference?

Click for Click

A few words about today's hot Internet auction houses and galleries.

The eBay site (www.ebay.com) is a great place to begin. There is so much there to explore, and the volume of goods and bids is great. You might try bidding on a small item with your *disposable* income to try out the process. These are person-to-person auctions, in which you are buying from an actual person rather than from a business. In these types of auctions, the company, such as eBay, functions as a host rather than the seller.

AntiqInfo

Online shipping sources include the U.S. Postal Service (www.usps.gov), Federal Express (www.fedex.com), and United Parcel Service (www.ups.com).

AntiqClue

A secure site will utilize Secure Socket Layer (SSL) encryption. The site will tell you whether it has this encryption, and if so, most people believe that you can feel safe.

AntiqInfo

Well, it isn't exactly info about antiques, but in today's Internet world, business is being conducted customer-to-customer (meaning private party to private party), business-to-business, and business-to-customer.

123

The eBay site Great Collections (www.ebaygreatcollections.com) is still growing. The regular site has more period pieces on it than this site. As mentioned before, Great Collections are business-to-customer auctions.

The Sotheby's site (www.sothebys.com) is another well-known and popular site. Here you have the assurance of the experts' opinions on pieces. That's lacking at some other sites. However, as other auction houses join related Web sites, more good pieces accompanied by expert opinions are expected. An example is www.antiqnet.com, which lists members and dealers, and has a link to Sloan's Auctions Web site (sloansauction.com) from its home page.

The antiqnet.com site provides many services, from reference materials and books to appraisal services, plus its connection to Sloan's expertise.

One Highway Leads to Many

As you explore these sites looking for some specific item, your eyes will likely stray to other antiques, or maybe even something brand new (like a computer!) that you may be interested in researching further.

Search and discover at will—and at your leisure. That's one good thing about browsing through antiques in cyberspace —you're not at risk of tripping on a Persian rug and falling into the display of Herend miniatures!

My Personal Take on Antiques Cyberspace

Having thought over the pros and cons of this brave new e-world, I've come to this conclusion. Ultimately the Internet will cause the value of commonplace items to decrease, and increase the value of rare ones.

The Least You Need to Know

➤ The Internet can open many doors and be your key to unlocking a great deal of knowledge about antiques.

➤ Virtual auction houses are many, and bidding can be fun. But you must exercise prudence.

➤ Gaining access to the Internet has become serious business for brick-and-mortar auction houses and museums—a fact that tells us the power of antiques cyberspace.

➤ You don't have to be a computer nerd to get hooked on shopping for antiques on the Internet.

Part 4

Getting Down to Brass Tacks

The casual antiques admirer and the true antiques lover have much in common. They subscribe to the same magazines. They buy the same books. They attend the same lectures. They visit the same museums. They even go to the same shops, sales, malls, and auctions.

There is one major factor that separates the casual antiques admirer from the true antiques lover, though—knowledge of the objects themselves.

In this part, you'll learn where to look and what to look for when examining antiques.

Furniture: The Lure of the Old

Historically, furniture as we think of it today—comfortable, practical, beautiful furniture—has been around for only about 300 years, or since the eighteenth century.

During those 300 years, there have been only seven or so major furniture designs. In fact, since the early to mid-twentieth century, not one single, truly original furniture movement has captured the general public's approval for any long-lasting period of time. Over the past 50 or 75 years, the majority of furniture companies have settled for turning out "remakes" of the old furniture designs.

What about Bauhaus and Art Deco and even 1950s modern furniture? you may be wondering. Yes, these are important furniture designs, but they never acquired the widespread public acceptance that the older, traditional styles had.

Early Warning Signs!

No area of antiques has been more faked and maligned than furniture. Why?

One reason goes back to what I've already said. Everyone needs a chair to sit on, a table to eat from, or a bed to sleep on. This means that more people are competing to collect antique furniture than any other category of antiques. This, in turn, means that furniture is where the big bucks are—except for art masterpieces (but those are considered the fine arts and antiques are classified as the decorative arts).

Another reason is that furniture, unlike *most* china, silver, and glass pieces, can be handmade by good craftsmen. This means it is possible to "re-create" pieces either copied after, or based on, furniture from the eighteenth and early nineteenth centuries. Clever craftsmen can also "alter" or "improve" a piece of furniture for whatever purpose. Remember, the original pieces were made in a workshop—*not* manufactured.

For all of these reasons, look closely before you buy.

Two Countries an Ocean Apart

The majority of antique furniture that you'll find for sale in most shops, malls, sales, and auction houses will be either American or English made. You may run into a fair amount of French furniture, but the best way to begin learning about antiques is to begin with the kind that you'll see the most of—American and English. These types of furniture are less complicated than French furniture, making it easier to get the lay of the land. For these reasons, we'll focus on English and American furniture.

Rule Britannia

Even if you didn't get an *A* in history, you probably remember that Jamestown, the first permanent English settlement in America, was settled in 1607. The brave souls who made it here obviously didn't bring any furniture with them on those tiny boats. But they did bring the tradition of English furniture design and the knowledge of how to make it.

Farther north, the Pilgrims and Puritans did the same. Many of these early stalwart adventurers may have come to America by way of other European countries, but they were basically of English heritage, and when they began making furniture for their homes, they followed the English tradition.

And so, north and south, the colonists preferred furniture with a distinctly English look.

Westward Ho!

It would take several years before the settlers in the Colonies had the leisure time and financial resources to build any but the most basic pieces of furniture. Even when they did, for decades, and generations, American craftsmen would continue to look to England to see what their furniture should look like.

In those days before airplanes, TV, and the Internet, months could elapse before England's latest styles reached American seaports. It then took still longer for pictures and examples of these designs to move farther westward and reach the hinterlands.

The British Invasion

There's one more consideration: the people who made the furniture in America and the people who were purchasing the pieces. For years, most of America's furniture craftsmen were immigrants who had learned their craft in England. Furthermore, the people who were ordering and purchasing these wares were usually of English background. Is it any surprise that English-looking furniture made in America was popular?

Come Together

To sum up, England's ongoing influence in the Colonies, plus the distance between the two countries, resulted in eighteenth- and nineteenth-century American furniture based on English designs.

Overlapping Timetables

Now everything would have been just fine, had not two factors come into play:

1. The time it took for new styles to travel from England to America and become popular here (remember, America has always been rather conservative)

2. America's desire to distance herself from the British crown once she began standing on her own two feet

AntiqInfo

Throughout the seventeenth century and also during the early years of the eighteenth century, Americans either ordered their furniture from England or had it made here, copying pieces shown in English pattern books.

AntiqInfo

Chippendale, Hepplewhite, and Sheraton weren't the only furniture designers making "Chippendale," "Hepplewhite," and "Sheraton" furniture. But they wrote the books and drew the pictures that caught the public's imagination, and thus their names have lived while other designers' names have been forgotten.

131

Without these factors, American furniture designs might have been called by the same names as the English ones: Jacobean, Queen Anne, Georgian, and so on. The English names were related to the names or reigns of the ruling British monarch at the time.

However, American-made furniture after the Queen Anne period, or around 1750 or 1760, is not known by the names of the ruling British monarchs. Instead, eighteenth- and nineteenth-century American furniture periods are known by the names of the Englishmen (commoners, mind you) who originated the designs: Chippendale, Hepplewhite, Sheraton, Eastlake, and so on. That's where the terms "Chippendale furniture" and "Eastlake furniture" come from.

Because it took so long for the new styles to reach America's shores, the old styles remained fashionable much longer than they did in England. This means, for example, that even though smaller, more delicate chairs were becoming popular in England in, say, 1770, the style didn't really become mainstream in American until around 1785. The fancy term for furniture made in the countryside in a style that has already become "old-fashioned" elsewhere is *retardetaire*.

Now you understand why American and English furniture can look very similar but be called by different names and actually vary a little in age. The following lists are quick references to the periods used in each country.

English Period Names and Dates	Ruling Monarchs
Jacobean, 1603–1625	James I
Carolean, 1625–1649	Charles I
Cromwellian, 1649–1660	Commonwealth
Restoration, 1660–1685	Charles II
Restoration, 1685–1689	James II
William and Mary, 1689–1694	William and Mary
William III, 1694–1702	William III
Queen Anne, 1702–1714	Anne
Early Georgian, 1714–1727	George I
Early Georgian, 1727–1760	George II

English Period Names and Dates	Ruling Monarchs
Later Georgian, 1760–1811	George III
Regency III, 1811–1820	George
Regency, 1820–1830	George IV
Regency, 1830–1837	William IV
Early Victorian, 1837–1860	Victoria
Later Victorian, 1860–1901	Victoria
Aesthetic Movement, 1860–1901	Victoria
Edwardian, 1901–1910	Edward VII
Aesthetic Movement, 1860–1901	Edward VII
Arts and Crafts, 1901–1910	Edward VII

Note that the reign of George III is associated with two different design eras, and the reigns of Victoria and Edward VII with three. Further, the Early Georgian, Regency, and Aesthetics eras extend beyond one monarch's reign.

American Period Names	Dates
Jacobean/William and Mary	1607–1702
Queen Anne	1702–1760
Chippendale	1750–1790
Federal (a.k.a. Hepplewhite)	1780–1800
Federal (a.k.a. Sheraton)	1800–1815
Empire (a.k.a. Classical and Duncan Phyfe)	1815–1850
Victorian Rococo	1830s–1890s
Victorian Gothic	1840–1860
Victorian Renaissance	1850–1880
Eastlake	1870–1900
Cottage	1840–1900
Aesthetic Movement	1880–1900
Art and Crafts	1890–1920

133

Put this all together and you come up with the following commonly used AntiqLingo and benchmark dates that will get you through almost any antiques scene until you become a real furniture expert:

Capsule Guide to Furniture Periods

Jacobean	American and English	Seventeenth century (1600–1700)
Queen Anne	American and English	Eighteenth century (1700–1760)
Chippendale	American	Eighteenth century (1750–1790)
Georgian	English only	Eighteenth/nineteenth century (1710–1810)
Hepplewhite	American	Eighteenth century (1780–1795)
Sheraton	American	Eighteenth/nineteenth century (1795–1815)
Federal	American only	Eighteenth/nineteenth century (1780–1815)
Regency	English only	Eighteenth/nineteenth century (1793–1830)
Empire/ Classical	American only	Nineteenth century (1815–1850)
Victorian	English and American	Nineteenth century (1840s–1900)
Aesthetic Movement	English and American	Nineteenth century (1860s–1900)
Arts and Crafts	English and American	Nineteenth/twentieth century (1880s–1920s)

Shortcut Aids to Understanding Furniture Periods

Now let's look at each one of these periods separately.

To make it easy to learn what makes, say, a Jacobean piece different from an Eastlake one, I'll give you some painless social and technological info about what was happening in the world at the time. Then I'll point out and describe those design elements that are special to the particular period. Finally I'll end with a short list of the furniture pieces made during that period.

However, before you read any further, here is a quick review of the names that experts give to the various furniture parts.

AntiqClue

It may not be politically correct, but the first place to look for clues about the style of a furniture piece is its legs and feet. Are they curvy, straight-lined, bulbous, or ball-and-claw? These are all distinguishing design elements that you'll soon be familiar with.

This quick review of names given to individual furniture parts may come in handy when you're discussing antiques.

AntiqInfo

Designs don't spring into being full grown. They evolve gradually with time. That's why you may see a chair with a "Queen Anne" back and "Chippendale" legs. Such pieces are called **transitional** pieces. Transitional pieces are usually named according to the design used for the legs. Thus, our hybrid chair with the Queen Anne back would be deemed a "Chippendale" chair because it has Chippendale legs.

Hefty Jacobean

The earliest period furniture that shows up in the antiques market is Jacobean furniture, the furniture made under the reign of James I (1603–1625) in England, and throughout the seventeenth century in America.

You aren't going to find much Jacobean (sometimes called William and Mary) furniture around. And even if you do, it may not be much to your liking—it's heavy, cumbersome, and uncomfortable. Seventeenth-century Jacobean furniture has a heft and bulk to it that you won't see again until the nineteenth century. This is the furniture made before chairs had springs and foam cushions. A wooden bed raised on legs was considered a luxury item, not a necessity, at this time. Remember also, the craftsmen of the era were working with large timbers and limited tools.

A good example of Jacobean furniture is the court cupboard—a multipurpose piece used to both store items (in the cupboard section) and to display them (on the top and open shelves).

The dominating Jacobean design elements include lots of straight lines, large panels and turned parts, and arches along cornices and at stretchers.

Representative pieces of the Jacobean period include chairs, joint stools, court cupboards, chests, trestle tables, gateleg tables, and chair-tables.

The boxy proportions, straight lines, large panels, and turned parts of this court cupboard are typically Jacobean.

(Photo courtesy of The Museum of Early Southern Decorative Arts)

During the seventeenth century, tables and chairs were the staple pieces of furniture in the Jacobean home. Just as the court cupboard was multipurposed, so was the table-chair (shown here as a table), which also served as a chair when the top was placed upright.

The few period Jacobean pieces that have survived often are better suited to historic restorations than to twenty-first century homes.

(Photo courtesy of Craig and Tarlton)

One Jacobean furniture form that has survived the centuries and remained popular is the gateleg table. The drop leaves makes this type of table versatile and easily moveable, a characteristic as useful today as 300 years ago.

The ball and ring turnings on the gates and legs plus the compact bun feet clearly identify this as a Jacobean piece.

(Photo courtesy of Craig and Tarlton)

137

Curvy Queen Anne

Many people call the Queen Anne era "the first modern furniture period." Furniture design was still in its infancy during this period. Nevertheless, the pieces that were made are showstoppers, and Queen Anne furniture retains its popularity yet today.

Before You Buy

The Jacobean look may not be very popular now, but it was *the* look in the late 1890s and early 1900s and was widely reproduced. Most of the reproductions are lightweight and spindly compared with the real period pieces.

In contrast to the straight lines of the preceding Jacobean era, curves became fashionable. In fact, it is the curved, cabriole leg that immediately labels a piece "Queen Anne." Cabriole literally means the bent shape of a leaping goat's leg, but when this shape is translated into a curve on a piece of furniture, the result is graceful and appealing.

The world was making many advances, socially and technically, in the early 1700s. Furniture was hand-made, of course, but stronger, newly designed tools made it possible to make more refined pieces more quickly. Greater wealth among the merchant class also created a greater demand for more furniture.

The chair is a good example of how quickly things were changing. In the seventeenth century, most chairs were wood. A few people could afford a little leather for a chair back, and the fabulously wealthy could afford some tapestry upholstery. During the Queen Anne period, upholstery seats and "overstuffed" chairs became fashionable, although only the privileged could afford them. Furthermore, the Queen Anne chair shown here clearly reveals how curving lines were used. This is in stark contrast to the straight lines of Jacobean furniture.

The rounded crest rail, the outswept cabriole leg, and the fiddle-shape of the back splat combine to give Queen Anne furniture a curving, feminine elegance.

Queen Anne design elements include graceful, curved lines, cabriole legs, vase or "fiddle" chair backs, carved shells, and acanthus motifs added for decoration.

Once the lighter, more graceful look of furniture became popular, older furniture forms were "reworked" to embrace the new style. For example, the dropleaf table of the Jacobean era was still serviceable. But its heavy lines and elaborately turned gates would have made it look out of place when used with the new, more feminine, Queen Anne chairs.

Luckily, the new tools and technology of the eighteenth century made it possible to support the heavy table leaves by pull-out brackets instead of the bulky load-bearing gates that had been necessary in Jacobean times. The solution was to keep the form but to change its design elements, and thus its appearance as seen here.

Notice the graceful scalloping along the table's skirt. This is a Queen Anne design element, as are the rounded, padded feet.

(Photo courtesy of Craig and Tarlton)

Representative pieces of the Queen Anne period include chairs, chests, highboys, lowboys or dressing tables, tea tables, gaming tables, candlestands, and dropleaf tables.

Interestingly, the changes occurring in everyday life and the accompanying lifestyles were strongly reflected in the new furniture forms of the Queen Anne era. Take, for example, the secretary/bookcase. This piece was perfect for businessmen in the newly emerging merchant class who needed a piece of furniture that could hold books and provide a writing surface where they could take care of correspondence and bookkeeping. Of course, only the wealthy could afford such a piece, but those who could wanted a lovely piece in the newest fashion, like the one illustrated next.

AntiqInfo

There are no period Queen Anne sideboards or extension dining room tables. The ones you see are reproductions.

The bold s-curve at the broken pediment cornice, the rounded "tombstone" paneled doors, and the compact cabriole legs are all strong Queen Anne design elements.

(Photo courtesy of Craig and Tarlton)

It was during the early eighteenth century that houses also began taking on a new, "modern," look. Earlier, one "great room" had functioned as the living and dining room. Now separate living rooms and dining rooms were being built. People were also gathering more possessions such as clothing, linens, and so on, around them.

One of the most desirable new pieces of furniture during the Queen Anne period was the highboy (shown next). It was both a serviceable storage piece and a beautiful form that allowed the expert craftsman a way to show off his skills.

Everything about this highboy characterizes the best of the Queen Anne period: fine proportions, the "bat-wing" hardware and keyhole escutcheons, elegant shell carving, and of course, the cabriole legs.

(Photo courtesy of Craig and Tarlton)

Straight Mr. Chippendale

Chippendale furniture is probably the best known and most easily identified of all the furniture periods. The designs were made famous when Thomas Chippendale published his book, *The Gentleman and Cabinet Maker's Director,* in 1754. Advanced students of eighteenth-century furniture divide Chippendale's design work into three groups: Rococo, Gothic, and Chinese Chippendale.

While pretty curves and cabriole legs say "Queen Anne," intricate carving and straight lines are the giveaway characteristic of the Chippendale period.

By the mid-eighteenth century, mahogany was being imported to America and Europe from the East and West Indies. Its dense grain and dark color were particularly well suited for the strong-lined, masculine Chippendale furniture designs.

The Chippendale chair clearly shows the changes introduced by the furniture craftsmen of the mid-eighteenth century. In the following figure, note how the crest rail is curved, but boldly so. Though the back is pierced, the design is contained within a basic rectangular shape. Gone are the sweeping, more feminine curves of the Queen Anne era.

Still there are some curving lines in Chippendale furniture, especially in the popular Chippendale tea table. As seen in the following figure, the table's round top and trifid base are proof of that. But when strong carving and ball-and-claw feet are added to those curving lines, the table takes on a new, stronger look.

The dominating Chippendale design elements include straight legs and stretchers, fret work, bold acanthus, gadroon carving, and larger-sized pieces.

Before You Buy

Think about it. Desks and secretary/bookcases serve a practical purpose but are expensive to make. During the Queen Anne period, only a few people in England and America would have had the money and the need for a desk or a secretary/bookcase.

AntiqClue

The English call the furniture made during the Chippendale period "early Georgian." Remember what Shakespeare said in *Romeo and Juliet:* "That which we call a rose/By any other name would smell as sweet."

The curves of the crest rail and back of the Chippendale chair are part of a strong and complex design element. Notice that the chair's legs and stretcher are straight and that the chair has lost the feminine look associated with Queen Anne pieces.

(Photo courtesy of Sloan's)

The cabriole legs of this high-style Chippendale tea table are a carry-over from the Queen Anne era, but the bold carving on the knees and at the feet, plus the dark mahogany wood, classify this piece as Chippendale.

(Photo courtesy of Craig and Tarlton)

By the 1760s and 1770s, the height of America's Chippendale period, the middle class was firmly in place. The slant-front writing desk, without the bookcase section, was becoming a necessity for the up-and-coming businessman's home. The following illustration is a very fine example of a Chippendale period piece.

There's not much fluff on this straight-lined Chippendale slant-front writing desk, but the shaped brasses and escutcheons, carved interior, quarter columns along the side, and ogee bracket feet make a strong statement.

(Photo courtesy of Craig and Tarlton)

Not all American-made Chippendale furniture was high style. By the 1760s, prosperous families were moving westward. They ordered "new-fashioned" furniture from local craftsmen who were not as skilled as their city counterparts. Furthermore, these craftsmen made furniture from the available native woods—cherry and walnut, even maple. Though simpler than "city pieces," these provencial antiques are often beautiful and very affordable.

A classic example of a strong, yet simple, Chippendale piece is this Pembroke table. Its simplicity is carried out in the bail brass pull on the drawer and its straight drop leaves. The additional molding of the legs and the cross stretcher add interest to this basic, and probably rural-made, period table.

(Photo courtesy of Craig and Tarlton)

143

Representative pieces of the Chippendale period include chairs, chests, tea tables, candlestands, and corner cupboards. This period also introduced Pembroke tables and saw the rise of desks and secretary/bookcases, which became more commonplace (but not common), as did upholstered chairs and sofas. Breakfronts became a popular English piece.

The Georges I, II, and III

These three Georges were on the throne from 1714 until 1811. When the English speak of Georgian furniture, they are referring to the furniture made between 1714 and 1795, when they begin using the term Regency. Thus, Georgian corresponds to the American Chippendale, Hepplewhite, and Sheraton periods.

The English further break this broad 1714 to 1795 time span into two sections: Early Georgian and Late Georgian. Unless you are going to be doing a lot of antiquing in England, or in highly specialized English antiques shops, just a nodding acquaintance with the term "Georgian" will probably get you by.

George I is credited with beginning the tradition of eating at a long dining room table set with matching silver, china, and glassware. But it wasn't until the second half of the eighteenth century that long dining room tables were made for the home.

> **Before You Buy**
>
> Fine upholstery, suitable for a Chippendale (or Queen Anne, for that matter) wing chair or sofa, was imported to America from Europe during pre-Revolutionary days. The British taxed the imports, remember? That's why very few upholstered pieces were made in America until the Federal period. If they cost a lot then, think what they cost now! Five and six figures worth.

You immediately see the similarities between this straight-lined, imposing mahogany Georgian-style breakfront bookcase and other Chippendale pieces. When you become a real expert you'll know that this is an English piece and should be called "Georgian," but it's okay to call it Chippendale for now.

(Photo courtesy of Sloan's)

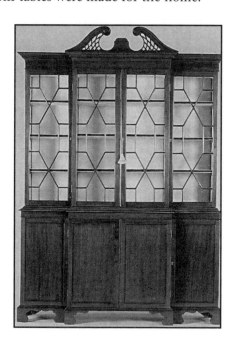

The Least You Need to Know

➤ Although much English and American furniture is very similar, the two countries use different period names. In addition, the dates that the furniture was made in each country will vary slightly.

➤ Seventeenth-century Jacobean furniture is sturdy, boxy, imposing, and rarely found.

➤ Eighteenth-century Queen Anne furniture is distinguished by its feminine curves and grace.

➤ Eighteenth-century Chippendale furniture is masculine when compared with Queen Anne pieces. Chippendale pieces are straight-lined and often made of mahogany.

➤ The English Georgian era encompasses about three quarters of a century of furniture styles.

Chapter 16

The Beginning of a Century of Change

In This Chapter

➤ Continue learning the names of the late eighteenth- and early nineteenth-century periods of English and American furniture

➤ Learn how Hepplewhite completely changed the look of furniture

➤ Find out how the changing nineteenth-century lifestyle led to new furniture pieces

➤ See how Empire furniture reverts back to a heavier, more massive style

If the eighteenth century brought furniture out of the dark ages, the nineteenth century brought furniture design into the light—at least for a while. Later in the century, when the stuffy Victorians brought red velvet and black bunting into fashion, things darkened up again. But for just a few years, what delicate and finely crafted pieces were made.

In studying the late eighteenth and early nineteenth centuries, it is helpful to know the background behind the term *Federal*, a name that rather recently has been applied to furniture of this period. Until about 30 or 40 years ago, American furniture pieces were classified as Hepplewhite or Sheraton or early Empire. Then, to bring attention to the special American post-Revolutionary era, these periods were consolidated into one large, all-inclusive category called "Federal."

Having one category for all these styles is handy, but it does tend to ignore the fact that there are many notable differences in the three designs. For that reason, each is individually described here.

Two Hundred Years and Counting

America's Revolutionary era was such a significant time in our country's history that it's easy to overlook the years between the arrival of the first settlers in 1607 and the Revolution of 1776. In truth, the world was just coming out of the Middle Ages back in 1602. Furniture was still scarce, and only basic pieces were available. The following quick look at America's population and its furniture styles will help put things into better perspective:

1607	Around 100 settlers reach Jamestown	Jacobean
1710	Population reaches approximately 375,500	Queen Anne
1750	Estimated colonial population is 1,207,000	Chippendale
1780	America's population exceeds 2,775,000	Federal/ Hepplewhite
1795	There are well over 4,000,000 Americans	Federal/ Sheraton

AntiqClue

Not every Hepplewhite piece is inlaid. Many Hepplewhite pieces have carved motifs, especially chairs. However, inlay is a *defining* characteristic of Hepplewhite furniture. For example, you'll never find a period inlaid Queen Anne chair or period inlaid Chippendale tea table.

Hepplewhite's Light Touch

In England, George Hepplewhite ushered out the eighteenth century. But in America, his designs bridged the gap between the eighteenth and nineteenth centuries.

Think back to the furniture styles described in Chapter 15, "Furniture: The Lure of the Old." Those earlier styles were mostly dark and large, and any decoration was always carved. It was Hepplewhite who lightened up furniture, slenderized it, and added contrasting, decorative inlay to it.

Those are a lot of changes. And they happened rather suddenly. That is why Hepplewhite furniture is so radically different from Chippendale, Queen Anne, and Jacobean furniture.

So what's the world picture at the dawn of the nineteenth century?

By now the Industrial Revolution had a firm grip in England and America. New power-driven tools made it easier and faster to turn out furniture, even in small, one- or two-person workshops. The middle class was growing like never before. Wealthy people living away from city centers wanted the same furniture as their city counterparts.

Add this all together and the time was right for a whole new look.

Compared with the furniture that came before it, Hepplewhite furniture is delicate in appearance and smaller in scale, and has lost some of that bulkiness, making it easier to transport from one place to another. The good news for the antiques collector is that a lot more furniture was made then than had been made during earlier periods.

The dominating Hepplewhite design elements include slender proportions, delicately carved urns, flowers, garlands, and intricate inlay motifs (bellflowers, urns, circles, and lines) executed in contrasting woods.

Just as the secretary/bookcase and slant-front desks had been highly desirable in the well-to-do early and mid-eighteenth-century home, so the secretary desk became a favorite during the later eighteenth century. Like those earlier pieces, the secretary desk provided a place to carry out business and correspondence. But its appearance was in keeping with the lighter, daintier Hepplewhite style.

AntiqInfo

Thomas Shearer, a contemporary furniture designer of Hepplewhite's, is little known in America. It is Shearer who is credited with the invention of the sideboard.

AntiqClue

Think Baltimore when you think "American Hepplewhite furniture." As the merchant class grew in the early 1800s, cities did, too. Smaller, elegant row houses began replacing large country homes. Large, dark Chippendale furniture just didn't look right in these new, scaled-down homes. Hepplewhite furniture was the perfect solution.

The delicately shaped chair back, open shield design, and square tapering legs immediately classify this as a Hepplewhite chair. What you don't see here is inlay that is more often found on other Hepplewhite pieces such as tables and sideboards.

(Photo courtesy of Craig and Tarlton)

The taller splay feet give this eighteenth-century Hepplewhite secretary desk a more delicate feeling than its Chippendale counterpart. The upper portion has letter cubbyholes and drawer compartments, and the hinged top folds out to make a writing surface.

(Photo courtesy of Sloan's)

Of all the furniture made during the Hepplewhite era, the sideboard emerged as the most popular new furniture form. Until now, serving tables and chests of drawers had been the usual dining room pieces. Now the longer sideboard (like the one shown next) provided even more display and storage space, while adding a beautiful addition to any dining room.

Delicate strips of inlay outline the shape of the sideboard, while inlaid ovals and bellflower drops show off the art of the craftsman. The lovely and practical Hepplewhite sideboard was—and still is—the pride of many a home.

(Photo courtesy of Craig and Tarlton)

Following the American Revolution, many changes affected the family's way of life. For example, there was no longer a high duty or tax on fabrics. Suddenly sofas and other upholstered pieces became affordable.

The shield back chair, inlaid card table, and upholstered seating furniture in the Baltimore Drawing Room at Winterthur exemplify the light, open look of Hepplewhite furniture.

(Photo courtesy of Winterthur)

In brief, the lighter, scaled-down furniture made for rooms in the smaller Federal homes have become antiques that are often ideally suited for some of today's houses, townhouses, and condos.

151

Before You Buy

Sideboards are beautiful, but they can receive a lot of hard use over the years. Hot serving dishes, coffee urns, and lighted candles can leave unsightly stains and damage. Be sure to check the sideboard top for major flaws or even repairs.

AntiqInfo

Sheraton is attributed with designing the first twin beds, roll-top desks, and kidney-shaped tables.

Representative Hepplewhite pieces of the period include chairs, sofas, chests, card tables, Pembroke tables, candlestands, work tables, sideboards, wardrobes, beds, and tambour desks.

Rounding It Off with Sheraton

Thomas Sheraton is known to have been a teacher, preacher, and bookseller. But there is some question about whether Sheraton was ever a practicing cabinetmaker. Little matter. His furniture design books secured his place in the annals of furniture history.

In America, Sheraton furniture is included in the large category known as Federal furniture. Like Hepplewhite furniture, Sheraton furniture has slender proportions, and it became popular at the end of the eighteenth century. But Sheraton furniture is often very different in appearance from Hepplewhite furniture.

Take the legs for example. Hepplewhite legs are square and tapering. Although straight legs were sometimes used (especially on side chairs), Sheraton legs are *usually* round, shapely, and often reeded. There's no place for inlay on a rounded Sheraton leg.

Sheraton furniture is lighter and more restrained than Chippendale furniture, yet it lacks the airy feel of Hepplewhite. You'll notice that the legs on Sheraton pieces begin to thicken a little, and without the inlay to lighten them up, Sheraton pieces start looking a little dark when compared with Hepplewhite pieces. The carving on Sheraton furniture also gives the pieces a slightly heavier aspect.

Look familiar? The pretty, turned legs and gracefully curving arms have made Sheraton sofas and settees a long-time favorite. Though reproductions abound, period Sheraton sofas can also be found.

(Photo courtesy of Craig and Tarlton)

Dominating Sheraton design elements include curved, slender lines; carved urns, ovals, and floral motifs.

You have noticed how the legs on the sofa are distinctly different from Hepplewhite legs. That becomes even more apparent on tables like the one shown next.

The ring turning and reeding on the legs quickly identify this practical, Pembroke table as a Sheraton piece. Notice also the shaped leaves.

(Photo courtesy of Craig and Tarlton)

The differences between Hepplewhite and Sheraton design elements and furniture forms become even more apparent when sideboards from the two periods are compared. In your mind's eye, remember the highly inlaid Hepplewhite sideboard that had long, tapering legs. Now compare that to this Sheraton sideboard (shown next) that was made only about 20 years later.

Turned legs, reeded half columns across the front and deep cabinet sections made this sideboard very fashionable around 1810. But notice the presence of inlay which is a carry-over from the recent Hepplewhite era. Still, the legs and general form of this sideboard clearly make it a Sheraton piece.

(Photo courtesy of Craig and Tarlton)

The Federal Deal

"Federal" furniture is furniture made between 1789 (when America established its Federal government) and 1810 or 1815. The term is a fairly recent one and is not always used by furniture experts. In fact, if you consult some of the older (but helpful) books on American antiques—the ones written before 1950 or 1960—you may not even find the term "Federal" in the index.

Here's an interesting quote from the bible on the period, *American Furniture: The Federal Period, 1788–1825,* written in 1966 by the great American furniture scholar Charles F. Montgomery.

Before You Buy

If Sheraton pieces appeal to you, you're in luck. Period pieces are often easily available and well priced.

As you read the following quote from the Introduction, remember that the name of the book is *The Federal Period*. Still, Henry Francis Du Pont, unquestionably the finest collector of American furniture in the twentieth century and the founder of the incomparable Winterthur Museum, wrote: "Over the years, I have bought many pieces of American furniture in the Hepplewhite and Sheraton styles for the furnishing of rooms, and I am pleased to see them brought together in this book …." Notice that Du Pont didn't refer to them as Federal pieces.

Regal Regency

English Regency furniture (1793–1830) is also called "late Georgian," but it in no way resembles the early Georgian pieces of nearly 100 years before—our Chippendale period.

Regency furniture is similar to that made in America during the early Empire period. It has much of the lightness found in the Hepplewhite era combined with the "Egyptian look."

The Regency period was a prosperous time in England, and the elegance of this furniture shows it. Satinwood and rosewood were favorite woods, and the pieces were dressed up with brass and ormolu ornaments, galleries, and grillwork.

American furniture makers didn't make pieces that looked like this English Regency table.

(Photo courtesy of Christie's)

The Empire Strikes Back

Here we go again.

American furniture made during the 1810 to 1850 era once was generally called "Empire." Except ...

In the early years of the twentieth century, many people called the furniture made in the *later* Empire era (1840s–1850s) Duncan Phyfe furniture, after the well-known Scottish-born cabinetmaker who worked in New York.

These days, many people use the term "Classical" when speaking of the furniture made in the *early* Empire era (1810–1830).

It is easy to understand how both "Empire" and "Classical" came to be applied to the furniture of this era. The furniture was definitely influenced by French *Empire* designs, which used *classical* motifs—animal feet, ornamental columns, lyres, sphinxes, and so on.

To confuse things further, another term is also sometimes used for the very early Empire years: American Directoire.

Before You Buy

Much Empire furniture is veneered. New machines of the time made it possible to cut thin sheets of beautifully figured and grained mahogany to be used on drawer and door fronts. Unfortunately, changing climates can cause veneer to loosen and pop over the years. Make sure that all the veneer is intact on any piece you purchase. It can be costly to restore lost veneer.

There are subtle nuances among *all* the names given to this era, but it's just too much for a novice to take in. The easy way out is to settle on the name "Empire" to cover the furniture made in America during the 1815 to 1850 time frame.

But what did it look like, you're wondering?

Recall that, following the light Hepplewhite era, Sheraton furniture began filling out a little more. Empire furniture continued that trend. The designers of the era returned to heavy, bold lines and dark woods.

AntiqInfo

What major event was occurring during the Empire years (1810–1850) that changed the way furniture was made? The Industrial Revolution. The first real furniture manufacturing factories were established during the Empire period.

Something else to keep in mind. This is the era immediately preceding the Victorian era, and much of the furniture made in the post-1830 years looks like Victorian furniture, but without the curves, scrolls, and flowers.

Sofas are among the most often seen Empire pieces. Now that you're familiar with the design elements of all the previous periods, a quick look at a piece like the sofa illustrated next should immediately tell you that this could not be an eighteenth century piece. To begin with, it doesn't have that "hand-made" look to it.

Though many steps involved in producing Empire furniture still involved hand processes—hand-carving some of the ornaments and hand-rubbing the finish for example—still, power-driven tools and machines were beginning to be used more.

Some people refer to this sofa as Classical, while others call it Empire. It was made circa 1815 to 1830, as identified by the rolled and scrolled lines at the crest rail, arms, and seat rail.

(Photo courtesy of Craig and Tarlton)

Dominating Empire design elements include bold scrolls used throughout, classical columns, thicker boards used in construction, very little decoration used—pieces mostly large and imposing.

The heavier, thicker lines of the Empire period are clearly seen when comparing a circa 1830 to 1850 sideboard (see the following figure) to a Sheraton one. Note also that pieces made during the Empire era appear much darker, thanks to the use of mahogany veneer which the new machines could cut with rapidity.

The cabinet sections that almost touch the floor give this piece a massive look. Add the dark mahogany veneer and elaborate carving and you have a fine example of high-style Empire furniture.

(Photo courtesy of Craig and Tarlton)

During the nineteenth century, high-ceilinged rooms and ever-increasing personal wardrobes gave rise to the armoire (see the following figure). Their tall paneled doors were the perfect showcase for long sheets of richly figured "flaming" mahogany veneer. No "modern" bedroom could be without one.

Armoires were not part of the eighteenth-century furniture vocabulary. This fine, circa 1830 armoire is distinguished by the veneer on the round classical Corinthian columns—a design element made possible by the new technology.

(Photo courtesy of Neal's)

Representative pieces of the period include chairs, sofas, chests, center tables, sideboards, dressers, wardrobes, armoires, beds, bookcases, and cabinets.

The Least You Need to Know

➤ Hepplewhite and Sheraton designs are often termed *Federal*.

➤ While Hepplewhite furniture is distinguished by its delicate inlay, Sheraton furniture is more often carved than inlaid.

➤ Regency furniture is English, not American.

➤ American Empire furniture typically is large, imposing, and undecorated.

Chapter 17

The Rest of the Nineteenth Century

In This Chapter

➤ Continue learning the names of the later-nineteenth-century periods of English and American furniture

➤ Learn how Victoria dominated the nineteenth century

➤ Master the varying style elements that change every few years with rapidly changing technology

➤ Understand why nineteenth-century period furniture is sometimes less revered than eighteenth-century furniture

➤ Discover the two new categories of antiques ushered in with the millennium

Victorious Victoria

Victoria was on the throne for so long—from 1830 to 1901 (some 71 years)—that many different furniture styles came and went during her reign. She was queen for so long, in fact, that, as another writer has said about her, "the problem is to know when to stop."

AntiqInfo

Queen Victoria considered Prince Albert to have such fine taste that *he* ruled in the area of home décor. After his death in 1861, Victoria still relied on his taste. When curtains or upholstery needed replacing, she had copies made of the patterns he had chosen and used those for the refurbishing.

AntiqClue

It was during the Victorian era that furniture "suites" became all the rage. Everything had to match. Needless to say, the remarkable new tools and repeating machines that made it possible to duplicate ornamental patterns and designs greatly contributed to this fad.

Truth is, you are probably more familiar with Victorian furniture than with any other kind of antique furniture. You've sat on Victorian chairs that your grandmother inherited from her grandmother, and slept on Victorian beds in cozy Bed and Breakfasts. That's going to make my job, and yours, easier.

As you begin this section, keep in mind that by the 1830s the entire world was changing rapidly, thanks to the Industrial Revolution. As fast-running machines and mass-transportation became part of everyday life, fashions on both sides of the Atlantic changed more quickly than ever before.

In fact, in the shrinking world of the mid-nineteenth century, British and American Victorian furniture designs were both popular at the same time. The lag time that had existed in the eighteenth century, and even in the early part of the nineteenth century, was no longer a factor.

These changes were considered great, positive, forward-leaping steps by the people of the time. But today, many antiques connoisseurs view with regret those wonderful advances brought about by the Industrial Revolution because they heralded the end of the tradition of fine craftsmanship. These connoisseurs consider 1830 to be a benchmark death-date of antiques of true quality and craftsmanship. For that reason, they do not revere pieces after the 1830s as highly as they do those made before then.

As far as furniture designs of the period go, there are four major substyles under the broad Victorian umbrella. They are: Rococo, Gothic, Renaissance, and Eastlake. These designs will be described and discussed here because they are the ones you'll see most frequently.

Rococo

Victorian Rococo furniture is distinguished by its gently curving lines and highly carved decoration. This is in stark contrast to the boxy, straight lines of the immediately preceding Empire period.

But note that densely grained, dark woods continue to dominate furniture during the mid-nineteenth century.

The Victorian Rococo style was so popular that it lasted through most of the Victorian era, from the 1830s through the 1890s, which explains, of course, why there is so much of it around. Its name, *Rococo,* refers to the floral, and often wavy, carving that dominates these pieces. These attributes show up in that most typical piece of the Victorian Rococo era: the floral-and-fruit carved side chair.

Dominating Victorian Rococo design elements: Floral carving, lots of scrolls, curving lines.

By the 1850s and 1860s technology was making quantum leaps forward. Repeating machines could cut out shapes and outlines that were then hand-carved into leaves, flowers, fruits—all the popular Victorian motifs. It was also possible to cut large pieces of glass inexpensively and without splintering them. These were then silvered and made into mirrors. This new technology made it possible to makes pieces like the armoire shown here.

AntiqInfo

Ever wonder why so many marble tops are seen on Victorian tables and dressers? Designers of the time were taking advantage of the newly invented steam-driven machines that were capable of cutting and shaping marble.

AntiqInfo

You may have heard the name John Belter. Belter was a New York cabinetmaker who developed a unique way of bonding sheets of wood together (laminating) so that they could be intricately carved. Belter's finest work exemplifies the height of Victorian Rococo fashion.

Everyone is familiar with the ubiquitous Victorian Rococo chair. Some are open-backed (often called balloon-back); others are fully upholstered. On both, the floral carving, rounded crest rail, and slightly cabriole leg are typical of the Victorian Rococo period.

(Photos courtesy of Neal's)

From the shaped cornice decorated with carved fruits and leaves, to the mirrored door, this large armoire is a prime example of the Victorian Rococo style.

Representative pieces of the period include chairs, sofas, tables of all sorts, chests, dressers, cabinets, étagères, beds, hall trees, washstands, ottomans, desks, bookcases, and secretary/bookcases.

Victorian Gothic

Victorian Gothic furniture is easily identified. If you can picture a window in a Gothic cathedral—with its pointed arches, rosettes, finials, and rugged lines—you can picture what Victorian Gothic furniture looks like. The furniture literally looks like it belongs in a medieval cathedral or in the pages of *Ivanhoe*.

Needless to say, the presence of machinery in the cabinetmaker's shop, and especially in furniture manufacturing plants, made it possible to cut out the intricate designs employed in this furniture.

Not much of this furniture is around, but it has such a strong presence that you need to be familiar with it. Just seeing one piece of Victorian Gothic furniture will impress its image on your mind.

AntiqLingo

Rococo is derived from two French words, *rocaille* and *coquillage*. In the decorative arts when the term "Rococo" is used, it refers to motifs taken from nature, such as rocks, flowers, leaves, or shells.

Seating furniture like this extraordinary settee made around 1840 with its architectural-type ornamentation can only be from the Victorian Gothic era.

(Photo courtesy of Neal's)

Even though there are scrolls in the lower portion of this bookcase, the Gothic arches and finials at the top of this 1840 to 1850 mahogany bookcase clearly dominate the entire piece.

(Photo courtesy of Neal's)

Dominating Victorian Gothic design elements include tracery, trefoil and quatrefoil rosettes, lancet arches, and finials.

Victorian Gothic furniture never really caught on in America the way it did in England. Of course, America didn't have the long-lived Gothic tradition of Britain, nor all its Gothic architecture. Victorian Gothic furniture is rare when compared to the other major. Victorian substyles—especially the large case pieces. But eye-catching Victorian Gothic side or hall chairs do show up frequently and are moderately priced.

As an interesting aside, some modern-day furniture historians think the Gothic Revival was inspired by a harkening back to religion in reaction to the "dilettantism" of some Victorians (Oscar Wilde, for example). Others think it was simply an alternative furniture design that used straight lines in reaction to all the flowery motifs of the Victorian rococo era. Whatever its source, Victorian gothic is a very distinctive style.

Renaissance Revival

You may have caught on to the importance of decoration on Victorian furniture. The ornamentation or decoration distinguishes one Victorian substyle from another. This is particularly important to know when

Before You Buy

Good period Victorian Rococo furniture is plentiful, though the best and most unusual pieces are pricey. Be wary of reproductions of Victorian Rococo seating furniture. Chairs and sofas were mass-produced in great numbers during the first half of the twentieth century.

you compare Victorian Rococo and Victorian Renaissance Revival furniture.

They both have lots of scrolls, curves, and robust carving. But the Renaissance Revival furniture designers used ornamentation not found on Rococo pieces—mainly sphinx heads, paw feet, and lots of classical medallions. That's because Renaissance Revival furniture was inspired by the architecture of the Renaissance, just as the Gothic Revival furniture was inspired by Gothic architecture.

When a furniture design is influenced by architecture, it makes sense that the furniture will be large and imposing. This is certainly true of Victorian furniture in general, and the Rococo and Renaissance furniture in particular.

To tell whether a piece is Victorian Rococo, or Victorian Renaissance Revival, look at the top of the piece—the crest rail of a chair, or the cornice of a bookcase, or the headboard of a bed, and so on.

AntiqClue

One way to remember the general dates of the Renaissance Revival is to think about the Civil War era. Renaissance Revival furniture began gaining widespread popularity in America during the 1860 to 1865 era and then continued to be a favorite into the 1880s.

Where a floral or foliage motif usually appears on Victorian Rococo pieces, on Victorian Renaissance Revival pieces there will be a medallion, shield, or raised, half-round cabochon motif surrounded by scrolls and curves.

Dominating Victorian Renaissance Revival design elements include squared-off lines, medallions, urns, carved ornaments.

A frequently seen Victorian Renaissance Revival decoration is a carved urn or other classical motif perched at the center of a stretcher base on a center table, as shown in the following figure.

The center egg motif topped by a carved shell and flanked by bold scrolls on the headboard are typical Victorian Renaissance Revival design elements. So are the urn-style finials on the posts.

(Photo courtesy of Neal's)

165

Modified cabriole legs are found on both Victorian Rococo and Victorian Renaissance Revival pieces. But the addition of the attention-getting carved urn is a Victorian Renaissance Revival trait. So are the sweeping pierced scrolls on the table apron.

(Photo courtesy of Neal's)

Bold decorations were particularly suited to the large, even monumental, Victorian Renaissance Revival furniture. Add several carved scrolls and a center design on a bookcase or armoire cornice and you've "crowned" an otherwise simple piece as seen in the next illustration.

The interwoven scrolls and center crest motif atop the arched cornice of this circa 1850 to 1860 Victorian Renaissance Revival bookcase add a dressy touch, like a fancy bonnet.

(Photo courtesy of Neal's)

Part of the charm of Renaissance Revival furniture is how well it captures the exuberance of the mid-Victorian era. Furthermore, the presence of classical motifs reflects the nineteenth century's interest in past times and cultures.

Representative pieces of the period include chairs, sofas, tables of all sorts, chests, washstands, dressers, desks, bookcases, cabinets, étagères, beds, hall trees, ottomans.

Eastlake

Charles Locke Eastlake made as big an impression on the British in the late nineteenth century as Thomas Chippendale did in the mid-eighteenth century. But Chippendale's beautiful designs were timeless and have never really gone out of style. That can't be said for Eastlake. Although his 1868 book, *Hints on Household Taste,* became a best seller on both sides of the Atlantic, Eastlake's designs remained popular for only a few decades, rather than for a few centuries.

Eastlake furniture swings a full 180 degrees away from the richly carved, elaborate, ornate, and dark furniture of the Renaissance Revival and Rococo eras. Eastlake-designed furniture was much simpler, less curvaceous, and lighter in feeling than those other two designs. Today, we may think Eastlake furniture is heavy because of its sheer size and bulk. But compared with those earlier styles, Eastlake furniture truly was a breath of fresh air to the Victorians.

Eastlake furniture is also very angular and straight when compared with the more fluid Rococo and Renaissance Revival furniture. Even Eastlake tables tend to be square or rectangular, rather than round. Straight, rectangular panels show up everywhere, from cabinets to high bed backs. And don't forget to look for the incised carving anyplace there's a thick straight board.

Before You Buy

A tape measure always comes in handy when you're considering purchasing a large Victorian Renaissance Revival piece. They're wonderful antiques, but they do tend to be tall and wide.

AntiqClue

The quickest clue to identifying Eastlake furniture is the carving. Instead of being relief-carved (raised from the wood), which is the method used in Rococo and Renaissance Revival, Eastlake decorations are carved into the wood. This is called incising and is a distinguishing characteristic of Eastlake furniture.

Suites of matching furniture became popular during the Victorian era thanks to a middle class who could afford to buy all the furniture for one room at one time, plus furniture manufacturers that could rapidly turn out matching sets. (This wasn't possible in the eighteenth century when a family bought one hand-made piece at a time.) To illustrate this nineteenth-century trend, the next figures show the bed and washstand that matched the dresser also shown.

Dominating Eastlake design elements include incised geometric and floral carving, panels, straight lines.

Incised carving at the mirror and drawer base clearly indicate that this dresser is a typical Eastlake piece. Note that this is a drawing taken from an 1880s furniture catalogue. By now almost all furniture was mass-manufactured.

Representative pieces of the period include chairs, sofas, tables of all sorts, sideboards, chests, dressers, cabinets, beds, wardrobes, washstands, hall trees, side-by-sides, chiffoniers, bookcases, and desks.

The large paneled head and footboards of the bed, and doors on the washstand, provided plenty of space for incised carving. The washstand was one of many new pieces of furniture that evolved to meet the new needs of the nineteenth-century home.

Aesthetic Movement

In every age, styles and designs are introduced that attract a lot of attention at the time but don't survive the test of centuries. Many years later, modern scholarly papers, beautifully illustrated magazine articles, and museum exhibits bring those same styles and designs back into fashion.

That's exactly what happened with the Aesthetic Movement, a design era in England and, to a lesser extent, in America, at the end of the nineteenth century. You won't see a lot of the furniture from this era unless you go searching for it. Yet, well-educated antiquers need a passing knowledge of this design.

The Aesthetic Movement is easy to grasp because a casual description of it might be "dressed-up and sophisticated Eastlake." The two periods occurred simultaneously, and the lines and motifs are rather similar. The major difference between the two can be summed up in the word "aesthetic."

Before You Buy

Once there was so much period Eastlake furniture available that no one made Eastlake reproductions. This has changed and "new" Eastlake-style furniture is now being manufactured. Real, period pieces are easily distinguishable by their thick wood and solid construction methods. Remember, comparing the old and the new will show the difference.

The dark ebonized wood and inlaid classical design on the cabinet doors, plus the Oriental-style brass pulls add "aesthetics" to the basically straight Eastlake lines of this parlor cabinet. The open shelves provided space to show off the cultured family's art glass collection.

(Photo courtesy of Neal's)

Eastlake furniture was primarily utilitarian and designed for the middle-class home. Aesthetic furniture put art and craftsmanship first. The general public thought this was a self-indulgent attitude, but many great artistic and intellectual names are associated with the Aesthetic Movement, including James Whistler, Oscar Wilde, and even Charles Lock Eastlake himself.

Dominating Aesthetic Movement design elements include artistic geometric and floral carving added to panels and other surfaces, straight lines. Representative pieces of the period include tables, dressers, cabinets of all sorts, music stands, wall cupboards, beds, seating furniture.

Cottage Furniture

Just as the Victorian Rococo era lasted and lasted, so did another fashion—Cottage furniture. It became fashionable in the 1840s and has never really gone out of style.

Before You Buy

There is currently a strong interest in American Aesthetic furniture and the prices are on the increase. But finding these pieces can take some effort. Because they were never in the "mainstream," they don't turn up everyday.

To get a handle on Cottage furniture, think about this. Not everyone lived in a large, 15-room Victorian mansion, and not everyone could afford the large furniture of the time. Smaller, cozier pieces had to be made for more-modest Victorian homes. In keeping with their reputation as romantics, you can be sure that the Victorians gave this style a lovely name—Cottage furniture.

Cottage furniture is light and open, often stenciled or painted. (The popular spool bed is a typical Cottage piece.) Cottage furniture was inexpensively mass-produced at the time and was never of exceptional quality. But if you're looking for the "country cottage look," this may be the style for you.

This typical mass-produced Victorian Cottage suite has the lines of Victorian Rococo pieces, but the cheerful paint lightens and brightens it, and makes it appear less massive.

(Photo courtesy of Neal's)

Dominating Victorian Cottage design elements include painted surfaces, floral designs, contrasting colors to bring out decorative motifs. Representative pieces of the period include bedroom pieces, including suites of furniture, occasional chairs and tables.

Much Victorian Cottage furniture has been repainted. Pieces retaining their original paint are much more valuable to the serious collector.

Arts and Crafts Movement

Following rapidly on the heels of the Aesthetic Movement at the end of the nineteenth century was the Arts and Crafts Movement. Just a few years ago, pieces from

AntiqInfo

Arts and Crafts furniture is now a "legal" antique.

AntiqClue

Remember, Arts and Crafts pieces were made in the twentieth century, so they were easily copied from the get-go by inferior furniture manufacturers, just as knockoffs of today's expensive name brands are. Never forget: age, quality, style, condition, and craftsmanship.

this era were almost giveaways, and they certainly weren't antiques. But lo and behold, Stickley pieces are now front and center on *The Antiques Roadshow!* They have come of age as of the year 2000.

The Arts and Crafts movement began in England with the formation in 1888 of the Arts and Crafts Exhibition Society, from which the movement took its name. Gustav Stickley, an American furniture designer and manufacturer, saw the furniture in Europe and began making it here in 1900.

Design-wise, the straight, low-slung, unadorned Arts and Crafts furniture was a reaction to the massive, lavishly decorated Victorian Rococo, Gothic, and Renaissance Revival furniture styles. The look of this furniture is unlike that of any other era, and you won't have any problem identifying it as Arts and Crafts when you see it.

Dominating Arts and Crafts design elements include straight, low-slung lines, absence of decoration, geometric shapes.

Representative pieces of the period include sofas and chairs, tables, dressers, cabinets, music stands, wall cupboards, beds, bookcases.

Everything about Arts and Crafts furniture is in total contrast to the designs of those that came before it. It is the straight, low, unadorned lines, large solid oak boards, and the leather cushion tag this piece as "Arts and Crafts."

(Photo courtesy of Skinner's)

172

The Colonial Era Comes 'Round Again

I make no bones about it. I think the Colonial Revival era is fascinating. I live in a Colonial Revival home. I buy Colonial Revival furniture and accessories, and I've even written a book on the topic.

Trouble is, most of the items made in the Colonial Revival era—which stretches from the late 1870s up until around 1950 when "modern" furniture began to dominate the home fashion magazines—aren't legal antiques. Furthermore, most of them are reproductions. And to make matters worse, the really well-made pieces of Colonial Revival furniture can look like period pieces.

You are going to learn most of what you need to know to distinguish a true period piece from a Colonial Revival piece in Chapter 18, "Chipping the Old Block, or the Chip Wood?" when you learn about the inner workings of furniture.

But here are some basic background facts about the Colonial Revival:

Before You Buy

Arts and Crafts furniture is currently so hot that Stickley labels are being reproduced and put on mass-manufactured Arts and Crafts pieces that have the "Stickley" look.

➤ The American Centennial (1876) created a new interest in America's early, or colonial, days.

➤ When period pieces were too scarce to go around, reproductions were made to look like the original, period pieces.

➤ The manufacture of Colonial Revival pieces hasn't slowed since the first Colonial Revival reproductions were made in the late 1870s.

➤ There is a tremendous difference in quality between faithful reproductions (see Chapter 2, "Antiques. Period.") and poorly designed pieces that combine elements from several different periods.

➤ Beautifully crafted, faithful reproductions—especially if they are now legal antiques—are rapidly increasing in value.

In a word, a vast amount of furniture that is offered for sale in antiques malls and "generalist" stores should be labeled Colonial Revival furniture, not "antique." Naturally, some of it is better quality than other.

This turn-of-the-century Queen Anne type writing desk takes great liberty with the Queen Anne period. First, there were no slant-front desks during the original Queen Anne period, and second, this carving is totally out of character for Queen Anne pieces.

In stark contrast to the previous illustration of a Queen Anne "type" or "style" writing desk is the following piece: a fine, late nineteenth-century copy of an eighteenth century highboy.

Well-made and faithful reproductions of period pieces are in great demand. The quality of wood and craftsmanship, as well as the attention given to the decorative motifs—shell carving, brasses, and ball-and-claw feet—of this highboy, give this Colonial Revival highboy great marks.

(Photo courtesy of Sloan's)

174

In addition to learning the construction techniques and design elements of period pieces, try to spend some time looking through old furniture catalogues and magazines. Public libraries often have old copies on file and sometimes you can find them for sale at the usual antiques haunts. With study, you will soon learn how different most Colonial Revival furniture looks from real, period pieces—as the following illustration shows.

Dominating Colonial Revival design elements include all motifs and designs associated with earlier, periods on which Colonial Revival pieces are based. Representative pieces of the period include literally every item made in earlier periods, plus the new pieces suited to early through mid-twentieth-century living: coffee or cocktail tables, telephone tables, cigarette stands, Victrola and TV stands, and bedside tables.

Before You Buy

There is nothing wrong with buying Colonial Revival furniture, especially the fine pieces. What you don't want to do is to pay a "period" or "antique" price for a not-so-old Colonial Revival piece. Before you buy the Colonial Revival copy, check out the cost of a similar period piece.

The glass in this display cabinet is an instant giveaway that it is not an eighteenth century piece. So is the small "Hepplewhite" inlaid oval motif used with Queen Anne and Chippendale design elements. This is a twentieth-century piece that combines several different eighteenth century motifs. If you look hard enough, you'll probably find its manufacturer's label attached somewhere.

(Photo courtesy of Bourne's)

The Least You Need to Know

➤ The Victorian era has four major substyles.

➤ By the 1830s and 1840s, the Industrial Revolution began to greatly affect how and how much furniture was being made.

➤ Victorian Rococo and Victorian Renaissance Revival are similar in their lavish carved motifs.

➤ Victorian Eastlake and the Aesthetic Movement are closely related.

➤ Victorian Cottage furniture was inexpensive when first made.

➤ Since Arts and Crafts and Colonial Revival furniture were mass-produced from their introduction, you will find vastly differing quality among pieces from those periods being sold as antiques.

Chapter 18

Chipping the Old Block, or the Chip Wood?

In This Chapter

➤ Learn where to look and what to look for to find positive evidence that a piece is a period piece

➤ Discover that technical information can be easily understood and mastered

➤ Find out why it's okay for drawers to have new brasses

➤ Understand how replacements, alterations, and enhancements affect value

Now that you've mastered the basics of furniture periods, let's strip away the real mystery of antique furniture and look at the telltale signs left behind by the craftsmen who made those pieces.

To do this, we'll peek inside a workshop from the eighteenth and early nineteenth centuries to see some of the tools these craftsmen used. Then I'll show you some tricks performed by crafty twentieth-century craftsmen.

Tooling Along

Don't close this book!

Even if you've never held a saw or operated an electric drill, you'll soon be able to understand the difference between the marks left behind by tools from the eighteenth and nineteenth centuries and those made by tools from the twentieth- and twenty-first centuries. Armed with this knowledge, you can make and save big bucks in the antiques world.

And remember to refer to the Appendix E, "Glossary," and Chapter 15, "Furniture: The Lure of the Old," as a quick reference to some of the furniture terms you are still learning.

Look for the Saw Marks

Every furniture workshop contained a saw. The distinctive marks left by a saw are one of the easiest-to-understand and most important tool marks to look for.

During the eighteenth century, two men sawed tree logs into rough planks, each holding one end of a long, unwieldy saw. Around 1810 a Shaker sister, Tabitha Babbitt, produced the prototype of the circular saw. It wasn't until the mid-1800s (or the Industrial Revolution days) that circular saws became commonplace, but once they did, they left behind a definite telltale sign—an arc.

When you see this distinct mark where a piece of wood would have been sawn—on the flat edge of a tabletop, on the backboard of a chest or cupboard, or on the bottom of a chair frame, for example—use the benchmark date of 1840 as the earliest this piece can be.

This picture shows arc marks left by the circular saw.

The Plane Facts

In the 1700s and early 1800s, up until about, you guessed it, 1830 or 1840, wood was finished by hand planing. The combination of the small planing blade and the varying pressure that the planer put on this simple tool left an irregular surface. Those little irregularities are like ripples. View a hand-planed surface in the light and you'll see them. Better yet, run your fingers over the surface of an eighteenth-century piece, and you'll probably feel them. In contrast, today's electric planers leave a totally smooth surface.

AntiqClue

When I'm giving talks, I always tell audiences to rub the fingers of one hand across the palm of the other hand. The smooth, slightly undulating feel of the palm closely resembles the feel of a hand-planed surface.

This picture depicts the irregular ripples left by hand planing.

Chisel Marks

Eighteenth- and early nineteenth-century workshops had another tool that left distinctive marks on furniture made before the 1830s and 1840s: the chisel. The old chisels left irregular gouged-out marks. You'll especially find these marks inside

179

drawer fronts where early craftsmen gouged out part of the board to make room for the nut needed to secure the drawer's handles or knobs.

AntiqClue

When you're not sure whether the dovetails are handmade or machine made, or if the shop is dark and it's hard to see them well, let your fingers do the walking! Run a fingernail along the dovetails. Your fingernail will slide right over recently cut, uniform dovetails. But it will almost always snag on irregular, hand-cut dovetails.

Making It Fit

In the eighteenth century, the art of fitting different furniture parts together was so highly regarded that the men who did it were called *joiners*—they joined the parts together. A weak joint meant a weak piece of furniture (read, one that might break).

Dovetails

Probably the best-known example of eighteenth- and nineteenth-century joinery is the *dovetail*, the construction device used to join a drawer front to the drawer's sides. But dovetails are also found on the fronts of pieces, especially on blanket chests. Early dovetails were cut by hand and are always irregular, even though masters of the dovetail technique could make them so perfectly that they may appear to be absolutely uniform. Machine-made dovetails, on the other hand, never vary. By the Victorian era, handmade dovetails had virtually disappeared.

It is essential that irregular, hand-cut dovetails be found in true early period antiques.

Mortise and Tenon Joints

Mortise and tenon joints are found where two pieces of wood meet at right angles, other than, of course, where dovetails are used in drawer construction. Look for mortise and tenon joints where table legs join the table skirt and where the chair crest rail meets the chair stiles. To keep these pieces securely in place, the mortise and tenon joint is often, but not always, locked in place by a wooden peg.

AntiqInfo

When a dovetail is visible from only one side it is called a half-blind dovetail.

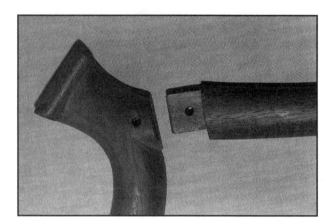

The rectangular block is the tenon and the cutout hole is the mortise. To firmly secure the joint, a peg is sometimes added.

The Modern Dowel

Hand-cut dovetails and modern dovetails look somewhat similar. But around the middle of the nineteenth century, machines began cutting round dowels, which replaced the mortise and tenon joint. It is this kind of shortcut that antiques connoisseurs object to in Victorian, and later, manufactured furniture.

Thin, round, machine-cut dowels are a positive sign of mid-nineteenth century, or later, furniture construction.

Hitting the Nail on the Head

Nails have long been an important part of furniture construction, but who wants to pull nails out of a valuable antique to check to see whether they are old?

Most important is knowing *where* nails were used by eighteenth- and early nineteenth-century cabinetmakers. A general rule is that nails were used where they wouldn't be seen—to attach a backboard or drawer bottom. No fine piece would have nails showing on an exterior surface. But country pieces would.

A safe way to verify that the nails in the piece are old is to look *around* the nail. Check for two signs. First, make sure that the wood around the nail has not been disturbed. Second, look for a dark area surrounding the nail; that indicates the nail has been in place for a long time. The dark area is oxidation, caused by humidity rusting the nail and bleeding into the wood grain.

Turning the Screw

Unlike nails, screws are seldom found in early antique furniture and, then, usually only in a high-stress place, such as where tabletops are attached.

The oldest screws were made of wood. Metal screws were hard to make by hand. The first screw-making machine was introduced around 1815, and the modern screw-making machine wasn't invented until the 1840s. The conclusion: When a piece has lots of screws in it, either it's a fairly new piece (post-1850) or else new screws have been put into the piece to give it added strength.

AntiqClue

Handwrought nails were used until around 1810. Square-cut nails were used from around 1800 until about 1890. Wire nails with round shanks, the kind we're still using today, became common in the 1890s.

The Truth About Hardware: It Takes a Beating

One of the questions the novice usually asks the antiques dealer is, "Are the brasses original?" There's much said about "replaced" hardware, such as the handles and knobs found on drawers. To my way of thinking, too much!

After all, the hardware takes the hard knocks that come with opening and closing overstuffed drawers year after year. That's why the experienced collector isn't concerned with whether or not a *fine* piece has its original brasses. If the piece does have its original brasses, then that's like getting money with the deal.

AntiqClue

Many a made-up piece has been wrongly deemed an antique because no one looked for screws.

How do you tell? Look on the inside as well as the out. If there is no evidence that the gouged-out area around the handle posts has been disturbed, it's a great sign. In such a case, leave the handles in place.

But if the gouged-out area shows lots of nicks, and the nut that is holding the post in place shows scratches and dents where it has been previously removed, then very carefully remove the nut and handle. (If you've never done this before, you might get some expert help.)

On the drawer front, you see what is called a ghost image—the outline of the handle or knob. If it matches up perfectly with the removed hardware, everything is fine. But if there is another "ghost" or outline, then you know this is not the original hardware.

Wood You Buy It?

One reason why people cherish antiques so highly is that they are made with beautiful, real wood. There's no place for chipboard, plywood, and wood parts in the antiques world.

You should know that two types of wood are used in antiques: primary wood and secondary wood. The *primary wood* is used on the exterior, whereas the *secondary wood* is used in the interior and unseen back.

The most commonly used exterior woods are mahogany, walnut, cherry, maple, pine, oak, and birch. Interior woods are most often poplar, pine, and oak. Furniture aficionados can quickly distinguish English pieces from American ones by the woods used, especially the secondary woods.

Patina: What It Means, What It's Worth

Most novices have heard antiques experts kick around that hundred-dollar word, *patina*. What they may not know is that the right patina can be worth thousands and thousands of dollars. You see, even though the old construction methods used to make an antique are highly treasured, no one can see them unless they open drawers or get down and look under a piece. The exterior proof of age is of tremendous importance.

When an antique is refinished, the accumulation of all the nicks and dirt and other evidence of its long life are removed. All that is left is a new-looking piece. Why bother to buy an antique when you could get a brand-new reproduction for less money?

AntiqClue

When you look inside a drawer, if you see an empty hole that doesn't match up with the hardware, you know the hardware is a replacement. Even worse is when you see signs of plugged-up holes on the front of the drawer!

AntiqLingo

Patina is the finish on a piece that has built up over years, including dents, scratches, wax, soot, oxidation, even spills, and that now glows with proof of age.

A rich exterior patina that has built up over time is so highly valued that everyone who copies eighteenth-century pieces—from the faker to mass-manufacturers—tries to give their new pieces the look of an old patina. You may even have seen new pieces that have been "distressed," meaning artificially banged up, to make them look old. But even modern science can't fake the natural, distinctive look that comes with age.

The Inside Patina

Because chances are greater that the exterior has been refinished, most people neglect to check the interior patina. But it, too, is important to the serious collector.

Telltale signs of changes and alterations are often found on the underneath and interior surfaces. Let's say, for example, that a Chippendale chest has lost one of its bracket feet in a move. A cabinetmaker can make a replacement foot and attach it. He may even be able to match the new foot's finish so closely with the rest of the piece that the casual observer will not be able to tell that the foot is new.

Until, that is, the piece has been turned over. Then the observer will notice that one foot is lighter and has a newer, fresher wood color than the other feet. This is why careful interior examination is a must when you are getting ready to spend a lot of money on antique furniture.

Unscrupulous antiques dealers and craftsmen, who want the customer to think a piece is in its original, pristine condition, will try to cover up *interior* repairs and alterations by staining new wood to look old. Think twice if you see stains or paint on an interior surface. Ask how they got there and what they might be covering up.

Faux Antiques: They Look Good But ...

It's sad, but true, that there is so much money in antiques, that faking them is big business, and it's been done for years. Years ago antiques expert Michael Gordon wrote these warning words: "Don't assume that because the shop you are buying it [the antique] in is reputable, it could not be a reproduction. The person selling you the piece may just not know what has been done to it or just when it was made."

For that reason, you, the buyer, have to be smart, on your toes, and in the know.

AntiqClue

The wise antiquer never buys an important piece of furniture without heeding Dr. Seuss's advice to look "inside, outside, upside down."

AntiqInfo

Because refinished antiques can look deceptively new, always examine the inside and back if you think the piece might be old. Wood darkens when constantly exposed to the air. The backboard of a truly old chest should be dark. Drawer backs will be slightly darker (where air will have circulated) than the drawer sides (where less air has circulated).

Born a Fake

Ironically, fewer out-and-out fakes (or pieces intended from the start to deceive the buyer) exist than do repaired and altered pieces. Nevertheless, the few "glamorous" fakes, the ones that end up in museums until they are finally exposed, are the ones that get lots of publicity. Well, if the fake is so well-made that it can get by museum experts, it will likely get by you, too. You can't spend your life worrying about those pieces. There are many more-dangerous wannabe antiques out there waiting to trap you. Those are the ones you need to know about.

AntiqClue

Among the most often "made-up" pieces waiting for the uninformed antiquer are: hanging shelves, plate racks, lowboys, highboys, huntboards (a Southern variation of the sideboard), and Pennsylvania spice cabinets.

The Made-Up Piece

One such type of piece is the *made-up piece,* which is created by combining old parts or old wood with new materials to make up a piece that looks like a period piece.

Some of the warning signs that a piece may be made-up, rather than genuine, are:

➤ **Size.** Made-up pieces will often be scaled down from the original to fit better in today's smaller, and lower-ceilinged rooms.

➤ **Material.** Eighteenth-century craftsmen used solid boards to make chests, secretaries, highboys, tables, etc., when wood was ample. Beware of pieces that look like eighteenth-century pieces but are veneered or made up of small boards glued or, worse yet, nailed together.

➤ **Color.** Watch out for a "new" outside look, or unexplainable stains and smudges on the inside.

AntiqLingo

A **married** antique is one in which two separate pieces, made at different times, have been put together to make one piece. This happens when a bookcase top is combined with a desk bottom to make a "married secretary/bookcase," or a lowboy is given a top that turns it into a more valuable highboy.

Mix-Matched Marriages

A special type of wannabe antique that you hear much about these days is the *married* piece.

One way to check out a possibly bad marriage (in antiques there are no good marriages) is to pull out the drawers of both the top and bottom parts. If you see a distinct difference in the dovetails, different kinds of woods, or a big difference in the interior patina in the two parts, beware!

186

Another, even more obvious, clue of a mix 'n' match is when the two parts show a difference in their exterior color.

Still another clue is when the two pieces are misaligned across the back. In original unaltered pieces, there is usually about a half-inch step-back where the upper case fits into the lower case. If you see considerably more or less than a half-inch difference, examine the piece very carefully.

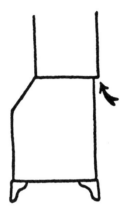

The misaligned top and bottom are bold hints that the two parts were made at different times and then put together.

Splitting Heirs

In today's market, large sets of eighteenth- and early nineteenth-century dining rooms chairs are scarce, and the ones that do exist are frightfully expensive, as was pointed out in Chapter 8, "Accumulator or Collector." One reason why so few of these sets exist can be traced to splitting heirs.

When the parents die, leaving 12 dining room chairs and four children, the 12 chairs are divided up and each heir takes 3 chairs. A couple of the kids may then have additional chairs made by a cabinetmaker to match the original ones and fill out a new set. Over the years, with the usual wear and tear given to the chairs, it may become hard to tell which ones are the old ones and which are the new—especially if the older chairs were refinished at the same time as the new ones were made. However, if you know the telltale signs of old construction, you won't be fooled. That's why, when buying a set of "antique" chairs, you need to examine each one carefully.

AntiqClue

Remember, anytime a set is broken up, duplicates can be made. For example, if a pair of twin beds is split up, and each heir has a matching bed made, the two beds quickly become four.

Repaired, Altered, and Enhanced Antiques

Now you're forewarned about the bunch of wannabe antiques out there waiting for a novice antiquer. Unfortunately, as bad as that situation is, an even worse one lies ahead: the hordes of repaired, altered, and enhanced pieces that will try to trip you up. That's what you're going to learn about next.

Before exclaiming, "Too technical for me!" remember, it's fun to become a detective of the decorative arts, and once you know where to look and what to look for, the search for the masquerading piece isn't so hard after all.

The Repaired Piece

Some types of repairs can drastically decrease an antique's value. Other repairs are almost expected on a piece that has survived for a couple hundred years. Knowing which repairs are acceptable, and which are unacceptable, can help you spend your dollars wisely.

To help you at this stage of the game, the following repairs are considered major, and pieces having these should be avoided as investment pieces:

➤ A replaced writing slant on a desk or secretary/bookcase

➤ A replaced drawer front that can be seen

➤ All four feet replaced

➤ A replaced cornice on a secretary/bookcase, breakfront, highboy, and so on

➤ The top board of a chest, sideboard, table, lowboy, candlestand, and so on

In fact, pieces having these repairs should be considerably less expensive than their unrepaired counterparts.

AntiqClue

Rarity should always be factored in when a repair is found. If the piece is truly a rare find, a repair or even replacement becomes more acceptable.

But if you find, for example, an eighteenth-century, American cherry secretary/bookcase that has a cornice with a repaired corner, that would be an acceptable, albeit undesirable, repair. Or, if you find a fabulous English, early Georgian chest with one back foot replaced, but otherwise perfect, you can buy the piece and still sleep at night.

The Altered Antique

Antiques have sometimes been altered over the years to accommodate changing fashions or different lifestyles.

Take the ubiquitous coffee table, for example. Back in the 1950s, Victorian Rococo furniture enjoyed a new burst of popularity. Everyone wanted a red velvet upholstered sofa and matching gentleman's and lady's chair. Trouble was, the 1950s hostess also wanted a Victorian Rococo coffee table to complete this suite of furniture. But there was no such thing as a coffee table during the Victorian Rococo era. The solution was simple. Take a small-ish Victorian Rococo occasional table with an oval top, take the legs off, cut them down, and voilà! a Victorian Rococo coffee table.

"But how do I tell?" you may be thinking. First, you would know that there is no such item as a period Victorian coffee table. But if you didn't know that, you would turn the piece over and look carefully where the top and legs are joined. There, underneath the table top, you would find evidence of where a different shaped base originally would have been.

AntiqInfo

The most common reason for altering an antique is to make it smaller so that it better fits today's lifestyle. Evidence of this can be found by closely examining a piece, looking for freshly cut wood, or paint or stain that would cover up these telltale signs.

The Enhanced Piece

Some crafty folks just can't leave well enough alone, especially if a little monkeying around can mean more money. That's what motivates some craftsmen to *enhance* a perfectly fine antique.

The craftsmen who tinker with pieces are well-informed about periods and correct decoration. They would never, for example, insert a line of inlay (a Hepplewhite decorative motif) along a straight Chippendale leg. Instead, they would carve a blind fretwork motif on the Chippendale leg, thereby turning the chair into the highly desirable and expensive Chinese Chippendale style.

AntiqLingo

An **enhanced** antique is one to which inlay, carving, scalloping, or other addition has been made sometime later in its life. The purpose of these changes is to embellish the plainer, original piece.

Among the most frequently encountered enhancements are ...

➤ Recarving a plain cabriole leg so it will be more glamorous.

➤ Recarving a straight Chippendale leg to give it blind fretwork.

➤ Adding inlay to a Hepplewhite piece.

189

AntiqInfo

If you are a novice, you need to know that this kind of deception is nothing new. During the early part of the twentieth century, many a period antique was made into two pieces (both sold, of course, as period antiques) by combining half old parts and half new parts.

➤ Scalloping originally straight skirt tops, leaves, shelves, and aprons.

➤ Reshaping or even adding a cornice to a case piece.

➤ Cutting down large pieces to a daintier, smaller size.

The Happy Ending

Despite the warnings about made-up pieces, alterations, enhancements, and the like, the good news is that absolutely wonderful antiques are being sold everyday through auctions, house sales, classified ads, antiques shops and malls, and even over the Internet. The information that you've just read will be your ammunition, and having that ammo is what defines a discriminating shopper and savvy collector.

So what do you do now? Visit every place possible where you can see, touch, and compare antiques. A picture may be worth a thousand words, but you can't put a dollar sign on the rewards of examining and analyzing actual pieces.

The Least You Need to Know

➤ The sum of the parts equals the total piece.

➤ Crafty woodworkers have been tinkering with old pieces for generations.

➤ A technical knowledge of antique furniture is essential to getting authentic pieces.

➤ Some repairs and even replacements are acceptable; other ones aren't.

➤ The interior of a piece is just as important as its exterior.

➤ In the end, it is always caveat emptor!

Chapter 19

Heavy Metal: Understanding Silver

In This Chapter

➤ Learn the difference between sterling, plated, and coin silver

➤ Practice identifying some of the English hallmarks

➤ Find out why valuable antique American silver is often thrown away

➤ Discover what distinguishes quality in silver pieces

Looking for an antique that has an intrinsic value and can be cashed in for real money? One that doesn't break, doesn't take up much room, and that appeals to an orderly, factual mind? Try silver.

Looking for the most romantic of all antiques, something that evokes images of kings and queens, romantic dinners, and flickering candles? Try silver.

Looking for some antiques that are plentiful, show up everywhere, can be used in every room in the house, and can be bought for less than a dollar or more than $100,000? Try silver.

AntiqInfo

In the late seventeenth and early eighteenth centuries, it became fashionable to cover wooden furniture frames with silver. Of course, only fabulously wealthy royalty and nobility could afford this, and little of it remains. Most of it was later melted down when hard times came.

AntiqLingo

Sterling silver is the standard of purity for silver, according to a statute set down in England in 1238, which is still adhered to today. It is 92.5 parts pure silver to 7.5 parts alloy (usually copper).

Once upon a time, silver was the dominion of the church and royalty, but beginning in the late 1600s, silver became a status symbol for the rising merchant class. By the nineteenth century, silver was considered a necessity in the proper household. Just a few pieces of antique silver in a twenty-first-century home give it a link to a rich history.

You Take a Ball of Silver

What does it take to turn a metal into an object of beauty? You start with the white, ductile alloy whose chemical symbol is Ag (from the Latin *argentum,* meaning silver).

The problem is that silver, in its pure form, is too soft to do anything with. But mix in another alloy, usually copper, and the silver becomes sufficiently strong to be shaped into usable, and very beautiful, objects—from teapots to coinage to furniture. Yes, furniture. Visit museums in Europe and South America and you'll see an occasional silver table or chair.

Long ago, silver was used for making coins. A rigid standard applied to how much silver and how much alloy could be used in coinage. Technically speaking, to get what we today call *sterling silver,* the ratio must be 11 oz., 2 dwt of pure silver to 18 dwt of alloy. (*Dwt* stands for pennyweight, the smallest measure of troy weight, which is how silver is weighed.)

All this technical talk boils down to a simple formula. It takes 925 parts of pure silver to 75 parts of alloy to equal a total of 1,000 parts. That mixture gives you a ball of silver that can be rolled, shaped, spun, pressed, molded, or hammered into forks, candy dishes, jewelry, goblets, and other pieces.

Mark It Well

Many would-be collectors say all those marks on silver frighten them away. Experienced collectors say all those marks give them the *confidence* to collect silver. Which category do you fit into?

Consider this: Because silver was once the basis for money, the system of *hallmarks* and manufacturing marks used on silver almost makes a science out of identifying silver. Once you know how to read silver marks, you'll quickly know whether a piece is English sterling silver, American sterling silver, silver-plated, or something else, and often exactly how old the piece is.

AntiqLingo

A **hallmark** is the mark that gives proof that a piece contains the correct amount of pure silver. The series of marks on an English silver piece that identify the silver content, town, age, and maker are its hallmarks.

The English Way

English silver is marked with four, and sometimes five, important symbols:

➤ **Lion.** A lion facing to the left is the symbol for the English standard of 925/1,000, or sterling silver.

Lion from the seventeenth century through 1821

Lion from 1822 through the present day

A lion, facing left, indicates that the piece meets the sterling standard.

➤ **Letter.** A letter in a shield or cartouche tells the year the piece is made.

The letter N in this script and in this shape of cartouche indicates that this piece of silver was made in 1728.

➤ **Initials.** These identify who made the piece.

The initials in this illustration are those of the great English silversmith Paul Storr.

➤ **Town mark.** This is a specific symbol that identifies where the piece was made.

Each town having a silver guild had its own symbol, which was stamped on pieces made there. This anchor represents Birmingham.

Other frequently seen English town marks.

London from the seventeenth century through 1821

Sheffield

London from 1822 to present day

Edinburgh

➤ **Sovereign's head.** This symbol is sometimes added to existing ones.

The profile of Queen Victoria.

If you are drawn to collecting silver, invest in a specialized book on silver and a small hallmark handbook like *Miller's Silver and Sheffield Plate Marks* by John Bly (Miller's Press, 1999). A hallmark handbook is handy because the letter, initials, and town hallmarks vary depending on *when* and *where* each piece of silver was made, and *who* made it. In a general book like this, it's impossible to list every year, maker, and city that each location has used since the seventeenth century.

However, the following presentation of hallmarks and illustrations of how to use them explains how to quickly and easily match up the marks you see on a piece of silver with the marks you will find in specialized silver books.

AntiqClue

Why bother to learn how to read English silver hallmarks? $$$, that's why. Every weekend savvy antiquers pick up antique English sterling pieces that some unknowing person is selling for silver plate because, "Well, they're not marked sterling."

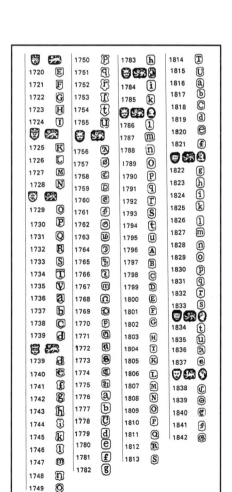

How many of these marks match marks you've seen on pieces or in books?

The chart for London hallmarks begins with the city's symbol, a leopard's head. The leopard originally wore a crown, but beginning in 1822 the leopard appears bare-headed. Next comes the lion facing left (notice that it changes slightly over the years). Finally there is a run of 20 consecutive letters contained in a cartouche—from *a* to *u*. The letters *j, v, w, x, y,* and *z* are never used. To make the years distinguishable from one another, the letters are printed in different typefaces inside cartouches of various shapes.

Along the rim of a silver goblet you see the lion, an uncrowned leopard's head, and this letter and cartouche. These marks match up with the year 1832.

Try this one: the lion, a crowned leopard's head, and this letter and cartouche. These marks match the year 1727.

Now try these two series of marks:

These marks match up with the year 1756.

These marks are for the year 1836.

Notice, though, that the letters and even the cartouches surrounding them are almost identical. It is the absence of the crown on the leopard's head in the second series that clearly tells you that this piece can't be from 1756 (remember, the crown was removed in 1822).

Another quick way to find out whether those marks were from 1757 or 1836 would be to look up the maker's initials in your handy hallmark guide—which you should always carry with you—as shown in this illustration:

Let's say that the initials *WB,* looking like this, appear on the piece. A quick check will show that initials like this were used by William Bateman when he was working in London between 1815 and 1840. Obviously, Bateman couldn't have made a piece in 1756.

But what if you find a piece with the following marks:

You won't be able to find it in the hallmark illustration. The lion means sterling, of course. The date mark looks like the one used in London in both 1756 and 1836. But what about the town mark? You saw only leopards' heads on that chart because it's the chart for London. But the mark I gave you (yes, this was a trick question) was for Birmingham. A quick check under Birmingham marks in your hallmark book would identify the date of this piece as 1824.

It is very important to know where these hallmarks are found on a piece of English sterling silver. Unlike American silver, which is almost always marked on the bottom of the piece, English hallmarks can appear around rims, edges, and handles, as well as on the bottom, of a piece.

Furthermore, each hallmark is punched in individually and so can appear in any order. Where there

AntiqClue

To become familiar with English hallmarks, visit an auction preview where English silver is being sold. Look at the hallmarks on a piece; find them in your hallmark guidebook. If the date you determine for the piece is different from the one given by the auction house, ask the silver expert to help you.

is ample room on the silver piece, a full set of hallmarks will appear. But some small pieces don't have enough space for all the marks. Be sure, though, that the lion is always present.

AntiqClue

Avoid putting fine silver in the dishwasher. The hot water and drying process can loosen hollow handles from knife blades. Further, many dishwasher detergents, especially the gels, leave a dull gray finish and take away silver's natural luster.

AntiqClue

When a piece of silver is made up of individual parts—say a removable top on a sugar bowl, or even a handle on a basket—be sure that all the parts have corresponding marks. Otherwise, the piece may have been mixmatched (like a piece of married furniture).

Finally, one last word about the highly revered English tradition of the silversmith. Not just anyone could use the English hallmarks. Hallmarks were reserved for members of the most highly honored Guild of Goldsmiths (which included silversmiths). Additionally, every piece of silver made by the Guild had to be tested before it could be marked, thereby guaranteeing that it was indeed sterling silver. It took years of apprenticeship and mastery of the craft to become a member of the Guild. That is why English silver is synonymous with fine quality.

The American Way

American sterling silver is much easier to identify than British sterling silver. It's usually marked "sterling"—after 1860 or 1865, that is. Having said that, there are a couple of exceptions.

The first exception is the American silver that was made before that benchmark date of 1860 or 1865. That silver will be discussed shortly in the section, "Coin Silver in the Home." The other exception you will immediately understand.

On occasion, a piece of American sterling silver will be marked "925," or "925/1000." You now know that those numbers signify that 925 parts of pure silver have been used and that the piece meets the sterling standard.

American sterling silver made from around the time of the Civil War to the present will be clearly marked either "sterling," or with the number "925," which indicates that the silver meets the sterling standard. The silver made prior to the Civil War, however, is a little different, and it provides the knowledgeable person with a great chance to make some remarkable finds.

Coin Silver in the Home

From colonial times until the middle of the nineteenth century, the best silver made in America fell just slightly short of the English sterling standard. This silver is called *coin silver*. Instead of being made of 925 parts of pure silver, this early American coin silver was made of 900 parts of pure silver. That was the standard used in American coinage. Get the connection? Coinage. Coin silver.

America's early silversmiths marked their wares differently from their British counterparts. In addition to the word "coin," some of the letter marks they used were ...

➤ *C* for coin.

➤ *D* for dollar.

➤ *S* for standard.

> **AntiqInfo**
>
> The word **weighted** sometimes appears on pieces also marked "sterling." This means that a dark, powdery, leadlike substance has been put into the base of the piece to give it extra weight and balance. That's what makes the piece weigh more—not any additional silver.

But old ways are hard to give up. Many Americans wanted their American-made silver marked to look like English hallmarks. As a result, some silversmiths developed *pseudohallmarks*—marks implying that American silver was just as fine as English silver. That might have worked for eighteenth-century Americans, but those pseudohallmarks can confuse the twenty-first-century silver collector.

These frequently used pseudohallmarks may resemble the English leopard's head, sovereign's head, lion, and date year, but they miss the mark.

Eighteenth-century coin silver was sometimes marked by the maker with his name or initials and, at times, his location. These marks can be the only marks on the piece, or they can be used along with other coin-silver marks.

Here's an example of how American coin silversmiths marked their wares.

R&W.WILSON
PHILADA.

AntiqInfo

That best-known of all American silver makers, Tiffany & Company, actually made many fine pieces using the 925 standard and marked "sterling" in the 1850s. With the onset of the Civil War, silver production dropped sharply. When the war ended, the sterling standard became widely accepted.

Because this early American coin silver is not marked with the word "sterling," and its marks don't match up with English hallmarks, it is often thought to be plated. In fact, I'd wager (if I were a betting woman) that more antique American coin silver has been discarded than any other single category of antiques. This should send up flags for you.

Learn what the marks look like. Learn what the pieces look like (see Chapter 21, "Silver: No Home Should Be Without It"). Then start pawing through every box of tarnished silver you see at flea markets, house sales, thrift shops, country auctions, and antique shops and malls. Remember that bit of advice I gave you earlier: Not all antiques dealers know about every kind of antique.

The European Way

There's a saying about English and European silver and gold that goes like this: The English are cheap with their gold, and the Europeans are cheap with their silver. That's because the English often use 9- and 10-karat gold rather than 16- or 18-karat gold, whereas the Europeans use only 800 parts pure silver rather than 925 parts. That's the first thing you need to know about European (or Continental, as it is often called) silver.

One of the differences between English and European silver is their guilds. English silver guilds were mostly located in regional centers—London, Birmingham, Sheffield, Chester, and so on. European silver guilds, in contrast, were found in untold numbers of cities, towns, and villages throughout the European countries, from Paris and Moscow, to Holbaek and Beja.

As a result, there are literally thousands of European hallmarks, to say nothing of the number of maker's marks. That makes identifying European silver by individual countries almost impossible.

AntiqLingo

Coin silver is silver having 900 parts of pure silver and 100 parts of alloy, and thus not as pure as sterling silver. The term is used for any 900 standard silver but is most often associated with American colonial silver.

Commonly found European silver marks include (clockwise from left to right) an ornate B topped by a crown (France), a crescent moon and a crown (Germany), a tomb-shaped cartouche with numbers around a center design (Eastern European countries), and a classical profile (Italy).

This small, but essential, bit of information should alert you to the presence of European silver, and lead you to explore the area further if you're interested. Specialty shops and auction houses are the best places to see correctly identified European silver.

Intrinsic Value vs. Aesthetic Value

At the outset, I said that silver has an intrinsic value and can be cashed in for real money. That's

AntiqLingo

Pseudohallmarks are marks used by American colonial silversmiths that closely resembled genuine English hallmarks.

AntiqClue

Some coin silver wasn't marked at all! If, after closely examining a piece, you do not find a mark, examine the area where the silver would have received the most wear. If the piece is silver plate, you'll see another color of metal showing through—proof that the piece is *not* sterling.

AntiqInfo

American "coin silver" does not mean that the silver was made from coins. On occasion, some coins were given to the colonial silversmith to be melted down to make a teapot or porringer or spoon. Out-of-fashion English and European silver pieces met the same fate. Coin silver means 900/1,000 parts pure silver. Pure and simple.

true. But the silver connoisseur doesn't give a flip about how much a troy ounce of silver is selling for these days. It's the same old song of age, design, craftsmanship, and condition that excites the collector.

Crudely made pieces simply won't look as good as well-crafted ones. Poorly designed pieces are not well balanced. They appear to be too thick, or too large, in one place and too thin, or too small, in another.

Look at how the piece is decorated. Is the design too fussy, too ornate, or too large for the size of the piece? If it is monogrammed, is the style in keeping with the piece's decoration?

Antique silver that has aged beautifully will have a lustrous, mellow patina that is quite unlike the finish on new silver. Just as the patina on antique furniture is the result of years of dust, dirt, and grime all being rubbed into the wood each time it is dusted and polished, so is the highly desirable patina on silver developed after years of small scratches and little nicks. The wear that comes from use and from polishing builds up a surface that silver lovers say resembles a piece of soft, blue-gray velvet. This is why old sterling silver should never be machine buffed but rather lovingly polished with a soft cloth.

Altered States

Check all pieces carefully for any repairs or alterations. Yes, there have been cases of hallmarks being cut out of one piece (usually a damaged one) and being put into another piece. Such surgery can usually be detected by the difference in the color.

Also check for signs that a monogram or coat of arms might have been removed. You'll see a thinned out, or rippled, area on the exterior surface where engraving would have been.

Look for these commonly found signs of damage or repair:

➤ Feet or bases that have been bent or damaged

➤ Handles that have pulled away from the body and repaired

➤ Attached lids that have been broken and reattached

➤ Stems on goblets or compotes that have been twisted or seriously bent

➤ Any raised ornamental decoration that has been damaged

➤ Split seams where the silver piece is joined

➤ Tears or splits where spouts are joined to the pitcher or pot body

Through Thick and Thin: Content or Gauge

Most important of all, don't fall for the old line: "Feel how heavy this piece is! That's because it's got more silver in it."

The truth is, the silver *marks* are going to tell you how much silver the piece has in it—925, 900, or 800 parts of pure silver. The weight of the piece has nothing to do with how much *pure* silver is in it. One piece will weigh more than another piece because the silver ball has been rolled thicker or thinner to make the final piece, just as a ball of dough is rolled thicker or thinner to make cookies or biscuits. The thickness of silver is called its gauge.

Yes, a heavier piece of silver (made of thick gauge) can be much finer—if the design, quality, and condition make it better. But weight alone will not a fine piece make.

So what should that line about the heavy piece of silver be? "Feel how heavy this piece is! That's because it is made of a thick gauge."

Silver Threads Among the Gold

You now know that the hallmark on a piece of English silver tells you the year it was made. And you know that the American changeover from coin silver to sterling silver came in the 1860s.

AntiqLingo

European silver is silver made throughout Europe (or the Continent) having a silver standard of 800 parts silver and 200 parts alloy.

AntiqInfo

Although the silver content of European silver is 800/1,000, or slightly lower than England's and America's 925/1,000 standard, European silver is still highly regarded. Its value lies in its age, design, and quality.

AntiqInfo

What's the best and cheapest silver polish? Your fingers Just rub the silver between your thumb and the tip of your pointer finger. It will become lustrous in no time!

But how, pray tell, can you tell the 1880 sterling silver piece from the 1980 sterling silver piece?

Design is as important a factor in dating silver as it is in dating furniture. Victorian silver has a look all its own. It has notably heavy decoration—lots of scrolls, flowers, exotic scenes, many of the same motifs you saw used on Victorian furniture. Likewise, twentieth-century silver has a "modern" look that is sleek and restrained when compared with later-nineteenth-century silver. And luckily, most twentieth-century American silver copied or reproduced from eighteenth-century silver is marked "sterling" (remember, eighteenth-century American silver was coin, not sterling), and is identified as a copy.

Now you understand why I said that identifying silver almost becomes a science once you can read and understand the marks.

Ready to learn more about silver? Chapter 21 illustrates many silver pieces that are commonly seen. That is where you will learn about eighteenth- and nineteenth-century silver designs. But first a short chapter on silver plate.

AntiqClue

About to pass up a piece because it is monogrammed? Don't. Until recent years, *all* fine silver was monogrammed. Remember, before banks, silver was a form of currency. It was monogrammed as a sign of ownership.

The Least You Need to Know

➤ English hallmarks tell you when, where, and who made the piece.

➤ Before the benchmark dates of the Civil War, America's finest silver was coin silver.

➤ After the Civil War, American silver switched over to the English sterling standard (925/1,000).

➤ European silver, though of a lower standard (800/1,000) standard, is valued for its aesthetic qualities.

➤ Silver must be carefully examined for repairs and restoration.

➤ Silver is one of the easiest categories of antiques to conquer.

Chapter 20

A Twist of Plate: Understanding Silver Plate

In This Chapter

➤ Learn the difference between Sheffield plate and electroplate

➤ Find out the pros and cons of replating silver plate

➤ Become acquainted with the various names and initials associated with electro-plating

All silver plate is not the same. It comes in all shapes, sizes, qualities, and conditions.

A set of four exceptional nineteenth-century Sheffield plate candlesticks can easily cost $4,000 or $5,000, or more. A badly worn nineteenth-century electroplated hand mirror can cost $5.00. As you can see, silver plate varies greatly in value and, contrary to what many people think, not all silver plate is bad. In fact, much mid- to late-nineteenth-century Victorian silverplate is seeing a strong revival.

Rolled Over: Sheffield Plate

You might recall from Chapter 19, "Heavy Metal: Understanding Silver," that wooden furniture frames were covered in silver during the late seventeenth and early eighteenth centuries. Silver adds a sheen to everything it touches. Little wonder that the hard-working middle classes who saw tables set with gleaming sterling silver wanted the same look in their more humble homes.

Modern silver plate began in 1743 when a layer of silver was *fused* onto a sheet of copper. For many years, sheets of this combination were rolled over copper frames or shapes, making them look like they were solid silver on the outer surface. Traces of the rolled-over edges on the undersides gave them away, however. Further, once the silver on the top surface began to wear off, the golden copper color began to come through. This is called *bleeding*.

A sample of old Sheffield pieces offered for sale around 1910.

At the mention of copper coming through, everyone who owns a piece of bleeding Sheffield asks antiques dealers and appraisers: "Should I have my old Sheffield silver plate replated?" Should you? There are two schools of thought.

When I asked a highly respected dealer of fine old Sheffield silver that very question, he explained it this way. Silver plate was meant to look like silver. If the maker had wanted the piece to be copper, he would have left it copper.

But another school of thought says that the silver plate on the very old Sheffield pieces was applied quite differently from the way it is today. Furthermore, it takes years and years for a rich silver patina to develop on newly applied silverplate. Replating, therefore, destroys the look and beauty of the old.

Which course should you take? I suggest that you weigh both responses and decide for yourself. Of course, if you're buying eighteenth-century Sheffield plate, the ideal situation is to find pieces that are still in very fine original condition and avoid the question entirely. But these pieces are hard to come by—and when you do find them, they are costly.

New technology and techniques perfected this fusing process. Soon, sheets of these fused metals could be stamped into shapes (like handles and feet) and soldered together. The die-stamping process eventually made it possible to mass-produce strips of decorative motifs. These were stamped out, cut, and applied onto trays. This process produced inexpensive look-alike pieces to satisfy the masses.

AntiqInfo

Just as Lambert Hitchcock set up an assembly line to make chairs, Benjamin Huntsman used interchangeable die-stamped parts—bases, decorative motifs, spouts, handles, and so on—to mass-produce Sheffield silver pieces for the middle class.

Marks, but No Hallmarks

Making silver plate became such a thriving industry in Sheffield that several companies were formed. Very little early Sheffield plate is marked, but by the late eighteenth century the companies began putting identifying marks on their wares. Under British law, these marks could in no way resemble the hallmarks used on English sterling.

Among the most often encountered early Sheffield marks are crossed keys and an open hand.

Plated for the Privileged Class

Large Sheffield plated trays were so outstanding that even well-to-do people began buying them. Although the plated trays were fairly expensive, just think how expensive a sterling silver tray large enough and strong enough to hold an entire coffee and tea service would have been! Plated trays had a problem, however. When a wealthy family wished to have their new possession engraved with their monogram or coat of arms, the engraving tools revealed the copper underneath. To avoid this, a sterling silver inset was put in the center of the tray, and this became the engravable area.

AntiqClue

To find out whether an old Sheffield tray has a sterling inset, look for the monogram or coat of arms. Then breathe heavily (puff) on it. The thin seams around the edge of the sterling inset will show up.

Electroplate: The Modern Way

It took almost a century to modernize the time-consuming and expensive method of fusing silver plate, but in the 1840s (there's the magical date again!) a new method of plating pieces with silver was developed, *electroplate*.

Nothing about this electroplated nineteenth-century piece resembles a piece of early-eighteenth-century fused old Sheffield silver.

Electroplating was less expensive and time-consuming than the old fusing method. It was now possible to silver plate over metal bodies other than copper—a fairly expensive metal.

Peeling Away the Outer Coating

Soon, everything from coffeepots to hand mirrors was being silver-plated atop one of two very inexpensive white base metals, *Britannia metal* and *German silver*. Suddenly, not only were silver-plated items affordable, but if the thin silver coating should wear away, a white metal would show through instead of a contrasting copper color. Hopefully, the color of the worn area wouldn't even be noticeable.

AntiqLingo

Electroplate is the method whereby a metal shape, or metal body, and silver are both immersed in an electrolytic solution, which makes the silver adhere to the metal.

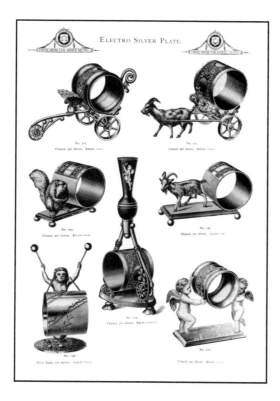

Silver companies produced an endless variety of electroplated pieces, as illustrated by this page from the Meriden Britannia Company's 1882 catalogue.

Silver Plating Comes to America, Big Time

The technology behind electroplating quickly moved from England to America in the 1840s. With companies like Reed and Barton and Gorham making plated wares by the 1860s, such pieces were so popular that often the same pieces were made in both sterling silver and silver plate. The plated ware sold so well that soon manufacturers were bragging that no one could tell the difference.

Making the Second Best as Good as the Best

Trays and baskets, coffeepots and tea urns, all pieces known as *hollowware*, weren't the only silver pieces made in silver plate. Table flatware patterns were also flooding the market. One

AntiqLingo

Britannia metal is an alloy much like pewter, but without the lead content. When used for silver plating, it is identified as the base, or underneath, metal by the mark "EPBM" (short for ElectroPlated Britannia Metal).

German silver (also known as Argentine and nickel silver) is an alloy of nickel, zinc, and copper. It's not used as frequently in electroplating as Britannia metal.

nineteenth-century magazine writer even wrote, "almost anyone may possess needed articles … being equal in appearance to the solid silver ware."

AntiqLingo

Hollowware is the name given to silver pieces having a hollow shape, for example, pitchers, pots, vases, jugs, cups, tankards, goblets, butter dishes, and even trays and platters. In other words, silver that is not flatware, such as knives, forks, spoons, ladles, and so on, falls into the hollowware category.

AntiqClue

Are there small dark dots on the silver-plated piece (or sterling piece, for that matter)? Those are the result of **pitting**. It occurs when dirt or food particles, especially salt, are left on the silver and eat through it. Gentle polishing sometimes removes pitting if it isn't too deep. Otherwise, it can ruin a piece. Remember to clean silver before putting it away!

When silver flatware patterns began to be manufactured in plated silver, the tables of the middle class could now look almost like those of the upper classes. All told, silver plate had a tremendous social impact during the later nineteenth century.

Yesterday's Demand; Today's Supply

The result is a plethora of silver plate, both flatware and hollowware, available to collectors—and much of it at reasonable prices. That's why, just as with sterling silver, you can be a discriminating collector.

But what happens when you have an old family piece from the 1870s or 1880s in which the white under-metal is beginning to show through? That's when the question already discussed in the Sheffield section arises: "Should I have it replated?"

Because today's method of replating—electroplating—is the same one used when the piece was made, the concern about replacing the old silver-plating technique with a modern technique doesn't apply.

Mark Those Marks

In the nineteenth century, there were scores of silver-plate manufacturers in England, and even more in America, but over the years their numbers shrank as one company bought another, and others went out of business.

If you love looking things up, you can look up silver-plate marks all day long. Two books will be especially helpful if this is your cup of tea: Dorothy Rainwater's *Encyclopedia of American Silver Manufacturers* (Schiffer Publishing, 1968) and the Kovels' *American Silver Marks* (Crown Publishers, 1989). Both books also have information about manufacturers in England and Canada.

Here, though, is a quick reference of some of the nineteenth-century companies that made electroplated wares and identified the pieces as being silver plate, not sterling silver:

Marks Appearing on Electroplated Silver Wares

A1

Silver plate

Plate

Sheffield Reproduction

Triple plate

Quadruple

NS (nickel silver)

EPC (electroplate on copper)

Silver on copper (silver on a copper base)

EPNS (electroplate silver on nickel base

EPWM (electroplate silver on nickel with white metal mounts—usually the feet, handles, and finials)

EPBM (electroplate on Britannia metal)

AntiqInfo

Some names used for silver plate sound a little more exotic: German silver, Nevada silver, Alaska silver, Argentine silver, Craig silver, and Inlaid silver. This is the time to remember what Gertrude Stein said, "A rose is a rose is a rose." Electro silver plate is electro silver plate is electro silver plate.

Here are a few of the marks commonly used by American manufacturers of electroplate:

Reed and Barton

Gorham

Meriden Silver Plate Company

International (Wilcox division)

W. & S. Blackinton

F.B. Rogers

Getting the Most for Your Money

Knowing that there is a lot of silver plate on the market, here are some points to keep in mind when you're getting ready to make a purchase:

➤ **Remember condition.** Silver plate wears with use. The cost of replating a piece of silver can run well over $100. And the new silver plate is very shiny. Before buying a piece of worn silver plate, ask yourself if you can live with the piece in its "as is" condition first and if you can afford to have it replated.

➤ **Look for a unique design.** A silver-plated butter dish can be just another silver-plated butter dish, or it can be a wonderful example of period design with sphinx heads (like Victorian Renaissance furniture) or with a cow atop it (get it?), or it can be in the shape of a Gothic building! Unique and interesting design makes for value in silverplated items.

Before You Buy

Before purchasing any piece of silver that is designed to hold liquid, fill it with water. Tiny punctures can be missed with the naked eye, as can damage around the pouring spout.

➤ **Look for the rare piece.** If you have not looked at nineteenth-century silver plate before, you may think that a tilting water pitcher is rare when you see one for the first time. Because silver plate was so immensely popular, thousands and thousands of almost every possible piece were made in silver plate. Don't buy the first piece you see. Do research on the Internet, in books, in shops, and so on to learn whether or not the piece really is rare. This will also familiarize you with fair prices.

➤ **Enjoy!** Silver was made to be enjoyed and used, just as furniture was. Don't buy it and then pack it away.

The Least You Need to Know

➤ Not all silver plate is alike.

➤ The electroplating process made it possible for the middle class to have pieces that looked like sterling silver.

➤ Check the marking on a piece to find out whether it is silver plate or sterling silver.

➤ There is so much nineteenth-century silver plate around that it should be used and enjoyed even though it is over 100 years old.

Silver: No Home Should Be Without It

Serious antiques collectors take great pride and delight in differentiating a piece of eighteenth-century American coin silver from, say, a piece of late-nineteenth-century English silverplate. Being able to make that distinction helps collectors decide which pieces to buy and which ones to walk away from. Once you become proficient in reading silver marks, you, too, will be able to make wise decisions and often, great finds.

However, to my way of thinking, knowing a little of the history behind silver's popularity and understanding why it was so treasured by our ancestors makes silver come to life.

Put Your Money Where Your Teaspoon Is

In the seventeenth and early eighteenth centuries, a man's home was his bank. That's where he kept his treasures. The problem was, one man's coins looked like the next man's coins. How could you prove whose coins were whose?

To get around this problem, the well-to-do merchant or professional gentleman would visit the local silversmith, taking along a handful of coins and some old silver that was no longer "fashionable." The silversmith would then figure up how much silver the gentleman had. Then they'd strike a deal.

AntiqInfo

America's first bank was chartered in 1781. Before then, keeping a family's wealth on the sideboard or in the dining room cupboard was a custom that the rising middle class learned from royalty and the church. From the earliest days, both the court and ecclesiastical groups measured their wealth in silver, gold, and gems.

If there was ample silver, the smithy would take his design and labor fee out of the silver that the gentleman had brought to him. With the remaining silver, he would create a spoon, porringer, tankard, teapot, or whatever piece was desired.

On the other hand, if the gentleman were a little short on silver, the silversmith would charge him for additional silver from the smithy's stock, add on a fee for design and labors, and when the silversmith's bill was paid, the client would walk away with forks or a plate or a mug.

As you can imagine, this practice created many wonderful pieces of early silver for today's collectors, but unfortunately it also led to the melting down of earlier pieces.

Well, we can't do anything about that, but we can treasure and enjoy the antique silver that is still around. And there's plenty of it because silver has long been a measure of real wealth.

The English Tradition

Oh, those English! They have always loved silver—so much so that travelers to sixteenth-century London said that more silver (and gold) was to be found in the shops of London than in all of Rome, Venice, Milan, and Florence put together. The trouble was that every time a war would come along, silver was one of the first things to go. It was confiscated as taxes and melted down to pay debts. As soon as conditions improved, though, more silver would be commissioned to take the place of the old.

AntiqInfo

Dining became much more refined in the seventeenth century than it had been in medieval days. In wealthier homes, the fork appeared during this time, as did a separate room devoted to dining.

By the seventeenth century, domestic (as opposed to ecclesiastical) silver pieces included basin sets, beakers and cups, tankards, porringers, punch bowls, teapots, spoons, and candleholders (both in the form of sconces for the wall, and candlesticks for the table). Now don't expect to find many of these pieces around, but they do exist.

Much more available to the collector is eighteenth-century silver. Add to the seventeenth-century list complete silver tea and coffee services, including waste bowls, sugar bowls, creamers, sugar tongs, tea caddies or boxes, caddy spoons, tureens, sugar sifters (for powdered sugar), plates, dishes, cake baskets, sauce boats, and brandy saucepans; plus snuff boxes, vinaigrettes, bells, snuffers and stands, cruet sets, mustard pots, cake baskets, epergnes, wine funnels, ladles, serving pieces of all types, inkstands, and boxes for patches and seals. Well, you're beginning to get the picture.

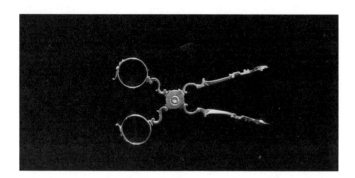

Small silver items like these circa 1800, sterling silver sugar nips are great conversation pieces, as well as being fun to collect.

As if that weren't enough, the opulence-loving Victorians joined forces with the machines of the Industrial Revolution to produce total excess. If they could think of it and make it, they made it in silver. From presentation pieces, such as horse trophies shaped like horses, to entire traveling toilette sets made of silver, the sky was the limit. In fact, silver has been called *the* Victorian status symbol.

Not only was the fashionable table set with scores of knives, forks, and spoons to eat or serve every type of food—from individual fish forks to lettuce serving forks—but the centerpiece had to be silver (electroplated, of course), too. In his novel *Our Mutual Friend,* Dickens describes an ornamental silver centerpiece for the table in which "a caravan of camels take charge of the fruit and flowers and candles, and kneel down to be loaded with the salt." 'Nuff said.

These are the wonderful English silver treasures that await you—sterling and plated, inexpensive and costly.

America's Silver Fever

You know about the great California gold rush. What you may not know about is America's silver rush.

In 1860, before he was a famous novelist, Mark Twain was a newspaperman in Virginia City, Nevada. The search for silver mines there was so frenzied that Twain wrote that people were "smitten with the silver fever."

That silver fever was nothing new, considering how much our English ancestors valued their silver. In fact, during Colonial days, American silver, like American furniture, mostly imitated English silver. There was also a strong Dutch influence in New York State, and some of America's greatest early silversmiths were of Dutch lineage.

America's best-known silversmith, however, was that midnight rider, Paul Revere. You already know how America's early coin silver was marked. If you see a piece with the initials "P.R." or "P. Revere," grab it up. *If,* that is, it has been authenticated and you receive a highly detailed sales receipt so that you can return the piece if there's a problem, or *if* you dig it out of a box of giveaways and you can buy it for nothing. Why?

Because, as with all the famous names in the annals of antiques, Paul Revere's silver was forged at the first part of the twentieth century when another silver fever hit the country—this time for collecting antique American silver.

The legend of Paul Revere is so much a part of America's Revolutionary history and silver tradition that the Towle silver company named a pattern in his honor.

Colonial Americans wanted and had the same silver pieces as their English counterparts. Needless to say, wealthy Americans abroad purchased the newest style of English (and European) pieces and then brought them home. Since American eighteenth-century silver was, in general, simpler and less ornate than its English counterpart, many Colonists preferred the English pieces.

A Silver Picture Is Worth Its Weight in Gold

To familiarize you with the changes in silver shapes and styles over the decades and centuries, this section has a quick reference picture book of silver pieces made through the years. Since the pieces are given chronologically, you'll get a sense of the time and the natural evolution merely by looking at the pictures and reading the captions.

And while you're studying this section, think of these silver pieces in relationship to the furniture of the era.

Table It, or Shelve It

The dining room has always been the silver chest of the home!

The majority of eighteenth-century silver was intended to be used in conjunction with food and drink, especially tea. In the early part of the eighteenth century, the years that correspond to the Queen Anne and early Chippendale furniture periods, silver is simple and most often of two shapes, slightly tapering or pear-shaped.

AntiqClue

Around 1975, I was shown a small oval-shaped standing salt with a pedestal base and handles at the side. And the marks "P.R." The problem was that the oval-shaped body had originally been an eighteenth-century spoon. Further, the handles were crudely attached. Paul Revere was a master craftsman and would never have done that. But a forger will do almost anything.

AntiqInfo

It looks like a piece of eighteenth-century silver. But is it American or English? How do you tell? Marks. Always remember to look for silver marks first.

At the end of the century, the shapes had begun to thin. A total "room" look was becoming popular as well. The examples of later-eighteenth-century silver shown in the following figure have the look and feel of the Hepplewhite furniture that was currently in vogue.

These are typical examples of the type of silver pieces used in the well-to-do home of the early eighteenth century.

The garland motif found on inlaid late-nineteenth-century furniture also showed up on silver pieces.

By the Victorian era, the trend in which furniture and accessories complemented one another was here to stay. Note the floral motif on the cream pitcher illustrated here. Doesn't it remind you of the carving on Victorian Rococo furniture?

In the late nineteenth century, high ceilings, large rooms, and massive furniture were matched with large silver pieces. One of the most popular pieces of the time was the silver-plated tilting pitcher. It reflects the same heft and feeling as Eastlake furniture.

By the middle of the nineteenth century, the silver was much more exuberant and less restrained than the silver of the early eighteenth century. Silver like this piece could never be mistaken for a 1720s piece, for example.

Victorian silver reflects the era's love affair with things, especially since the new machines made it possible to produce goods quickly and inexpensively.

The flatware used at mealtime at the end of the nineteenth century boggles the twenty-first-century brain. From the early-eighteenth-century days when only a simple all-purpose silver spoon and fork were required, life had changed so radically that by the 1890s a set of silver flatware might include both a grapefruit spoon and an orange spoon, an ice cream spoon, plus a chocolate spoon. And heaven forbid that a hostess would use a morning teaspoon instead of an afternoon teaspoon at afternoon tea.

A page from one company's list of available flatware silver pieces— just in case you think you've run out of things to collect.

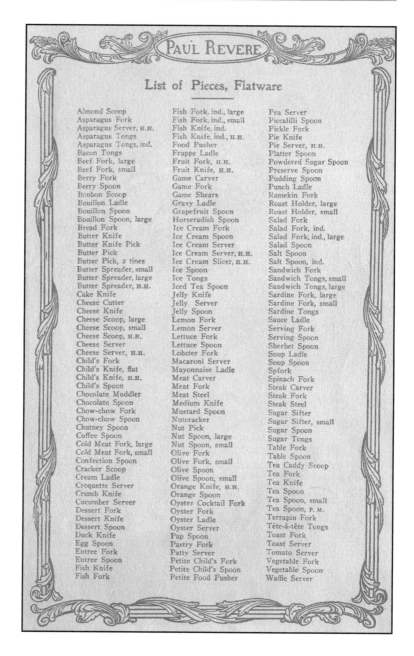

PAUL REVERE

List of Pieces, Flatware

Almond Scoop	Fish Fork, ind., large	Pea Server
Asparagus Fork	Fish Fork, ind., small	Piccalilli Spoon
Asparagus Server, H.H.	Fish Knife, ind.	Pickle Fork
Asparagus Tongs	Fish Knife, ind., H.H.	Pie Knife
Asparagus Tongs, ind.	Food Pusher	Pie Server, H.H.
Bacon Tongs	Frappe Ladle	Platter Spoon
Beef Fork, large	Fruit Fork, H.H.	Powdered Sugar Spoon
Beef Fork, small	Fruit Knife, H.H.	Preserve Spoon
Berry Fork	Game Carver	Pudding Spoon
Berry Spoon	Game Fork	Punch Ladle
Bonbon Scoop	Game Shears	Ramekin Fork
Bouillon Ladle	Gravy Ladle	Roast Holder, large
Bouillon Spoon	Grapefruit Spoon	Roast Holder, small
Bouillon Spoon, large	Horseradish Spoon	Salad Fork
Bread Fork	Ice Cream Fork	Salad Fork, ind.
Butter Knife	Ice Cream Spoon	Salad Fork, ind., large
Butter Knife Pick	Ice Cream Server	Salad Spoon
Butter Pick	Ice Cream Server, H.H.	Salt Spoon
Butter Pick, 2 tines	Ice Cream Slicer, H.H.	Salt Spoon, ind.
Butter Spreader, small	Ice Spoon	Sandwich Fork
Butter Spreader, large	Ice Tongs	Sandwich Tongs, small
Butter Spreader, H.H.	Iced Tea Spoon	Sandwich Tongs, large
Cake Knife	Jelly Knife	Sardine Fork, large
Cheese Cutter	Jelly Server	Sardine Fork, small
Cheese Knife	Jelly Spoon	Sardine Tongs
Cheese Scoop, large	Lemon Fork	Sauce Ladle
Cheese Scoop, small	Lemon Server	Serving Fork
Cheese Scoop, H.H.	Lettuce Fork	Serving Spoon
Cheese Server	Lettuce Spoon	Sherbet Spoon
Cheese Server, H.H.	Lobster Fork	Soup Ladle
Child's Fork	Macaroni Server	Soup Spoon
Child's Knife, flat	Mayonnaise Ladle	Spfork
Child's Knife, H.H.	Meat Carver	Spinach Fork
Child's Spoon	Meat Fork	Steak Carver
Chocolate Muddler	Meat Steel	Steak Fork
Chocolate Spoon	Medium Knife	Steak Steel
Chow-chow Fork	Mustard Spoon	Sugar Sifter
Chow-chow Spoon	Nutcracker	Sugar Sifter, small
Chutney Spoon	Nut Pick	Sugar Spoon
Coffee Spoon	Nut Spoon, large	Sugar Tongs
Cold Meat Fork, large	Nut Spoon, small	Table Fork
Cold Meat Fork, small	Olive Fork	Table Spoon
Confection Spoon	Olive Fork, small	Tea Caddy Scoop
Cracker Scoop	Olive Spoon	Tea Fork
Cream Ladle	Olive Spoon, small	Tea Knife
Croquette Server	Orange Knife, H.H.	Tea Spoon
Crumb Knife	Orange Spoon	Tea Spoon, small
Cucumber Server	Oyster Cocktail Fork	Tea Spoon, P. M.
Dessert Fork	Oyster Fork	Terrapin Fork
Dessert Knife	Oyster Ladle	Tête-à-tête Tongs
Dessert Spoon	Oyster Server	Toast Fork
Duck Knife	Pap Spoon	Toast Server
Egg Spoon	Pastry Fork	Tomato Server
Entree Fork	Patty Server	Vegetable Fork
Entree Spoon	Petite Child's Fork	Vegetable Spoon
Fish Knife	Petite Child's Spoon	Waffle Server
Fish Fork	Petite Food Pusher	

Personal Effects

When it came to silver, there was no reason to stop at the dining room. We are all familiar with pictures showing eighteenth-century ladies wearing "beauty patches."

Where did they keep the patches when they weren't wearing them? In silver boxes, of course. And no fine gentleman would carry his snuff in anything less than a sterling silver box. Remember, too, only silver buckles would do for both the lady's and the gentleman's shoes.

The tradition of using silver for lovely personal effects has been around since Renaissance days. But naturally this fashion reached its height in the Victorian era. Every fine lady's dressing table was expected to be "dressed" itself. A wealthy lady could not face the day without her sterling silver brushes, mirrors, powder boxes, button hooks, perfume and cologne bottles, bud vases, even hair-receivers and silver-handled curling irons. Although this indulgence may seem excessive to some, even the most jaded twenty-first-century minimalist will admit that these objects are fascinating, as well as lovely.

AntiqClue

Small silver items are the ideal collectible if you want something that reverberates with echoes of an elegant past, and you prefer small objects that can be bought when you're out-of-town on a business trip or can be easily moved across country when you're transferred.

Silver-mounted brushes were an essential part of every fine lady's boudoir furnishings.

(Photo courtesy Neal's Auction Company)

The Least You Need to Know

➤ Silver has been an integral part of family life since the eighteenth century.

➤ Although silver fakes are rare, they do exist.

➤ Silver is readily available to the collector.

Chapter 22

Coming Out of the China Closet

In This Chapter

➤ Learn when and how fine porcelain came to Europe and England

➤ Become familiar with the difference between porcelain and pottery

➤ Begin learning names and terms associated with antique ceramics

---

I'll never forget the day I opened a letter to find a picture of a beautiful plate in it. "Can you tell me who made the plate and how old it is?" the writer of the letter asked. I put down the letter, picked up the photograph, examined the front of the plate carefully, and then turned over the photograph so I could see the marks on the back of the plate.

Talk about feeling like an idiot! But the photograph was so clear and the plate so lovely that for just a moment I forgot I was looking at a picture and I did what anyone looking at a piece of china does. I instinctively looked for the mark. Like the marks on silver, the marks on a piece of china—or the lack of them—tell a great deal about the piece.

China China

Entire books are devoted to telling the history of china. What the novice needs to know is that what we casually refer to as "fine china" or porcelain was discovered by the Chinese during the Tang Dynasty (618–906).

On the Home Front

In the fourteenth century, Marco Polo and other explorers took back to Europe cups and bowls and other porcelain wares made by the Chinese for home use. It would be several hundred years before the Europeans learned how to make porcelain for themselves.

For the Foreign Trade

In the eighteenth century when the West established regular trade with China, whole shiploads of this precious porcelain commodity were taken to Portugal, Spain, England, the American Colonies, and even to South America. It served as ballast for the ships and was treasured in Western homes. This Chinese porcelain is known as *Chinese Export,* since it was made specifically for occidental homes and is different from that which the Chinese made for their own use.

Millions of pieces of Chinese Export china have been made through the years—but china breaks. Fine eighteenth- and even nineteenth-century pieces, recognizable by their shapes, decoration, and color, command high prices.

The three most highly prized Chinese Export patterns are Armorial (decorated with a family's crest or arms), Rose Medallion (brightly decorated in pinks and orange with Oriental scenes—people, places, ornithological specimens), and Canton (the familiar blue bridge and pagoda scene).

The Continental Touch

The Europeans had the best luck creating ceramics after they became familiar with the Chinese wares, but it was not without trial and error.

Delft: The Trying Dutchmen

The Dutch were unsuccessful in creating porcelain, but by the mid-seventeenth century they were successful in developing a ceramic ware known as *Delft*, named for a town near Rotterdam.

An example of the simple, but lovely, designs found on early Delftware.

German Alchemy Pays Off

The sixteenth and early seventeenth centuries are settings for wonderful stories told about alchemists who were imprisoned until they could … no, not spin gold from straw—until they could create porcelain!

When Johann Bottger discovered the correct formula for *hard paste* porcelain in Meissen, Germany, the Meissen factory became the standard bearer for fine European porcelain.

The French Connection

Competing with Meissen to make the first and finest continental porcelain was a factory in Saint-Cloud, France. But theirs was a soft paste porcelain, and Meissen soon took the lead.

AntiqLingo

Delft is the generic name for a thick, nontranslucent pottery or earthenware having a shiny tin glaze that makes it appear more chinalike. Delft was first made in Holland and in the eighteenth century in England.

Also on the home front was the famed Sevre porcelain. Sevre china became so highly prized that even Catherine the Great of Russia ordered a grand service for her court.

Even more memorable was Madame de Pompadour's association with the Sevre factory. That's how one of the Sevre colors, a beautiful rose-pink, came to be called "rose Pompadour."

Even though these handsome vases were catalogued as "Sevres," they are still stunning and are valued in the $20,000-plus range.

(Photo courtesy of Sloan's)

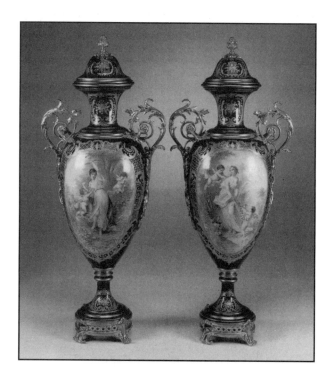

England Tries and Succeeds

England finally began producing real porcelain after a few false starts. But what false starts those were. In addition to Delft, which was created in Holland first and in England later, many other types of English pottery were created during those experimental years. Today they are highly prized. Among them are …

AntiqInfo

Chinese porcelain was so highly prized in Europe during the sixteenth and seventeenth centuries that pieces were mounted in precious silver and gold.

➤ Slip-decorated ware.

➤ Redware.

➤ Salt-glaze ware.

➤ Creamware, Queensware, Pearlware.

➤ Tortoiseshell ware (Whieldon).

➤ Any variety of vari-colored wares (agate, mocha, marbled, and so on).

➤ Jasperware.

The breakthrough in porcelain manufacture came in England during the mid-1740s and 1750s, and by 1800 there was a well-established industry. The names associated with early English porcelain are sometimes factories, and other times locations where china was made. They include Bow, Chelsea, Bristol, Derby, New Hall, Worcester, Liverpool, Lowestoft, Longton Hall, and Spode.

Much of the early English porcelain resembles Chinese Export ware. Also note how similar this shape is to silver teapots made at the same time.

America Lags Behind

Two names stand out in the annals of America's attempts to establish a porcelain factory: Bonnin & Morris and Tucker. Both were in Philadelphia, Bonnin & Morris in the 1770s, and Tucker in the 1820s. Examples of their wares are as rare as the proverbial "hen's teeth."

For the novice, America's porcelain history begins with the Lenox factory in the late nineteenth century, although a rich tradition of regional pottery—Redware, salt-glazed pieces, and of course the famed Bennington pottery from Vermont—existed as well.

But, you may protest, shelves in antiques stores are jammed with Fiesta Ware, McCoy, Roseville, etc. Yes, but these *collectibles* have a little more aging to do before they can be antiques.

AntiqLingo

Hard paste is the porcelain known as "true" porcelain. The glaze melds with the paste (or body) and becomes so strong that it cannot be marked with a file. **Soft paste,** on the other hand, can be marked or scratched.

The Great Pretenders

The experienced china collector will tell the beginner, "Beware the great pretenders." Historically, once a china design or pattern from a well-known factory became famous, imitators would spring up everywhere.

AntiqInfo

Sevre porcelain became so highly prized throughout Europe that, during the nineteenth century, porcelain factories everywhere imitated the Sevre colors, forms, and decorations. These imitations are denoted by putting the name in quotation marks: "Sevres," which means "Sevre-like."

Look-Alikes

For example, when Meissen's colorful flower motifs became all the rage in Germany, porcelain factories throughout Germany, Austria, and the rest of Europe came up with their own, ever-so-slightly-changed, Meissenlike, colorful flower motifs.

Or, when the exquisite Sevre sky blue, properly called *bleu céleste,* became *the* color, everyone else tried to imitate it.

The Name Game

The copies would be easy for even an idiot to recognize except for one thing. Often the copiers also imitated the original company's marks. For example, a quick look in a porcelain marks book will show first the familiar Meissen crossed swords and then the crossed swords used by other companies trying to imitate the original, authentic Meissen mark.

The top figure shows a crossed swords mark from a French factory. The bottom figure shows another crossed swords mark—a true Meissen crossed swords mark.

**Jacob Petit,
Fontainbleau,
(F)** *c1830–40*

**Meissen,
(G)** *Late 18C.*

228

Those Other China Types

Although porcelain is considered the finest, or most refined, of the ceramics, antiquers also seek out other ceramics wares and pay hefty prices for them. Pottery and its close cousin stoneware are fun to collect, especially if you like the unusual.

Pot-tery It Up

Pottery differs from porcelain by being thick, dense, and nontranslucent. It simply doesn't have the translucent white color of porcelain. But don't make the mistake of thinking that pottery is just clay pots crudely made. Many pottery pieces take on the dimension of folk art, particularly the nineteenth-century wares made in Pennsylvania and throughout the mid-Atlantic and Southern states.

> **AntiqClue**
>
> Stop and think about it. Whose name was on the back of your grandmother's best china? Haviland? Or was it Spode, Noritake, Limoges, Minton, or Wedgwood? But she had American-made silver. Why? Read on.

An example of highly sought-after nineteenth-century American pottery.

That Glazed Look

When a *glaze* is added to a pottery body or form, things get all fired up. Different kinds of glazes give different results, depending on which chemicals or metals are used to make the glaze, and at what temperature the ceramic piece is fired in the kiln. For example, when cobalt pigment on a red pottery body is fired at a high temperature, the surface turns a rich black. But when just a little cobalt is added to a white-colored glaze and put on a white pottery body, the surface takes on a bluish white luster.

AntiqInfo

Lenox china had its start in 1889 as the Ceramic Art Company in Trenton, New Jersey. In 1906 Walter Scott Lenox broke away and began his own company, Lenox. Thus, even the earliest pieces marked Lenox china need a few years yet to become antiques.

AntiqClue

To know fine antique china, learn what the real thing looks like—both the real surface design and colors, *and* the real mark.

AntiqLingo

Glaze is the coating put on pottery (and porcelain) that gives it a shiny appearance and makes the clay body nonporous.

A Stone's Throw

One of the very best known types of pottery is called *stoneware*, which is simply an earthenware body made from a more finely textured clay. This body is more compact and slightly more translucent than other earthenware material.

This is the same base that is frequently used to make English ceramics. You'll see many names given to stoneware: "stone china," "new stone," "ironstone," and "semiporcelain," among them.

Ultimately, though, it is the glaze and design that distinguish one stoneware from another and give it its charm, appeal, and quality.

The Exterior Design

The body or form of a plate or figurine can be made of either porcelain or pottery, but it is the exterior design that catches our attention.

There are two main ways to turn a molded lump of clay into a work of art: painting it by hand or transferring printed patterns onto it.

Hand-Painted Designs

Decorating china by hand is an exacting art that takes talent and precision. The exquisite figures made by the German and French factories in the eighteenth century are proof of this. At the Meissen factory, for example, entire services were painted, but this was neither time-efficient nor affordable for any but the wealthiest clients.

Transfer-Pattern Designs

The introduction of *transfer-printing* patterns as a means of decorating ceramic bodies in the late eighteenth century had the same impact on the china industries around the world that machines had on the furniture industries.

Transfer-printing made it possible for factories to quickly and efficiently create the untold numbers of semiporcelain dinner services needed by the large Victorian family. The services had plates of every size, cups and saucers—tea, coffee, and demitasse, of course—platters, tureens, serving bowls for every conceivable dish, pitchers, pots, sugars and creamers, and on and on.

Transfer-printing made it possible for the middle class to have affordable, attractive dinnerware. Combine this with the newly available silver-plated flatware and hollowware, and things were looking up by the middle 1850s.

By the nineteenth century, transfer-printing was commonplace, and it even began to be used on fine porcelains.

AntiqLingo

Transfer-printing is the technique of using a print made from a copper plate and transferring it directly onto the ceramic body.

All those wonderful blue-and-white historical motif pieces of china you see in antiques shops were made possible by transfer-printing.

231

> ### The Least You Need to Know
>
> ➤ The china we call fine porcelain originated in China.
>
> ➤ The majority of antique ceramics found in antiques shops comes from the Orient, the Continent, or England.
>
> ➤ America had no major porcelain industry until the twentieth century.
>
> ➤ Transfer-printed semiporcelain or ironstone brought affordable, attractive dinnerware to middle class tables.

The China Collector's Cabinet

What's the point in having a china cabinet if you don't have any china to put in it? Of *course* you need a Wedgwood pitcher, a Leeds plate, a handless Chinese Export cup, and a stunning Sevre vase to set the cabinet off. The flip side of that question is, what are you going to put your grandmother's china in? Of *course* you need a fine Pennsylvania corner cupboard, or maybe an elegant English breakfront would be better to hold her prized wedding china. In all truthfulness, antique china adds beauty and interest to every room in a home.

The Connoisseur's Choice

If you have a four-bedroom house, chances are you'd be hard-pressed to find room for more than eight beds. But there's always room to squeeze in just one more pretty platter or lovely cup and saucer. Once, when I was running out of room to store any more china in the cupboards and closets, and every flat surface was already stacked two high and three deep, I took to the walls and began hanging plates every place I could.

When you find yourself in that sort of situation, it's time to move from being a collector to becoming a connoisseur. Or, you could avoid getting to that point by being selective from the outstart. If china tickles your fancy, I highly recommend narrowing your sights rather than grabbing up every pretty plate you see.

The unusual shape of the sauceboat, plus its eighteenth-century origins, makes it an attractive choice to the china connoisseur.

Some connoisseurs will collect a particular company's wares—maybe Wedgwood Jasperware. Others will choose a particular kind of early ceramic ware—perhaps mocha ware. One collector may decide to search for different examples from just one factory—say, Sevres—or for pieces from a particular geographic region—say, North Carolina pottery. Color is an attraction to many connoisseurs—which explains why blue-and-white Staffordshire has been popular through the ages.

Looking, studying, and comparing examples from the widely diverse world of antique ceramics will help you decide what appeals to you and interests you. You will find a vast array of every sort of antique ceramics in museums, shops, auctions, and Internet sites.

AntiqInfo

Only one sauceboat or covered tureen will be made for literally hundreds of dinner plates. This makes antique serving pieces that are colorful and attractive highly collectible. Even a leaf-shaped or a scalloped dish is preferable to a plain round one.

What's Old and What's Not

You know that many copies have been made of the old china patterns and that some patterns have never ceased to be produced. Examples of these are the ever-popular Rose Medallion and Blue Willow patterns. When china is correctly marked, it can be easily dated with the help of the many general and specialized books on china marks.

By the end of the late nineteenth century, popular china patterns from the late eighteenth and early nineteenth centuries were being made and sold in fashionable shops.

Sometimes, though, imported modern copies of old patterns are intentionally left unmarked. Instead, an easily removable paper label will be attached to the bottom. The idea here is that, without the label, the unmarked piece can be sold to the unknowledgeable person as being older than it actually is.

As a starting point to understanding how china (fine porcelain and other ceramic wares) is marked, here's one of those important benchmark date clues.

If the name of a country, France or England, for example, appears on the piece, chances are it was made between 1891 and the end of World War I—which of course would mean that at this point it might, or might not, be a true antique.

But even if it's not, it is on its way. Before 1891, almost anything goes. Pieces might be unmarked, or marked with any of the following notations:

➤ The company's name

➤ The company's symbol or mark

➤ The company's name and symbol or mark

➤ The painter's symbol or number (if applicable)

➤ The pattern name

➤ The pattern number

➤ A registration mark, if English

If "Trade Mark" is impressed into the bottom of a piece of china, you can assume that it was made after about 1860 or 1865. And if the English term "Limited" appears, the piece most likely was made after 1885 or 1890.

Lastly, if the words "Made in" appear on the piece, you can be sure that it is a twentieth-century piece.

Figuring Out the Shape Things Are in, Literally

Other than marks and dates, a good guide to dating china is by its shape or form. Many books on antique ceramics have helpful tables and guides that show how the shapes of individual china pieces evolved and changed over the years.

Take the cup for example. Early cups had no handles. They really looked like small bowls. Around 1750 a simple upward-swept loop handle was attached. Fancier handles became fashionable during the nineteenth century.

1700   1750   1800   1850

Shapes can be an important guide to dating china, the same way that styles can date furniture.

Figuring Out the Shape Things Are in, Condition-Wise

Don't forget that other shape—the shape the china is in. Condition is of primary importance to the serious ceramics collector.

A chipped porcelain plate is a chipped plate. It will never be as valuable as one that is in perfect condition. On the other hand, pottery, which chips much more easily, is not held to that exacting standard. In fact, Delft pieces from the early and mid-eighteenth century are almost expected to have minor chips in the delicate tin glaze.

The China Collector's Name and Address Book

There are seemingly endless possibilities for the china collector to chose from. Knowing this, remember that quality is always important and that quality can vary within one company's wares. Meissen even marked its wares according to each piece's quality. Just as today we label pieces "seconds" and "thirds," so, too, did the Meissen factory score their crossed swords marks when a piece wasn't of first quality.

Few other companies followed those high standards, so it will be up to you to learn how to judge the quality of ceramics based on color, design, execution, and aesthetics.

With those words of advice, here is a name and address book of some of the best-known makers and most popular types and designs of antique ceramics. Some of these companies and designs continued into the twentieth century, and are even made today. Use this list to become familiar with unfamiliar names. Then, when you're out antiquing, ask, "Do you have any Imari (or Minton or Davenport or whatever)?" Or if you can't wait, log on to your favorite Web site and see what you can find.

AntiqClue

Do not be misled by numbers on china that read like year dates (1776 or 1832 or 1889). China patterns were often given identifying numbers, and china painters in factories were also assigned numbers. True, Victorian ladies who painted china dated many of their pieces, but those pieces do not resemble factory pieces.

A display of Victorian Belleek pieces dating from 1872.

Before You Buy

Chinese Export china is highly prized, partly for its looks and partly for its age. But people seem to lose sight of how *much* of it was made in the eighteenth century. There is no reason to settle for a handleless cup with age cracks or a repaired bowl.

➤ **Belleek.** Irish Belleek dates from the 1850s to the present.

➤ **Bow.** One of the earliest and rarest of English ceramic factories, Bow was established in the 1740s.

➤ **Bristol.** An English factory that began in 1750, Bristol sometimes marked its wares with crossed swords similar to those used by Meissen.

➤ **Chelsea.** One of the "golden" names in early-eighteenth-century English porcelain, Chelsea china and its golden anchor mark have been widely copied.

➤ **Chinese Export.** The name loosely used to identify and date eighteenth-century and early-nineteenth-century china exported from China to occidental countries.

➤ **Davenport.** Maker of fine-quality semiporcelain for almost 100 years, from 1793 to 1887.

➤ **Derby.** Eighteenth-century Derby ranks among the most precious of English ceramics, and the company continues today under the name Royal Crown Derby.

➤ **Doulton.** Begun in the mid-nineteenth century, the Doulton factory continues today as Royal Doulton.

➤ **Dresden.** A city in Germany filled with wonderful china factories, including Meissen; the name "Dresden" is used as a general, all-inclusive name for the china, including figurines, made in that historic city.

➤ **Imari.** The name given to Japanese ceramics (from plates to urns) decorated in cobalt blue and reddish orange colors, usually depicting flowers, fans, and geometric motifs; highly copied by occidental factories.

➤ **KPM.** Like Dresden, KPM is used to include all Berlin factories, but several eighteenth- and nineteenth-century German factories are also known by the initials KPM.

➤ **Kutani.** An area in Japan known since the seventeenth century for its fine ceramics, and now used as a generic name for thick-bodied, heavily decorated, colorful Japanese ceramics.

➤ **Lenox.** America's best-known porcelain manufacturer for twentieth-century wares.

➤ **Mason.** Makers of earthenware in the Staffordshire area of England; well known for patterns influenced by Oriental colors and motifs.

➤ **Mettlach.** A German city renowned since the mid-nineteenth century for its thick-bodied, richly detailed steins and plaques based on folklore scenes.

➤ **Minton.** Founded in 1793, the Minton factory produced exceptional ceramics throughout the nineteenth century, but particularly during the Victorian era.

➤ **Nippon.** Although a well-known name in Japanese ceramics, Nippon dates from only 1891. It is relatively new to the world of antiques and is not of exceptionally fine quality.

➤ **Old Paris.** Also known as "Vieux Paris." Old Paris is another generic name, like Dresden, that covers vast quantities of ceramics made in nineteenth-century France. It is very popular in America.

Typical examples of the form and decoration of Old Paris china.

(Photo courtesy of Neal Auction Company)

239

➤ **Satsuma.** Japanese ceramic ware originating in the eighteenth century and distinguished by its cream-colored body and brocadelike decoration.

Fine-quality nineteenth-century Satsuma china is becoming rarer and more valuable.

➤ **Sevres.** Exceptional-quality porcelain dating from the eighteenth century and made in Sevres, France; the crossed "L" mark on Sevres porcelain is one of the most famous, and most copied, of all porcelain marks.

➤ **Spode.** One of the first Staffordshire factories, Spode is famous for both its porcelain and its "stone" or earthenware, as well as a wide variety of motifs.

➤ **Staffordshire.** England's Staffordshire district has been a hub of porcelain and ceramics factories since the eighteenth century, but its name is also associated with the famed Victorian blue-and-white, Staffordshire transfer-printed historical scenes.

➤ **Wedgwood.** From its founding in the mid-eighteenth century, the Wedgwood factory has produced many different kinds of ceramics, from Queensware to "Fairyland" lustreware, but none is so well known as its various jasperwares.

Wedgwood's Jasperware began in the eighteenth century and has never gone out of vogue.

The Least You Need to Know

➤ Don't settle for a cracked or damaged piece just because it's old.

➤ Narrow your focus before grabbing up every piece of antique china you see.

➤ Look at the total piece—age, quality, rarity, and condition—before buying.

Chapter 24

The Glass House

In This Chapter

➤ Learn how to tell the difference between cut and pressed glass

➤ Become familiar with different types of antique glass

➤ Gain an acquaintance with many of the names and terms associated with antique glass

There are so many copies and fakes of old glass that when the real thing shows up it can be over-looked, or even dismissed, without a second thought. While that sort of sweeping statement frightens away the faint of heart, that's exactly the sort of situation the detective of the decorative arts lives for.

I still remember the day when I told the curator of china and glass at the Winterthur Museum that I had found a rare eighteenth-century American Amelung goblet. She gave me every reason imaginable why the goblet could *not* be authentic. But when I stuck to my guns, she agreed to examine it. In the end, the goblet was authentic and, best of all, it was a piece Winterthur had been looking for and was thrilled to add to their collection.

That's the stuff dreams are made of.

Early Glass: Blowing It Off

Speaking of antiques being old, blown glass is one of the oldest objects that falls into the category of antiques, dating to ancient Syria and Rome. The way glass was made didn't change much from that early period until late in the eighteenth century.

AntiqLingo

A **pontil mark** is the rough, irregular mark or scar left on hand-blown glass when the object is removed from the **pontil rod**—a solid iron rod that the glassmaker uses to hold the hot glass object in place while he continues working on it.

When in Rome

For centuries, glassblowers have gathered hot "liquid" glass on a long blowpipe and "blown" and sculpted the glass into the desired shape. When satisfied, the glassblower would attach the bottom of the still-hot glass object onto a rod to draw the heat to that point. With the rod holding the object in place, the glassblower "finished off" the other end. That completed, he removed the goblet or bowl from the hot rod, leaving a *pontil mark* on the bottom of the object.

This method of blowing glass was invented during the first century B.C.E. in Syria. Roman glassblowers later perfected the technique during the first centuries C.E. It wasn't until around 1780 that the pontil mark became "polished" or smoothed over. This mark is the age-old sign that identifies the piece as being hand-blown, and it's the first thing that the glass collector should look for.

The Venetian Way

By the thirteenth century, glassblowing was so important that the Venetian blowers formed a guild (about the same time that English silversmiths formed their guild). Naturally, working together, these craftsmen began refining their trade, and soon Venetian glass (jugs, goblets, plates, and so on) was as treasured as china from China.

From the Rhine

As you've figured out by now, after one European country found out that a neighboring country was able to produce a new product, the competition became fierce. German glass factories began springing up in the forest regions (maybe that's the *real* reason the witch in *Hansel and Gretel* had the oven going). This tradition eventually gave rise to the highly sought-after colorful Bohemian glass developed in the nineteenth century.

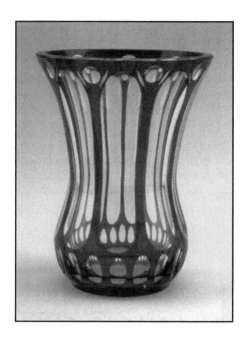

The combination of the deep color (usually red, blue, or green) contrasting with the clear crystal makes antique Bohemian glass interesting and collectible.

In England—in Like Flint

Meanwhile, in England, the clear, sparkling brilliance of glass was enhanced by George Ravencroft. While experimenting with different native materials to make a better-quality and less-expensive glass than Venetian glass, Ravencroft added ground-up flint stone to the glass mixture. The result was *flint glass*.

This stronger and brighter glass made England the dominant leader in glassmaking during the eighteenth century, and it paved the way for the great Irish glass industry, which continues today in Waterford crystal.

An example of the restrained design typical of the flint glass made by the English glassmakers.

(Photo courtesy of Neal Auction Company)

As Time Goes by: Cutting It Up

The technique of using a sharp wheel to cut into a glass object, thereby bringing out its refractive qualities, was practiced by the early Romans. The Germans became so expert at glass cutting that during the eighteenth century the English hired them to train English glass-cutting apprentices in the techniques for creating *cut glass*.

AntiqLingo

Cut glass is glass that has been decorated by grinding and polishing in order to make the glass reflect light and to make it sparkle.

In Deep Relief

Cut glass reached its heyday in the later nineteenth century when the advanced technology of the Industrial Revolution made the cutting process much easier. However, the glass cutter's job still required extreme care and the skill of a true craftsman, for he controlled how deeply the cutting wheel went into the glass. On a large, thick piece like a punch bowl, he might be able to cut in as deeply as half an inch, but on a delicate champagne glass, the glass itself might be no deeper than an eighth of an inch.

Cut glass is familiar to almost everyone, and this assortment is typical of the pieces made at the turn of the century.

(Photo courtesy of Richard S. Brunk Auction Services, Inc.)

Cut glass became a symbol of the opulence of the Victorian era, especially for the wealthy. The craze began when a 17-foot-high fountain made of cut glass was exhibited at the Centennial Exposition of 1876 in Philadelphia. By the 1880s, the number of cut-glass patterns available was mind-boggling, as every glass factory tried to outdo the others.

Acid Takes Over

The real change in how cut glass was made occurred about 1900 (a convenient date for those looking for benchmark dates). The advent of an acid dip process eliminated the need for a craftsman to smooth or polish the rough edges left on the glass body by the cutting tools. Because the craftsman no longer had to polish the edges by using a wooden wheel and jeweler's rouge or pumice, the art of cut glass lost a step in the hand-made process. Serious collectors generally look for pieces made before this time.

Later Yet: A Pressing Matter for the Table

AntiqClue

To distinguish a fine piece of cut glass from an inferior one, hold the glass up to the light. Inferior glass will look slightly yellow when compared with fine glass. Also note that the cutting of the fine piece will be precise and sharp, while the cutting of the inferior piece will be irregular.

While cut glass was being made for the wealthy, developments to bring affordable glass to the masses were also underway during the nineteenth century. Molds and machines that would press glass, rather than a craftsman hand-blowing it, made it possible to mass-produce glass.

In the 1820s, the English developed a pressing machine that would forever change the way glass was made. Hot glass now could be poured into a machine that pressed the liquid into a pattern plate or goblet or other object. Additional technological advancements around mid-century made it possible to produce whole sets of table glass, candlesticks, bowls, and vases even less expensively.

Just a few samples of the seemingly endless patterns of nineteenth-century pressed glass goblets.

(Photo courtesy of Garth Auction House)

Within the enormous realm of pressed glass, there are three specialized categories of objects made in the nineteenth century that attract a lot of attention: three-part mold pieces, historical bottles and flasks, and cup plates.

Three-Part Molds

If you get into antique glass collecting, you'll hear a lot of talk about "blown three-mold glass." This term refers to a method of making glass during the years 1815 to 1835, before pressing machines became widely used. Glass was actually blown into a mold, which had patterns inside the mold. Bottles, goblets, decanters, and other items were made by this procedure, which was less expensive than fully blown glass. Eventually the pressing machines replaced this technique.

Flasks: History on a Bottle

Two of the most popular forms of nineteenth-century molded glass are historical bottles and flasks. Molds were made with all sorts of pictures and patterns depicting the events and the tastes of the day. Bottles and flasks depicting busts of past and current presidents, Masonic emblems, log cabins, and even simple sunbursts and cornucopias were made from the early 1810s through the third quarter of the century.

Cup Plates: The Look of Lace

Bottles and flasks were, of course, a man's domain. But for the lady, pressed-glass cup plates were appropriate. These small plates usually ranged from approximately 2½ to 4½ inches across and had multiple purposes. They were coasters for teacups; they kept table linen from becoming soiled; they protected a bare tabletop from a hot cup; but most unusual of all, the little plates held milady's teacup while the hot tea or coffee that had been served in the cup was cooling off in the cup's saucer, where it had been poured! That's a long-lost custom.

The feminine look and practical purposes of cup plates made these lacy-looking, pressed-glass objects a Victorian favorite.

The center of the cup plate was decorated in any of hundreds of designs, including profiles of historical figures, historical monuments, and assorted fancy designs. But the borders or rims were almost always lacy-looking in appearance.

Glass on the Edge of Becoming Antique

We now move from the Victorian way of life, with its lacy cup plate, to the late nineteenth century, when everything became more "modern." This end-of-the-century period is the one from which we get the term *art glass*. Even though the word "art" suggests that all this glass is fine and of beautiful design, actually this term is a generic one that incorporates all types and qualities of decorative glass. Art glass became popular at the end of the nineteenth century, but the movement really took off during the Arts and Crafts era. Many of the "modern-looking" pieces are quickly becoming bona fide, legal antiques.

Although the look is modern, this art glass covered jar dates from the late nineteenth century and is now a legal antique.

Names Worth Noting

Glass has always provided so many objects for both practical and decorative purposes that it would take pages to list all the names you will come across. Like porcelain, many of the best-known manufacturers and types of glass are hanging around, gracefully aging, awaiting their magical 100th birthday. The following list will take you out of the idiot category:

➤ **Amelung.** A German immigrant, John Frederick Amelung, founded a large glass factory in Maryland in the eighteenth century, but his name is now used generically to refer to early American blown and etched glass.

➤ **Bohemian Glass.** A generic name, Bohemian glass refers to richly colored glass made originally in Bohemia and Germany.

➤ **Burmese Glass.** This type of glass was developed in the 1850s by the Mt. Washington Glass Company. Burmese glass is distinguished by its coloring, which gradually shades from a peach pink to yellow.

➤ **Cranberry Glass.** Made in the late nineteenth century, this glass turns "cranberry" when gold is added to the glass mixture.

➤ **Daum.** Founded in 1875, Daum produces fine-quality French glass, much of which meets the "antique" criterion.

➤ **Gallé.** Emile Gallé founded this French factory in 1874, and though it turned out pottery and furniture, Gallé is best known for its art glass.

➤ **Loetz.** A nineteenth-century Bohemian glass company that is known for fine-quality glass, much of which was similar to some of Tiffany's iridescent glass.

➤ **Milk Glass.** Although heavy white glass was known in ancient times, opaque white glass, generically called "milk glass," became an inexpensive household favorite, especially when molded as animal and bird figures.

➤ **Moser.** This Bohemian glass manufacturer was founded in 1857 and continued to make fine glassware in the twentieth century.

➤ **Peachblow.** Late-nineteenth-century art glass made by American glass companies in imitation of the rare and expensive Chinese "peachblow" porcelain, this glass is now expensive itself.

➤ **Pittsburg.** A broad term used to describe glass made in the early nineteenth century in the Pittsburg area, where there were several glass factories.

➤ **Sandwich.** One of America's best-known centers for making pressed glass was in Sandwich, Massachusetts. After Ruth Webb Lee wrote several books about the glass made there, Sandwich glass became a household name.

➤ **Satin Glass.** This late-nineteenth-century American art glass has a name that defines it well.

➤ **Tiffany.** Louis Comfort Tiffany was an immensely talented man whose nineteenth-century European studies greatly influenced his jewelry, glass, and furniture designs. However, it is his art glass for which he is best known; therefore, we speak of "Tiffany glass."

➤ **Vaseline Glass.** Vaseline glass was made in glass factories in Europe and America in the late nineteenth century and is recognized by its slightly oily yellow sheen.

➤ **Waterford.** Founded in 1783, Waterford Glass Works began by making flint glass but, by the mid-nineteenth century, was best known for its cut glass; today's new Waterford carries on this tradition.

Under the Glass Dome

Any mention of glass would not be complete without a quick note about the wonderful glass domes made during the Victorian era. Victorians had a passion for putting things under glass—from stuffed birds to flowers made of shells and wax to Staffordshire figurines to clocks. These decorative still-life novelties are a real statement of a time in history.

Weighting Around: Paperweights

Another truly Victorian glass item is the paperweight. Once the merchant class became successful and "proper," and ladies became more widely educated, the desk or secretary/bookcase became both a focal point and a practical piece of furniture. Well, now that you have it, what are you going to put on it?

By the mid-nineteenth century, paperweights were the answer. They served the dual purpose of providing beauty and a way of holding papers in place. The two most revered names in paperweights are French: Baccarat and Clinchy. The buzz word for paperweight design or motif is *millefiori*, a decorative design having many small flowers. Put this combination of name and design together, and you have a winner.

By the later nineteenth century, the shape of paperweights became fanciful. Plymouth Rock, books by famous authors, animals, and bouquets of fruits or flowers—these are just a few of the motifs the Victorians thought of.

AntiqLingo

Millefiori, from the Italian word meaning "thousand flowers," is a type of ornamental glass in which canes of colorful glass rods are arranged to look like flowers and are encased in a paperweight.

Seeing Through the Fakes

Almost every pressed or molded nineteenth-century glass object has been reproduced. How do you tell the real thing? Read. Look. Touch. Feel. Volumes have been written warning about reproductions. If you see the same object at every mall or flea market, *beware!* Finally, compare the old with the new. Differences in color, weight, and quality will soon be obvious.

The Least You Need to Know

➤ A pontil mark can be a clue for dating glass.

➤ Hand-blown glass was largely replaced by pressed glass in the nineteenth century.

➤ Nineteenth-century cut glass required great skill to create.

➤ If you see the same piece or form of antique pressed glass for sale in several different places, think "reproduction."

Part 5

Here Today, Still Here Tomorrow: Protecting Your Investment

Owning antiques is thrilling. Appreciating their history and craftsmanship takes understanding. And preserving them requires attention. That's why, once these pieces are in your possession, you need to assess how you will care for them to ensure their safety and well-being.

Sometimes—whether it is because you tire of certain pieces, you refine your tastes, you run out of room, or you decide to scale back—you may want to dispose of some of your treasures. In such circumstances, you have a responsibility to the pieces: to find a good and proper home for them. You also have a responsibility to yourself: to ensure that you will reap their full monetary value.

Chapter 25

It's Mine! Now What Do I Do?

In This Chapter

➤ Learn why you need to have a record of your prized possessions

➤ Find out why collectors lose track of valuable objects

➤ Become prepared to hire the right appraiser for your needs

➤ Discover how to keep down the cost of an appraisal

You bought it. You inherited it. You were given it. In short, it's yours.

Now it's your responsibility to guard and protect this antique treasure for yet another generation. Remember, it's a dear old thing with a long history, and it's probably getting more valuable year by year.

Unfortunately, valuable, beautiful, historically important antiques have their needs. They need to be polished and cleaned, protected from too much sun, kept away from too much moisture or dryness, and, of course, displayed or stored out of harm's way.

You don't need to obsess about proper care of your antiques to the point that you can't enjoy them. Look, they've made it this far. On the other hand, when you properly care for your antiques, you may be protecting a present or a future investment. It only takes a trip to an antiques shop, a Web site, or an auction sale, or to the travelling *Antiques Roadshow,* to remind you of that.

They've Been in Good Hands

For a piece to have survived down through the years, it has either been lovingly cared for or been packed away. Pieces that didn't have such smooth sailing are now broken or repaired—or lost forever. It is those *less* fortunate pieces that have made the lucky pieces, the ones that have survived in excellent condition, desirable and rare.

It's Up to You

These remaining pieces are now *your* responsibility. Probably the best way to describe your caretaker role is that of being a steward—someone responsible for property that, eventually, will be passed on to yet another generation.

That's a big role, but look at the enjoyment these pieces will bring you, whether the piece is your great-grandmother's Haviland china or Uncle Bob's Stickley desk chair or the silver-plated tilting pitcher you bought just because you liked it.

The Collector's Pitfalls

Sometimes, though, even collectors can take for granted those very objects they once had to have. Or they become interested in a new area of collecting and pack the old things away to make room for the new, old things. You know what happens then: out of sight, out of mind.

Other people just aren't aware of the prices that antiques bring today. Tom Porter, of Garth's Auctions, tells the story of the woman who, each time she would receive a fat check for the items Garth's had sold for her, would call and ask if there hadn't been a mistake. She just could not understand how the items she had lived with and used could bring so much money—hundreds of thousands of dollars, in fact.

The trouble is, many antiques can lose their value if they are neglected or aren't checked on every so often. Eighteenth-century furniture can split, shrink, and swell if exposed to temperature extremes. Fine silver will turn black with tarnish and can become pitted if stored under the wrong conditions. Antique textiles and paper goods are prey to all sorts of insects and critters.

Look at it this way. You take care of your stocks, real estate, and other monetary investments. In today's climate, antiques have gained the right to be labeled "investments," too.

AntiqClue

It's hard to believe, but some people don't realize that they have collections. If you've inherited a few things here, and bought a few things there, you may just think you've got a lot of things—while, in reality, you have a valuable array of antiques.

Facing the Fact of What Might Happen

Everyone knows that displaying your beautiful Chinese Export teapot on the same sideboard where your cat likes to land is chancing a flying teapot or that pouring very hot liquid into a cut glass bowl is risking a crack. In most instances, these types of accidents don't have to happen.

But other situations may be out of your control—though hopefully they will not occur. As unfortunate as some disasters may be, it is possible to prevent them or at least be prepared if they should happen.

Thieves Shop Around

Life is a double-edged sword. As antiques go up in value, more burglars figure out how to make them theirs—at least until they sell them. At the same time, we enjoy sharing our antiques with others by displaying them where they can be seen.

In the late 1970s and 1980s, burglars went straight for the silver; they bagged it and melted it down. Why not? Silver was selling for $30, $40, even $50 an ounce. The pieces that were stolen, but not melted, still brought a pretty penny when people paid premium prices to replace their lost pieces.

AntiqInfo

My many years as an appraiser have taught me that there are three, and possibly four, times when you need to know what you *own* and what it's *worth*: when you're buying insurance, assembling your financial portfolio, making your will, and, believe it or not, contemplating marriage—or divorce!

Silver prices have dropped and leveled out since then. Wholesale burglaries of prized antiques are now uncommon enough that we aren't frightened. Not many people are sufficiently knowledgeable about rare glass or have a way to take an eighteenth-century highboy out of a house, without being seen, to frighten us about wholesale burglaries of our prized antiques. Nevertheless, thieves are smart, and they shop around. They find out who is going on a cruise, who goes to a second home every weekend, and who has things worth stealing.

If you enjoy the thrill of the chase, just think how much thieves enjoy the thrill of the catch.

Fireman, Fireman! Save My Antiques!

Theft is devastating, but a fire is even worse. Besides losing the piece itself, you may also have lost photographs, videos, and other records that would be proof of ownership. Even a minor fire can be traumatic. Often the very best-intentioned firefighters can cause breakage with their hoses and inflict permanent water damage.

When Nature's Way Isn't Better

Natural disasters can bring rack and ruin to those very items that have escaped without even a scratch over the years. Thanks to the Weather Channel, hurricanes and storms aren't the threat they used to be, and people in threatened areas usually have time to prepare. However, there's no way to protect against a tornado or major flash floods.

AntiqInfo

Who thought about prenuptial agreements 50 or even 25 years ago? Royalty and the fabulously wealthy. Well, times have changed, and I can tell you that the worst appraisal situations I have ever faced involved property disputes in nasty divorces.

AntiqClue

This theory of mine has no guarantee. In fact, it's probably just coincidence. Maybe it's nothing but silly superstition. However, over the years, I've concluded that a good insurance policy can sometimes provide an invisible protective shield for your treasured possession.

Planning for the Future

Assuming that you will never be plagued with theft, fire, or natural disasters—and most people aren't—you still need to think about the future. Do you plan to sell your collection at some point? Whom do you want to inherit your pieces? Should you donate some things to a museum? Chapter 26, "To Market, to Market," discusses disposal of your objects, but let's start thinking about some of these matters now.

Money Heals a Lot

Burglary. Fire. Death. Divorce. Yikes! This sounds like the coming of the Four Horsemen of the Antiques Apocalypse!

It isn't that bad, I assure you. But I have learned one thing in dealing with people who have faced the loss of valuable personal property and antiques: The loss of the objects themselves is distressing enough, especially if they have been family pieces. When you also lose their potential, the loss is even more catastrophic.

That's why personal property insurance is important.

Ensuring That You Won't Need to File an Insurance Claim

During the height of the silver burglaries, if one house on the block didn't have adequate personal property insurance—that's where the burglars hit. Recently, when flood damage was widespread, a house that had flood insurance received less damage than one across the street that didn't have it. Go figure.

Insurance policies vary tremendously. To get the right insurance policy, you have to get a handle on all that "stuff." The question is when, and how, do you do it?

When? If you're facing an upcoming move, you have a natural opportunity. Otherwise, you'll just have to make the time.

How? Have an appraisal made.

Appraising Appraisers

An appraisal is only as good as the appraiser who makes it. And appraisers are good only if they know the objects they are appraising.

All appraisals are not the same. The kind of appraisal that you need is another factor to consider. For example, an *insurance appraisal* should state what it would cost to replace an item. But according to the courts, an *estate appraisal* should state the cash value of a piece. There can be a considerable difference between these two figures. A fine, circa 1860, Victorian Rococo sofa, beautifully upholstered and in mint condition, bought from a New Orleans antiques shop in the French Quarter might cost $5,000 or more. But that same sofa, teetering on only three legs, with its old red velvet upholstery hanging in shreds, might bring only $300 or $400 in an estate sale.

To locate a good, highly experienced, qualified appraiser, check with museums in your area, insurance professionals, and appraisal societies. There are no national or state licensing bodies for personal property appraisers, but some national societies do provide courses and examinations, which most true professional appraisers take.

AntiqInfo

It is considered unethical for appraisers to offer to purchase items that they appraise. If this happens, be wary. At the same time, if you are having items appraised in order to sell them, do not offer them to the appraiser.

The Least They Need to Know

Getting the best appraiser is up to you. It isn't going to do you any good to have a coin expert appraise your French porcelain. So here are a few questions what it would cost to replace an item. But according to the courts, an *estate appraisal* should state the cash value and hints to keep in mind:

1. Find out from the appraiser what his or her area of expertise is and how long the person has been an appraiser.

2. Inquire whether the appraiser belongs to a professional society.

3. Tell the appraiser the types of antiques you will need to have appraised, for example, Eastlake furniture, American nineteenth-century glass, eighteenth-century coin silver, and so on.

AntiqClue

People tend to be modest about their collections until the appraiser is on site. Then they begin bringing out the "might-as-wells." You know, "Well, while you're here, you might as well appraise this." Remember, time is money; not everything has to be appraised.

AntiqInfo

Never, ever, under any circumstances, pay an appraiser a percentage of your property's value. Ethical, professional appraisers charge by the hour.

4. Inform the appraiser of the reason for the appraisal—insurance, potential sale, divorce, estate, and so on.

The Price of Protection

Appraisals aren't done for free, and fine appraisers are in high demand. A general gauge for a good appraiser's fee is the same hourly fee charged by young professionals—lawyers, financial planners, CPAs, and so on—in your area.

To keep the cost of your appraisal down, organize your property before the appraiser arrives. This also helps you remember items you might otherwise overlook. Eliminate pieces that don't really need appraising. Here are some organizing tips:

1. Take silver, china, and glass out of drawers and down from shelves, if appropriate.

2. Gather any earlier appraisals or paperwork (including bills and receipts), and place with the items.

3. Separate silver into two groups, sterling and silver plate.

4. Group patterns (flatware, china, crystal, linen sets) together, and count them in advance.

5. Flag furniture and accessories with bright string or Post-Its to help the appraiser know which pieces are to be appraised.

The Proper Paperwork

After the appraiser's inspection of your property, you should receive two copies of the appraisal document. The importance of this document cannot be overstated. The appraisal will be the basis for your insurance. It can help establish proof of ownership. In these litigious times, appraisal documents can be used in court. For those reasons, your appraisal document should read like an auction house catalogue and state the age, full description, condition, measurements, and value of each item.

Beyond this, the proper appraisal must also include:

1. The appraiser's name, qualifications, or professional designation.

2. The appraiser's business address.

3. The purpose for which the appraisal was made (insurance, estate, and so on).

4. The client's name.

5. Page numbers stated individually and collectively (for example, page 4 of 26).

6. The appraiser's statement of disinterest in the property.

7. The appraiser's signature.

8. The date of the property inspection and the date of the appraisal document.

I'd Rather Do It Myself

Can you make your own appraisal? Yes. I wrote an entire book, *Emyl Jenkins' Appraisal Book* (Crown, 1998), to help people who may not have ready access to a good appraiser or who, for various other reasons, may want to make their own appraisals.

Of course, your own appraisal cannot be considered a truly professional appraisal. After all, it wasn't done at "an arm's length." It's more of an inventory. However, some record of your personal property is much better than no record at all. And thanks to today's digital cameras, Internet auctions, auction catalogues, and TV "discovery," it's possible for you to gather a lot of information about your personal property.

AntiqClue

Most professional appraisals will be accompanied by photographs of the pieces and close-ups of any significant damage or outstanding ornamental or decorative details that might affect a piece's value.

AntiqInfo

Whether you have a professional appraisal or a homemade inventory, you need to keep this information in a secure place. Do this. Keep one copy in a safe place at home. Then mail the other copy to your most highly trusted relative or friend to be put, *unopened*, in his or her safe deposit box. This ensures access to that copy if something happens to yours.

The Least You Need to Know

➤ Serious collectors need good insurance.

➤ It's easy to take your possessions for granted until it's too late.

➤ Getting the right appraiser is serious business.

➤ If an appraisal isn't possible, it's better to have a good inventory than no record at all.

Chapter 26

To Market, to Market

In This Chapter

➤ Learn about available options for selling your antiques

➤ Discover when you should *not* sell a collection all at one time

➤ Find out the terms and agreements that different businesses have

➤ Weigh options that relate to your particular situation

Eventually almost everyone sells a few antiques. The first time you sell some pieces they may not be your own pieces. Perhaps they belonged to parents or a grandparent, or perhaps an elderly friend was seeking your help in selling pieces. There's no sin in passing on beautiful treasures. It's much better than being a pack rat and storing them away where heaven-knows-what can happen to them.

By nature, some people like to squirrel things away. If that's the case with you, a sudden surge of guilt may strike at selling time. I can't do anything about that because, you see, I suffer from that same ailment myself. But I can help you think about alternative ways to handle the dilemma—the selling part, not the guilt.

Knowing the Market

Before any selling decisions are made, you need to explore the market: Learn what's hot, what's glutting the market, what's hard to find these days. You can start this research by picking up current copies of the more-expensive shelter magazines—*Architectural Digest, Veranda, House Beautiful,* and so on. Their pages are filled with the objects everyone wants for his or her home.

Getting a Second Opinion

Of course, you'll also want to do on-site research by checking out shops, malls, antiques shows, and sales. Trouble is, you have to keep focused on your purpose: scouting the market—not buying more things. This is also the time to start making inquiries about the market by asking, What's selling well? Is there any interest in blue-and-white Staffordshire? What's the market for a collection of nineteenth-century perfume bottles?

Buy Low, Sell High

Hopefully, you, or your family, bought these treasures before they became hot, and you are now able to cash in on their value. However, there are two factors to remember. First, if you sell them to a dealer, you can't expect to be paid a retail price for them. Second, antiques, just like men's ties and women's shoes, have fashions. That's why you need to do market research before you sell. Your investigations may lead you to sell some things now but not others.

AntiqClue

If only every antique lover had a special crystal ball for antiques-market forecasting. But if you love antiques, chances are the crystal ball would itself be an antique—cracked and crazed, and out of touch with today's e-world. That's why you should buy what you like and can afford. If, later, you make money on your pieces, that's a bonus.

Antique Crystal Balls

The ever-changing, even fickle, public taste is why it never works to buy antiques solely for investment purposes. Forty years ago, I knew a young couple living in Connecticut who used their wedding money to buy a very fine eighteenth-century, English trestle table from a well-known dealer—not because they loved it, but because "It's going to be a great investment." They have enjoyed the table, and its value has increased. The time has come to sell the table, but now they are living in a small town in Oregon that has a very limited market for antiques. To get full dollar for the piece, they are going to have to incur added expenses they wouldn't have had if they were in a different location.

Look Before You Leap, or Sell

The combination of many factors—where you live, what the current market for your pieces is, how quickly you must sell them—will influence your final decision. That's why, before you make any final decisions, you need to give yourself sufficient time to …

1. Assess the market.
2. Assess the collection.

Bit by Bit

Oftentimes when an entire collection, especially a highly specialized one, is sold all at once, it can glut the market.

How many collectors are there for helmet-shaped, Georgian silver cream pitchers? A good example would be expected to bring around $800 to $1,500 at auction. But if 50 helmet-shaped, Georgian silver cream pitchers were suddenly offered in one auction, there wouldn't be enough buyers to support that price for all 50 of them.

One or two helmet-shaped Georgian silver cream pitchers add interest to a general auction, but too many will glut the market.

(Photo courtesy of Neal Auction Company)

Conversely, sometimes an auction house will build an entire auction, or portion of an auction, around a specialized collection—especially if the items are currently hot and there is much variety among the items. For example, a collection of eighteenth-century Wedgwood china ranging from a transfer-pattern teapot to a monumental jasper urn would attract collectors from around the world.

AntiqClue

Before selling a highly specialized collection, inquire whether another collection of the same objects has recently sold. If so, the market for these pieces may be saturated.

Clearing Everything Out

In certain circumstances, it is financially wise to sell everything at once. This is particularly true when a family's name is associated with the collection. Your name doesn't have to be Rockefeller to attract buyers to your collection. Collectors love to have pieces from other collectors' collections. And people who don't even own an antique will pay top dollar for a piece associated with a dear friend or locally well-known person.

Where to Sell?

Where should your pieces be sold? Certainly a rare and important collection needs high visibility, possibly at a national, or international, dealer or auction house. Antiques belonging to a locally well-known person will do best where that person has lived. Items of regional interest will bring more money if sold where they are highly treasured. Also, certain antiques do best in a geographical area where they are collected. Here again, it's research time.

AntiqInfo

If you're cleaning out an entire household at one time, there may not be one solution that works for everything, especially if you want, or need, to get top dollar for each item. Be forewarned, though; it takes time and trouble to send large or fragile items out to several different specialized markets.

Back to the Dealer

If a dealer has helped in assembling the collection in question, definitely consider selling the objects back to that dealer. He or she will know the value of the pieces and be able to cash in on having sold them years earlier.

It goes without saying that dealers are an obvious and important way to dispose of antiques. Like every business, sometimes a shop is low on merchandise and other times it will be overstocked. Telephone various dealers and antiques malls, telling them what you have to sell. Antiques dealers are a friendly sort and often will make other suggestions, even if they aren't interested in your things for their shops.

A Percentage Deal

Individual dealers will vary in the way they pay for their merchandise. Because there is no guarantee how quickly pieces will sell, many like to work on a *consignment basis,* whereby they take a percentage of the selling price and you, the seller, receive your money when the piece is paid for.

If you enter into such an arrangement, be sure that you have a written contract and agreement that includes:

1. A full description of all pieces, including condition at the time they are received by the dealer.

2. Mutually agreed-upon prices for each piece or lot.

3. A statement of the percentage split of the selling price between the seller and the dealer (see the accompanying AntiqInfo for more on this).

4. A statement that you will be consulted before the agreed-upon prices are changed.

5. An established time limit for selling the pieces, after which they will be returned to you, or the prices renegotiated.

6. A clear statement of any additional charges the dealer will make, like insurance, advertising, transportation to shows, and so on.

AntiqClue

You're a novice. Suddenly you must dispose of a collection that you know nothing about. Consider hiring an appraiser for an hour's consultation. Ethically, the appraiser cannot buy the pieces, but the appraiser can suggest the best markets for your further investigation.

Taking the Cash

Proper consignment agreements require a lot of time and paperwork, and they place restrictions on the sale. Most dealers prefer to pay outright for new merchandise if they have the cash on hand. This gives them more flexibility in pricing, less paperwork to contend with, and more options on how to sell the pieces.

As long as the price offered is satisfactory, outright payment may also be the easiest, quickest, and cleanest deal for you.

AntiqInfo

Dealers often sell merchandise at a discounted price. Be sure that you have a written record of each piece's mutually agreed-upon price and your percentage of that price. If the dealer reduces the price for any piece without your prior agreement, you will be entitled to the percentage of the agreed-upon price, not the reduced price.

Auctioning It Off

Auction houses are just as hungry as dealers are for great pieces. And, like dealers, auction houses have their faithful clientele.

One major difference between selling to a shop and through an auction is that the auction house has the option of placing antiques in specific sales, where the house thinks the pieces will do best. Of course, this means a delay in payment to the owner, but it can be worth it.

The Terms of the Deal

Auction houses prefer to take in large groups of items rather than just a piece or two. They like being able to advertise "The Collection of a Lady" or "Formerly the Property of Dr. and Mrs. John Doe," for example. Furthermore, the moving and handling of the objects themselves, and the paperwork required for just a few pieces, can be exceedingly expensive.

For this reason, the percentage of the selling price that auction houses charge their clients will vary, depending upon the total worth of the property. Auction houses may charge as much as 25 percent of hammer price for pieces selling for under $1,000, whereas they may offer to sell all the antiques in a million-dollar estate for 10 or 15 percent.

Who sets the prices for your pieces? Before any deals are sealed, the department experts will discuss the price range that they believe your pieces will fall into at auction. Usually they will show you similar pieces that they have sold and tell you what they have brought. Then they'll explain how your pieces compare, better or worse, with those pieces so that you'll know what to expect.

If you discuss selling a collection through an auction house, be sure to get specific information about their packing, handling, and transportation charges; advertising fees (for photographs in the catalogue); insurance costs; and any other miscellaneous charges.

AntiqInfo

Cell phones and absentee bidding can help bring great prices at auctions, even if there's a snowstorm that day, a competing auction, or even a basketball game going on.

Reserving Your Goods

Also discuss the least amount of money you will accept for certain items. As you learned in Chapter 13, "Playing for Keeps," owners sometimes put a *reserve* (the price beneath which the object will not be sold) on valuable or highly treasured pieces to ensure that they will sell for a fair price. The auction house experts will discuss reserves with you.

Why should a piece fall short of its reserve? Circumstances or just plain bad luck—the same way a great piece can sit, unnoticed, in an antiques shop for weeks, months, or even years. It doesn't necessarily mean that the auction house fell down on its job.

Same Time, Next Auction

For those pieces that didn't sell, or didn't meet the buyer's reserve, most auction houses will hold them in storage until a later auction, when a better mix of circumstances will bring their full price. Usually such pieces are "held out" for a few months. Then, when they reappear, their first appearance will have been forgotten.

Having It Your Way

In selling your antiques to a dealer or through an auction, one factor is missing—you. Once the pieces are turned over to an auction house or dealer, you fade into the background. If you want more control, you might consider a house sale or the Internet.

Home Sweet Home Sale

If you're just clearing out a few items, you can have your own garage or yard sale and price the items yourself.

For a large sale, professional house-sale conductors can do a great job of disposing of everything from fine period pieces to unused kitty litter boxes.

Anyone selling antiques for a living is interested in getting the highest dollar for the good pieces. Thus, house sale conductors will sometimes call in experts to help identify and price the finer pieces. Further, these on-site sales attract big crowds.

If you want to get rid of certain pieces, regardless of what they bring, but you also want to sell other pieces for no less than a given price, a house sale lets you have the best of both worlds.

First, you can instruct the sale conductor as to what price (within reason, of course) to mark the pieces you're hesitant about selling for less than a specific price. Second, since the sale is in your home, you don't have to worry about moving these pieces back and forth if they don't sell.

Unraveling the Web

For total control, use the Internet. That way you get to do it all, from listing your item with an

AntiqClue

The house sale has many advantages, but it also has drawbacks. Someone has to clean the items and the house to make a good impression. After the sale is over, there is additional cleaning up to do. Keep this in mind when acquiring a professional house-sale conductor.

online auction house, to taking the pictures to put on the Web page, to packing and shipping the items to the buyer. And, as is so often noted, you can do many of those tasks in your pajamas.

The cost of Internet selling is less than using the services of a dealer or auction house, but remember that you are the one responsible for collecting the money. Always know ahead of time what the terms are for selling on that particular site and what the online seller's agreement is.

Giving It Away

Don't overlook giving away, rather than selling, some of your antiques.

Your Noble Intentions

Say gifts and charity, and you may immediately think of church bazaars or charitable thrift shops. There are many other possibilities.

Museums, especially regional historic societies and house museums, even colleges and universities, depend on gifts—not just of money, but of objects as well. Some antique items aren't really suited to home settings. Further, such pieces are *needed* and welcomed by institutions that are constantly changing their exhibits and displays.

I'm not suggesting that you can give away just anything to museums. Curators and Acquisition Committees prevent that from happening. But if you have items of possible interest and value to such places, this option could be worth pursuing.

The IRS Is Here to Help You

You may get a tax deduction for your noble intentions.

The IRS allows deductions for donations of gifts "in kind" (objects rather than money, stocks, or bonds) to be taken on your federal taxes. However, this privilege can, and has been, abused, so there are strict rules and guidelines.

AntiqInfo

Want to begin a whole new generation of collectors? Take an antique that you, or someone in your family loved, write up its history—factual and fanciful—and give it to a young person. You may begin a lifelong love affair with antiques. I know several serious collectors who began in just that way.

Playing by the Rules

A CPA or tax attorney will assist you in filling out the proper forms. But two considerations you should know about now are (1) items of substantial value ($500 or more) must be appraised, and (2) the value allowed for such gifts must be substantiated by the price that other, comparable items have sold for.

AntiqInfo

Donors, not the receiving institutions, are responsible for paying for the appraisal of property given to nonprofit or charitable organizations.

To ensure that a fair appraisal is made of such property, the IRS will hold the appraiser of the property liable and subject to fines if the item is overvalued.

Despite the red tape and regulations accompanying these nobly intended donations, in my many years of appraising, I know that such donations are appreciated by museums and institutions. The IRS is not unfair in their requirements. They are preventing art and antiques scam artists from getting excessive tax breaks.

Now That You Have Some Room—Starting Over

No matter which avenue you use to dispose of antiques, once you've cleared out a little space …

In my book, that's as good as a license to go shopping.

The Least You Need to Know

➤ There is more than one way to sell antiques.

➤ Time restraints and money needs can influence your choice of seller.

➤ Gifts of personal property can benefit the receiving institution—and you—financially.

➤ With some empty spaces and extra cash, it's time to start anew and buy, buy, buy! Happy antiquing!

A Guide to Furniture Periods and Styles

Eighteenth- and nineteenth-century periods are discussed in detail in Chapters 15 through 17. But it helps to have an at-a-glance reference. That's what you have here.

Style	Period	Characteristics
Jacobean	Seventeenth century; American and English	Hefty, boxy, large panels; turned and spiraled legs
Queen Anne	Early eighteenth century; American and English	Graceful, curved lines, cabriole legs, fiddle-shaped backs, carved shell decorations
Chippendale	Mid-to-late eighteenth century; American only	Straight lines and legs; strong, masculine appearance; bold carving, usually mahogany
Georgian	Eighteenth/nineteenth century; English only	The "Chippendale" look
Hepplewhite	Late eighteenth century; American and English	Slender proportions, straight lines, light-colored wood inlay, occasional delicately carved motifs
Sheraton	Late eighteenth/early nineteenth century; American and English	Curving lines, rounded legs, carved motifs, seldom inlaid
Federal	Late eighteenth/early nineteenth century; American only	A composite name for the Hepplewhite and Sheraton periods
Regency	Late eighteenth/early nineteenth century; English only	Contrasting light and dark woods, often decorated with brass and ormolu

continues

continued

Style	Period	Characteristics
Empire/ Classical	Early-to-mid nineteenth century; American only	Large, often oversized, decorative panels and scrolls
Victorian	Mid-to-late nineteenth century; English and American	Made up of four major designs:
		Victorian Rococo—curving lines, floral carving, scrolls
		Victorian Gothic—architectural-like with corresponding Gothic motifs
		Renaissance Revival—squared, straight lines; carved medallions, urns
		Eastlake—straight, large, incised carved floral and geometric motifs
Aesthetic Movement	Nineteenth century; English and American	The look of Eastlake, but more exotic and artistic
Arts and Crafts	Nineteenth/twentieth century; English and American	Straight, low-slung, unadorned

Where to Go

Never pass by an interesting-looking shop, mall, yard sale, or auction. And to help you get going in the right direction, here's a short list of some of the many sources, actual and virtual, available to you. Don't forget, many of the "real" auction houses can be accessed through their own Web sites—time to crank up one of those search engines.

Brick 'n' Mortar Auction Houses

The following auction houses vary in size and are located across the country. Some are classified as regional houses, while others are national, even international, in scope and audience.

Boos
420 Enterprise Court
Bloomfield Hills, MI 48302
248-332-1500

Brunk's
Box 18294
Asheville, NC 28814
704-254-6846

Butterfield's (Los Angeles)
7601 Sunset Blvd.
Los Angeles, CA 90046
213-850-7500

Butterfield's (San Francisco)
220 San Bruno Ave.
San Francisco, CA 94103
415-861-7500

Christie's
502 Park Ave.
New York, NY 10022
212-546-1000

Christie's East
219 East 67th St.
New York, NY 10021
212-606-0400

Doyle's
175 East 87th St.
New York, NY 10129
212-427-2730

DuMouchelle
409 East Jefferson Ave.
Detroit, MI 48226
313-963-6255

Farmer's
105A Harrison St.
Radford, VA 24141
540-639-0939

Freeman's
1810 Chestnut St.
Philadelphia, PA 19103
215-563-9275

Garth's
2690 Stratford Rd.
Delaware, OH 43015

Neal's
4038 Magazine St.
New Orleans, LA 70115

New Orleans
801 Magazine St.
New Orleans, LA 70130
504-899-5329

Phillips
406 East 79th St.
New York, NY 10021
212-570-4830

Skinner's (Bolton, MA)
357 Main St., Route 117
Bolton, MA 01740
978-779-6241

Skinner's (Boston)
63 Park Plaza
Boston, MA 02116
617-350-5400

Sloan's (Washington D.C.)
4920 Wyaconda Rd.
North Bethesda, MD 20852
301-468-4911

Sloan's (Miami)
8861 NW 18th Terrace
Miami, FL 33172
305-592-2575

Sotheby's (Chicago)
215 West Ohio St.
Chicago, IL 60610
312-592-2575

Sotheby's (New York)
1334 York Ave.
New York, NY 10021

Wolf's
1239 West Sixth St.
Cleveland, OH 44113
216-575-9653

Virtual Auction Houses

Virtual auction houses are not just for buying; some, like icollector.com, are a great resource, too:

www.circline.com

www.ebay.com

www.ebaygreatcollections.com

www.icollector.com

www.sothebys.com

www.sothebys.amazon.com

Antiques Portals

Antiques portals will be your Internet link to upcoming events, more auction houses, journals and other antiques "hot spots." Try one of these if you're looking for education, appraisers, and so on. Have fun exploring these informative sites:

www.antiqcast.com

www.antiqnet.com

www.antiqueresources.com

www.antiquestradegazette.com

www.bmark.com/aq

www.eppraisals.com

www.rubylane.com

www.seriouscollector.com

www.supergavel.com

Live Internet Bidding

If you're feeling really brave, try one of these sites for a virtual experience that can have instant results.

www.auctionchannel.com

www.livebid.com

www.realbidder.com

Publications

For listings of local, regional, and national shops, malls, flea markets, shows, and calendars of events, refer to these publications:

Antique Gazette
6949 Charlotte Pike
Nashville, TN 37209
615-352-0941

Antique Monthly
2100 Powers Ferry Rd.
Atlanta, GA 30330
404-955-5656

Antique Trader
P.O. Box 1050
Dubuque, IA 52001
319-588-2073

Antiques & the Arts Weekly
(The Newtown Bee)
5 Church Hill Rd.
Newtown, CT 06470
203-426-3141

Antiques Week
P.O. Box 90
Knightstown, IN 46148
317-345-5133

Antiques West
3315 Sacramento St., #618
San Francisco, CA 94118

Art & Antiques
2100 Powers Ferry Rd.
Atlanta, GA 30339
770-955-5656

Collectors News
P.O. Box 156
Grundy Center, IA 50638
319-824-6981

Magazine Antiques, The
575 Broadway
New York, NY 10012
212-941-2800

Maine Antique Digest
P.O. Box 1429
Waldoboro, ME 04572
207-832-7534

MidAtlantic Antiques
P.O. Box 908
Henderson, NC 27536
919-4920-4001

Mountain States Collector
P.O. Box 2525
Evergreen, CO 80439
303-987-3994

New England Antiques Journal
P.O. Box 120
Ware, MA 01082

New York–Pennsylvania Collector
Drawer C
Fishers, NY 14453
716-924-7734

Southern Antiques
P.O. Drawer 1107
Decatur, GA 30031
404-289-0054

What to Read

Only one thing is better than buying a new antique for your collection. That is buying a book about antiques for your library. My personal library is filled with literally hundreds of out-of-print, used, and yes, antique books on antiques. But an unopened book on the shelf isn't going to do you any good. You have to read and study to become a connoisseur. That's why I'm giving you a short list of some of the very best books about antiques. These are worth having and reading.

Furniture

Butler, Joseph T. *Field Guide to American Antique Furniture*. New York: Roundtree Press, Facts on File Publications, 1985.

Dubrow, Eileen, and Richard Dubrow. *American Furniture of the 19th Century, 1840–1880*. Exton, Pennsylvania: Schiffer Publishing, 1983.

Marsh, Moreton. *The Easy Expert in Collecting and Restoring American Antiques*. Philadelphia and New York: J.P. Lippincott, 1978.

Philp, Peter, and Gillian Walkling. *Field Guide to Antique Furniture*. New York: Houghton Mifflin Co., 1992.

Sack, Albert. *The New Fine Points of Furniture: Early American*. New York: Crown Publishers, 1993.

Glass

Bogess, Bill, and Louise Bogess. *American Brilliant Cut Glass*. New York: Crown Publishers, 1977.

McKearin, Helen, and George McKearin. *Two Hundred Years of American Blown Glass,* rev. ed. New York: Crown Publishers, 1966.

Revi, Albert C. *American Cut and Engraved Glass*. Exton, Pennsylvania: Schiffer Publishing, 1982.

Swan, Martha L. *American Cut and Engraved Glass*. Lombard, Illinois: Wallace–Homestead Books, 1986.

Pottery and Porcelain

Godden, Geoffrey. *Encyclopedia of British Pottery and Porcelain Marks*. Exton, Pennsylvania: Schiffer Publishing, 1983.

Gordon, Elinor. *Collecting Chinese Export Porcelain*. New York: Main Street Press, 1977.

Schiffer, Herbert, Peter Schiffer, and Nancy Schiffer. *Chinese Export Porcelain*. Exton, Pennsylvania: Schiffer Publishing, 1975.

Silver

Hogan, Edmund P. *The Elegance of Old Silverplate*. Exton, Pennsylvania: Schiffer Publishing, 1980.

Kovel, Ralph, and Terry H. Kovel. *Kovels' American Silver Marks*. New York: Crown Publishers, 1989.

Luddington, John. *Starting to Collect Silver*. Woodbridge, Suffolk, England: Antique Collectors' Club, 1984.

The Meriden Britannia Silver Plate Treasury. New York: Dover Publications, 1982.

Rainwater, Dorothy T. *Encyclopedia of American Silver Manufacturers,* 3rd ed., rev. Exton, Pennsylvania: Schiffer Publishing, 1986.

Wyler, Seymour B. *The Book of Old Silver*. New York: Crown Publishers, 1937.

General Marks Pocket Guide

Miller, Judith, and Martin Miller. *Miller's Pocket Antiques Fact File*. London: Miller's Publications, 1994.

Antiques Series

Macdonald Guide to Buying Antique Furniture. Field, Rachael. London and Sydney: Macdonald & Co., 1986.

Macdonald Guide to Buying Antique Silver and Sheffield Plate. Field, Rachael. London and Sydney: Macdonald & Co., 1988.

Macdonald Guide to Buying Pottery and Porcelain. Field, Rachael. London and Sydney: Macdonald & Co., 1987.

Miller's Antiques Checklists: Furniture. Davidson, Richard. London: Miller's Publications, 1991.

Miller's Antiques Checklists: Glass. West, Mark. London: Miller's Publications, 1994.

Miller's Antiques Checklists: Porcelain. Lang, Gordon. London: Miller's Publications, 1992.

Miller's Antiques Checklists: Silver and Plate. Wilson, John. London: Miller's Publications, 1999.

Miller's Collecting Furniture. Payne, Christopher. London: Miller's Publications, 1996.

Miller's Silver and Sheffield Plate Marks. Bly, John. London: Miller's Publications, 1994.

Miller's 20th Century Ceramics. Atterbury, Paul and Ellen Paul Denker. London: Miller's Publications, 1999.

Sotheby's Concise Encyclopedia of Furniture. Payne, Christopher, ed. London: Conran Octopus, 1995.

Sotheby's Concise Encyclopedia of Glass. Battie, David. London: Conran Octopus, 1994.

Sotheby's Concise Encyclopedia of Silver. Truman, Charles. London: Conran Octopus, 1996.

Starting to Collect Antique Furniture. Andrews, John. Woodbridge, Suffolk, England: Antique Collectors' Club, 1998.

Starting to Collect Antique Glass. Sandon, John. Woodbridge, Suffolk, England: Antique Collectors' Club, 1999.

Starting to Collect Antique Porcelain. Sandon, John. Woodbridge, Suffolk, England: Antique Collectors' Club, 1998.

House Museums

Experiencing life as it was lived in another time, another place, is always a learning experience. Whether you are visiting an eighteenth-century plantation or a nineteenth-century town house, being in close proximity to the furniture, silver, china, and glass that our ancestors used tells us much about how these objects enhanced their lives. Even when the rooms are roped off, often you can get a closer look at furnishings here than you can in some museums.

But house museums can be hard to find—certainly more so than better advertised and publicized art museums and state and county historical society collections. For that reason, I've included this index of house museums and restored villages scattered around the country. Of course, many have Web sites. Also, if you visit one such house in an area, the guide will know of other house museums and decorative arts collections in the vicinity.

Abigail Adams Smith Museum
421 East 61st St.
New York, NY 10021
212-838-6878

Adams Thoroughgood House
1636 Parish Rd.
Virginia Beach, VA 23455
757-664-6283

Alexander Ramsey House
265 South Exchange St.
Saint Paul, MN 55102
612-296-8760

Ashland, The Henry Clay Estate
120 Sycamore Rd.
Lexington, KY 40502
606-266-8581

Ash Lawn
100 James Monroe Pkwy.
Charlottesville, VA 22092
804-293-9539

Barton Country Historical Society Village
85 South Highway 281
Great Bend, KS 67530
316-793-5125

Bayou Bend
#1 Westcott
Houston, TX 77007
713-639-7750

Beauvoir, The Jefferson Davis Home
2244 Beach Blvd.
Biloxi, MS 39531
228-388-9074

Belle Meade Plantation
5025 Harding Rd.
Nashville, TN 37205
615-356-0501

Betsy Ross House
239 Arch St.
Philadelphia, PA 19106
215-627-5343

Bigelow House Museum
918 Glass Ave., N E
Olympia, WA 98506
360-357-6198

Biltmore Estate
One North Pack Square
Asheville, NC 28801
828-255-1776

The Bishop's Place
1402 Broadway
Galveston, TX 77550
404-762-2475

Bowers Mansion
4005 U.S. 395 N
Carson City, NV 89704
702-849-0201

Cozens Ranch
77849 U.S. Highway 40
Winter Park, CO 80482
970-726-5488

The Henry Francis Du Pont Winterthur Museum
Route 52
Winterthur, DE 19735
302-888-4600

Henry Morrison Flagler Museum
Cocoanut Row
Palm Beach, FL 33480
407-655-2833

Hermann-Grima House
820 St. Louis St.
New Orleans, LA 70112
504-525-5661

Isabella Stewart Gardner Museum
280 The Fenway
Boston, MA 02115
617-278-5125

Kelton House Museum
586 East Town St.
Columbus, OH 43215
614-464-2022

Limberlost
200 Sixth St.
Geneva, IN 46740
219-368-7428

Mark Twain House
351 Farmington Ave.
Hartford, CT 06105
860-247-0998

Mary Washington House
1200 Charles St.
Fredericksburg VA 22401
540-373-1569

Monticello
Route 53 Thomas Jefferson Pkwy.
Charlottesville, VA 22902
804-984-9801

284

Point of Honor
112 Cabell St.
Lynchburg, VA 25405
804-847-1459

Rockwood Museum
610 Shipley Rd.
Wilmington, DE 19809
302-761-4340

Rothschild House
Franklin St.
Port Townsend, WA 98368
360-385-4730

San Simeon
750 Hearst Castle Rd.
San Simeon, CA 93452
805-927-2020

The Sargent House Museum
49 Middle St.
Gloucester, MA 01930
978-281-2432

Shrewsbury Windle House
301 West First St.
Madison, IN 47250
812-265-4481

Tryon Palace
610 Pollock St.
New Bern, NC 28562
252-514-4900

Tudor Place
1644 31st St., NW
Washington DC 20007
202-965-0400

Walnut Grove Plantation
1200 Otts' Shoals Rd.
Roebuck, SC 29376
864-576-6546

Wilton Museum House
South Wilton Rd.
Richmond, VA 23226
804-282-5936

And don't forget these centers of restored historical homes:

Charleston, South Carolina
Historic Charleston Foundation
40 East Bay
Charleston, SC 29401
843-723-1623

Natchez, Mississippi
Natchez Visitor's Center
640 South Canal St.
Natchez, MS 39121
1-800-647-6724

Newport, Rhode Island
Newport Historical Society
127 Thames St.
Newport, RI 02840
401-846-0813

Old Salem, North Carolina
Old Salem
P.O. Box F
Winston-Salem, NC 27108
336-721-7300

Savannah, Georgia
Historic Savannah Foundation
P.O. Box 1733
Savannah, GA 31402
912-233 7787

Williamsburg, Virginia
Colonial Williamsburg
134 North Henry St.
Williamsburg, VA 23185
757-229-1000
(Also inquire about the homes along the famous Plantation Highway, Route 5, between Richmond and Williamsburg.)

Glossary

absentee bid   A bid that is left with the auction house rather than made in person.

antique   (1) To the connoisseur, a piece made prior to the onset of the Industrial Revolution, or before circa 1820 to 1840. (2) Legally, according to U.S. Customs, a piece made "prior to one hundred years before the date of entry." (3) Anything that belonged to your grandmother. Don't bank on it.

auction catalogue   A detailed listing of items to be sold at auction at a given time. Usually illustrated.

blown in the mold   Glass that is hand-blown into a decorated mold.

case piece   A piece of furniture intended to store or hold items. Examples of case pieces are cupboards, chests, and armoires. Beds, chairs, and tables (even ones with drawers) are not case pieces.

Canterbury   A stand to hold sheet music and music books.

cellaret   A stand with divided interior to hold wine bottles.

cheval mirror   A long, free-standing mirror contained within two upright columns.

circa   Also written as *ca.,* and *c.* A word meaning "approximate date," as in "The teapot was made circa 1830."

coin silver   Silver having 900 parts of pure silver and 100 parts of alloy. Also the name of American colonial silver.

collectible   An item that is less than 100 years old, was mass-manufactured, and in expensive when it was originally produced.

connoisseur   An expert who recognizes the very best.

corner or wash stand   A triangular stand designed to hold a wash bowl, thus also called a basin stand.

cut glass   Glass decorated by a grinding and polishing process.

dovetail   A method of joining two pieces of wood.

étagère   A stand having several open shelves to display objects on.

faithful copy   A copy that follows the original design, line for line, inch for inch, material for material, decoration for decoration.

fake or fraud   A piece made with the specific intent to deceive the purchaser.

flatware   Silver pieces, such as knives, forks, spoons, and ladles, that are used for eating or serving food. *See also* hollowware.

hallmark   A mark used on English silver since approximately 1300 that provides proof that a piece contains the correct amount of pure silver. Also, the series of marks on English silver identifying the silver content, town, age, and maker.

hammer price   The final bid taken by the auctioneer, at which time the auctioneer bangs the hammer on the podium. The hammer price is, therefore, the selling price.

hollowware   Silver pieces of a hollow shape, for example, pitchers, pots, vases, jugs, cups, tankards, goblets, and even trays and platters. *See also* flatware.

lot   A numbered unit of merchandise sold at an auction. May be composed of a single or multiple pieces.

maker's label   Designates the manufacturer of a piece.

méridienne   A day bed or chaise lounge.

out-of-period   A term denoting that a piece was made several years after the original time frame of the design. *See also* style.

ottoman   Originally named after a low, wide cushioned Turkish bench, but now used to describe an oversized footstool.

patina   The finish on a piece that has built up over years, including dents, scratches, wax, soot, oxidation, even spills, and that now glows with proof of age.

period   The term used in the antiques world to denote that a piece was made during the original time frame of the design.

picker   A knowledgeable person who wanders about "picking" antiques out of unlikely places and then reselling the wares for a profit.

pontil mark   The rough, irregular mark or scar left on the bottom of hand-blown glass when the object is removed from the pontil rod.

porcelain   Fine-quality china that is translucent. *See also* pottery.

pottery   An opaque, thick-bodied ceramic. *See also* porcelain.

price guide   A book that lists prices that antiques and collectibles are known to have sold for. Price guides are intended to be guides, not bibles.

prie dieu   A prayer stool with cushion for kneeling and high shelf for prayer book.

primary wood   The wood used on the exterior of a piece.

provenance   The source or origin of a piece; who owned it.

pseudohallmarks   Marks, used by American colonial silversmiths, that closely resembled genuine English hallmarks.

reproduction   Recently made pieces copied from earlier designs and never intended to deceive the public as original antiques. *See also* period and fake.

récamier   A day bed or chaise lounge with scrolled ends.

secondary wood   The wood used in the interior, underneath, and back of a piece.

secrétaire à abattant   A straight-fronted desk with fall-front writing surface.

settle   A seventeenth-century panel-fronted bench with a hinged seat which, when raised, opens to provide storage space.

sterling silver   The widely accepted standard of 925 parts of pure silver and 75 parts alloy (usually copper).

style   The term used to denote that a piece was made several years after the original time frame of the design, as in a Chippendale-style chair. *See also* out-of-period.

tête-à-tête   A serpentine, or S-shaped bench which allows two people to face one another. Also called a confidante or sociable.

trestle table   A seventeenth-century table with a long board supported by a trestle, or saw-horse base.

work or sewing table   A small, easily moveable table with drawers or a pouch used to store sewing implements and needlework.

Index

X–Y–Z